Eternally One, Eternally Three

A Journey from Atheism to Catholicism
Through the Most Holy Trinity

Eternally One, Eternally Three

A Journey from Atheism to Catholicism
Through the Most Holy Trinity

MATTHEW D. ARISTONE

CRUAChAN
HILL PRESS

𝔑𝔦𝔥𝔦𝔩 𝔒𝔟𝔰𝔱𝔞𝔱:
MSGR. ROBERT LUNSFORD
Censor Librorum.

ℑ𝔪𝔭𝔯𝔦𝔪𝔞𝔱𝔲𝔯:
✠ EARL BOYEA
Episcopus Lansingensis.

Printed with Ecclesiastical Permission
Most Reverent Earl Boyea. December 12, 2023
Lansing, MI.

Copyright © 2024 Cruachan Hill Press & Matthew D. Aristone

All rights reserved—no part of this work may not be reproduced, transmitted, or stored in any form by any means—electronic, mechanical, recorded, photocopy, or otherwise—without prior written permission from the publisher, except for brief excerpts in articles or critical reviews.

ISBN: 978-1-957206-22-6
Cover Design by Jessica Fellmeth

Published by

Cruachan Hill Press
12552 E Michigan Ave.
Grass Lake, MI 49240
www.cruachanhill.com

Printed and Bound in the United States of America

O my Jesus, you have said: *"Truly I say to you, ask and it will be given you, seek and you will find, knock and it shall be opened to you."* Behold I knock, I seek and ask that You open my heart to truth."

~Saint Pio of Pietrelcina,
Efficacious Novena to the Sacred Heart

TABLE OF CONTENTS

BOOK I: PATREM OMNIPOTENTEM 1
   1. The Human Condition 3
   2. The Nature of God & Divine Simplicity.. 7
   3. The Limitations of Scientific Inquiry... 11
   4. The Argument from Contingency.. 15
   5. The Teleological Argument 19
   6. The Argument from Objective Moral Truths............................... 23
   7. The Argument from Human Desire.. 27
   8. The Complementarity of God and Science 31
   9. Scientific Considerations: The Big Bang Theory......................... 35
   10. Scientific Considerations: Fine Tuning of the Universe 39
   11. Scientific Considerations: The Signature in the Cell................ 43
   12. Scientific Considerations: The Cambrian Explosion 49
   13. Conclusion 53
   Book I Bibliography 61

BOOK II: FILIUM DEI UNIGENITUM 63
   1. Religious Pluralism... 65
   2. Spiritual, But Not Religious... 69
   3. The Necessity of Grace 71

- 4. The Trinity.. 77
- 5. The Problem of Evil and Innocent Suffering.................... 81
- 6. The Historicity of Jesus Christ 87
- 7. Christ in the Gospel Accounts 93
- 8. The Historical Reliability of the Gospel Accounts.......... 101
- 9. The Fittingness of the Cross 113
- 10. The Historical Case for the Resurrection...................... 117
- 11. Conclusion.. 143
- Book II Bibliography.. 147

BOOK III: SPIRITUM SANCTUM, DOMINUM 149
- 1. The Role of the Holy Spirit... 151
- 2. Scripture, Tradition, and the Magisterium 153
  - Early Christian Witness for Scripture, et. al 163
- 3. The Papacy.. 171
- 4. The Primacy of Simon Peter... 175
  - Early Christian Witness for the Primacy of Peter 181
- 5. Peter in Rome... 187
  - Early Christian Witness for Peter in Rome 189
- 6. Papal Succession.. 193
  - Early Christian Witness for Papal Succession.................... 199
- 7. Papal Infallibility 205
  - Early Christian Witness for Papal Infallibility 209
- 8. The Seven Sacraments 215
- 9. The Sacrament of Baptism.. 219
  - Early Christian Witness for the Sacrament of Baptism 223
- 10. The Sacrament of Confirmation..................................... 227

  Early Christian Witness for Confirmation............................231
11. The Eucharist/Holy Communion 235
  Early Christian Witness for the Eucharist 241
12. The Sacrament of Confession..247
  Early Christian Witness for Confession 253
13. The Sacrament of Extreme Unction...257
  Early Christian Witness for Extreme Unction 261
14. The Sacrament of Matrimony 265
  Early Christian Witness for Matrimony...............................269
15. The Sacrament of Holy Orders 273
  Early Christian Witness for Holy Orders.............................277
16. Justification by Grace, Through Faith, Formed by Charity...283
  Early Christian Witness for Justification, et. al. 287
17. Purgatory..291
  Early Christian Witness for Purgatory 295
18. The Communion of Saints 301
  Early Christian Witness for the Communion of Saints 305
19. The Uniqueness of Mary..309
  Early Christian Witness for the Uniqueness of Mary 313
20. Conclusion 319
Book III Bibliography..323

BOOK I:
PATREM OMNIPOTENTEM

(THE FATHER ALMIGHTY)

I. THE HUMAN CONDITION

As famed French mathematician, Blaise Pascal, quite rightly stated: *Man is an enigma*—for, in one sense we are the most fortunate species to have ever existed, yet in another the most accursed.[1] To be sure, our intellectual capacity and the ability to grasp abstract concepts allows us to experience aspects of life that all other creatures simply cannot: we are able to express ourselves through literature and art; able to dialogue with one another; able to continuously acquire knowledge and collectively grow in understanding; we experience sensations such as humor, awe, and wonder; we love deeply, and in turn, we are loved. Nevertheless, despite these appreciable advantages, we are also the only species that is acutely aware of its own mortality, that grapples with its own existence, and ponders its meaning and consequence. In fact, from the very foundation of life on earth, mankind alone has been able to

---

1. "What sort of freak then is man! How novel, how monstrous, how chaotic, how paradoxical, how prodigious! Judge of all things, yet a feeble earthworm; repository of truth, yet a sink of doubt and error; glory and refuse of the universe!" (Blaise Pascal, Pensées 434, A.D. 1670)

ask himself: Why? Why am I here? Where am I going? Is there a purpose to my existence? [2]

In truth, the mystery of the cosmos, and our place within it, is one of the most intriguing and important questions we can ask ourselves in our search to lead a meaningful life. However, it is also one of the most frightening. So much so, that in today's postmodern world, many prefer to distract themselves with facile entertainment and other such superficialities, to avoid the anxiety and despair that often come hand in hand with questions of life's ultimate purpose. For if we acknowledge our mortality, without a reason to hope for a continuation and exaltation of human consciousness, we must then come to terms with how fleeting and meaningless our lives truly are. Or, as philosopher Dr. William Lane Craig explains it:

> Insofar as his scientific world view is correct, man learns that he is an inconsequential speck, lost in the immensity of time and space. His brief life is bounded on either side by eternity, his place in the universe is lost in the immeasurable infinity of space. [3]

And yet, notwithstanding our efforts to the contrary, avoidance of or indifference to our human condition appears to be nothing but an exercise in futility, in that questions of ultimate purpose so often arise both during times of elation and gratitude and in moments of travail and suffering. To be sure, whether it is a moment of gratitude, such as the birth of a child, or an experience of tragedy, like the loss of a loved one—no matter the cause—all of us are eventually forced out of the monotony of everyday life. Indeed, sooner or later, we are each confronted with the mystery of our existence, and the frightening reality that we will all one day cease

---

2. William Lane Craig, *Reasonable Faith: Christian Truth and Apologetics*, 3rd ed. (Wheaton, IL: Crossway, 2008), 71
   3. Ibid., 66

to exist.⁴ As such, the question then becomes: what can give objective purpose to our lives, in the face of certain extinction?

If living a meaningful life is possible—if there is, in fact, a solution to our human condition—then we must first discover an entity from which objective meaning can be derived; that is to say, we must make a case for the existence of God. Indeed, for in the absence of a providential design, humanity, our world, and the entire universe are unquestionably rendered objectively meaningless, as everything we have ever done, said, or accomplished, both collectively and individually, would be destined to expire and be forgotten, in a dying universe that cares not of our experiences, achievements, sacrifices, relationships, and memories.⁵ In fact, all of existence would be similarly rendered both arbitrary and inconsequential, as it sprang from nothing, without a purpose, and into nothing it will inevitably return. Correspondingly, as much as we may be inclined to assign a subjective purpose to our lives, to give ourselves incentive and direction, the universe does not acquire meaning at the behest of our desires, and to think otherwise would be delusion.⁶

Wherefore, irrespective of our varying walks of life—our principles, persuasions, and convictions—each of us must ultimately choose between three philosophical worldviews. Admittedly, each of these worldviews is multifaceted and contains its own subset of

---

4. Ibid., 71

5. "I see the terrifying immensity of the universe which surrounds me and find myself limited to one corner of this vast expanse, without knowing why I am set down here rather than elsewhere, nor why the brief period appointed for my life is assigned to me at this moment rather than another in all the eternity that has gone before and will come after me. On all sides I behold nothing but infinity, in which I am a mere atom, a mere passing shadow that returns no more. All I know is that I must soon die, but what I understand least of all is this very death which I cannot escape ... As I know not whence, I come, so I know not whither I go. I only know that on leaving this world I fall for ever into nothingness, or into the hands of a wrathful God, without knowing to which of these two states I shall be everlastingly consigned. Such is my condition, full of weakness and uncertainty." (Blaise Pascal, *Pensées* 194, A.D. 1670)

6. William Lane Craig, *Reasonable Faith: Christian Truth and Apologetics*, 3rd ed. (Wheaton, IL: Crossway, 2008), 79

questions, they can nevertheless be distilled down to three basic propositions:

1. A theistic worldview, and the affirmation that there is a purpose and consequence to our lives.

2. An atheistic worldview, and the subsequent acceptance that everything is objectively meaningless.

3. An agnostic worldview, yet ultimately living as if one of the aforementioned two worldviews is true.

II. THE NATURE OF GOD AND DIVINE SIMPLICITY

The nature of God has been one of the most contentious subject matters in the entirety of human existence, for, since the dawn of mankind, countless deities have been ascribed disparate and contradictory characteristics by people of different creeds, cultures, languages, localities, and different historical eras. It would thus be impossible to offer a convincing case for the existence of God without first establishing what theists historically meant when invoking the divine, for "God" has stood for many things. For instance, many modern opponents of organized religion envisage a tyrannical supreme being, an omnipotent dictator who rules over and above the world. However, for Saint Gregory of Nazianzen,[7]

---

7. "For in Himself He sums up and contains all Being, having neither beginning in the past nor end in the future; like some great Sea of Being, limitless and unbounded, transcending all conception of time and nature, only adumbrated by the mind... The Divine Nature then is boundless and hard to understand; and all that we can comprehend of Him is His boundlessness; even though one may conceive that because He is of a simple nature, He is therefore either wholly incomprehensible, or perfectly comprehensible. For let us further enquire what is implied by "is of a simple nature." For it is quite certain that this simplicity is not itself its nature, just as

Saint Augustine,[8] and Saint Anselm,[9] and others, this is precisely what God was not. On the contrary, what these classical theologians instead proposed, is that God is the necessary consequence of a distinction between essence and existence; that is, a distinction between WHAT a thing is, and THAT a thing is.[10]

Case in point, simply consider a scenario in which an unenlightened child is presented with the accurate depictions of a lion, a pterodactyl, and a unicorn; by nature, he would soon begin to recognize each creature's essential characteristics, and to distinguish them, one from the other.[11] However, what if we were to ask this same child to identify the animal which exists today, the one which had once existed, but is now extinct, and the one which

---

composition is not by itself the essence of compound beings." (Saint Gregory of Nazianzen, *Oration 38*, A.D. 363)

8. "There is, accordingly, a good which is alone simple, and therefore alone unchangeable, and this is God. By this Good have all others been created, but not simple, and therefore not unchangeable." (Saint Augustine of Hippo, *The City of God 11:10*, A.D. 426)

9. "What are you, Lord, what are You; what shall my heart understand You to be? You are, assuredly, life, You are wisdom, You are truth, You are goodness, You are blessedness, You are eternity, and You are every true good. These are many things, and my limited understanding cannot see them all in one single glance to delight in all at once. How then, Lord, are You all these things? Are they parts of You, or rather, is each one of these wholly what You are? For whatever is made up of parts is not absolutely one, but in a sense many and other than itself, and it can be broken up either actually or by the mind – all of which things are foreign to You.... Therefore, there are no parts in You, Lord, neither are You many, but You are so much one and the same with Yourself that in nothing You are dissimilar with Yourself. Indeed, You are unity itself, not divisible by any mind. Life and wisdom and the other [attributes] then, are not parts of You, but all are one and each one of them is wholly what You are and what all the others are. Since then, neither You nor Your eternity which You are have parts, no part of You or of Your eternity is anywhere or at any time, but You exist, as a whole, everywhere and Your eternity exists as a whole always." (Saint Anselm of Canterbury, *Proslogion 18*, A.D. 1077)

10. Edward Feser, *Five Proofs for the Existence of God* (San Francisco, CA: Ignatius Press, 2017), 13

11. Ibid., 117

had never existed at all?[12] Would he be able to tell which was which? Would his newfound knowledge of the essence of each animal somehow equate to knowledge of its existence? If not, then the existence of an entity and the essence of an entity must be regarded as two distinct properties, whereupon for any entity to exist within reality, existence must be added or imparted to its essence.[13] And yet, from where can existence be derived apart from an independent external source? For, in the absence of self-causation, any entity's existence is necessarily derived from something beyond itself.[14] In point of fact, nothing in nature creates itself; everything we experience is contingent.

However, given that any external entity must also derive its being from a further external source, we must eventually arrive at a foundational source whose essence and existence are *one*; whose only essence is existence itself. Wherefore, for those who subscribe to classical theism, God is neither an item nor an individual who is directly discoverable through exploration or the physical sciences; that is, He is not just another "thing" in the universe, nor is He the greatest "being" among many. Conversely, God is the subsistent act of being itself, upon which all existence is dependent. He is the foundation of all existence.

What is more, if we grant that God is the subsistence of being, with no potential, privation, or contingency, then by acting in accord with His limitless nature, He is also subsistent potency, goodness, and wisdom. Foreseeably, this has profound implications for how we understand God and our relation to Him. For instance, given that God is neither an individual being nor a competing entity, one must consider that humanity is neither in rivalry with nor are we enslaved to Him. As such, unlike the fictitious gods of antiquity—the polytheistic deities who both diminished and

---

12. Ibid.
13. Ibid., 124.
14. Ibid.

consumed the world—the classical theistic concept of God holds Him incapable of such things. Instead, as Saint Irenaeus of Lyons so astutely notes in his treatise, *Against all Heresies,* "The glory of God is a human being fully alive." [15]

---

15. Saint Irenaeus of Lyons, *Against All Heresies 4:20:7,* A.D. 189

III. THE LIMITATIONS OF SCIENTIFIC INQUIRY

From modern medicine to lunar landings, to alterations of the human genome, it is undeniable that the scientific method has produced a vast array of innovations and discoveries over the past five centuries. Nevertheless, as much as humanity has unquestionably reaped the rewards of advancements in scientific knowledge, the success of the sciences has also unfortunately given rise to bias and partiality. Case in point: many now claim that science is sufficient to explain the totality of finite reality. Or, in other words, many now claim that all truth and knowledge is reducible to scientific truth and knowledge. However, there are several glaring problems with said assertions.

 Firstly, the very concept of an omnipotent scientific method is a self-defeating position, for it cannot be tested, quantified, compared, or verified, and, as such, is not the least bit scientific. Furthermore, finite reality is not entirely reducible to just material objects and events. In fact, to commit oneself to a strict materialism is to completely discount a host of abstract realities, such as logical absolutes, mathematics, ethics, and esthetics, as well as many other commonly held metaphysical presuppositions. What is more, not only are these realities as much a part of human existence as any physical object or event, but they are also realities that the scientific method cannot even begin to evaluate.

For example, insofar as the scientific method is capable of evaluating the chemical composition of paper and ink, it could never decipher the meaning or significance of a single piece of literature.[16] Likewise, even as science could sufficiently explain the biological makeup of the human brain and body, it could never determine what renders an act morally virtuous or repugnant.[17] Further still, we could certainly extract the various compounds of paint which adorn the Sistine Chapel ceiling; however, this data could not begin to explain why it is universally considered it a masterful work of art.[18] To be sure, this is not to suggest the scientific method is underdeveloped or incomplete, but rather, that by its nature it is inadequate to reach beyond the physical/material realms.[19] Or in other words, just as a metal detector will inevitably fail to locate compounds of paper or plastic, so too do the tools of scientific analysis fail to evaluate the abstract. Indeed, for this we must turn to philosophy and theology.

Lamentably, theology has been frequently misrepresented as a pseudo-scientific intellectual discipline; however, it is nothing of the sort. In fact, at its best, theological inquiry does not even attempt to address the inner workings of the natural world; rather, it contemplates the reality and nature of God, as well as a proper mode of being. Accordingly, as much as the heterogeneous writings within ancient Scripture authoritatively prescribe a finite beginning and a providential design, they also predate modern science and its methods by some 1500 years. Subsequently, any notion that these

---

16. Source: Bishop Robert Barron, "Why Science Will Never Disprove God," Word on Fire Catholic Ministries, October 1, 2012, https://www.wordonfire.org/articles/barron/why-the-sciences-will-never-disprove-the-existence-of-god/
17. Ibid.
18. Ibid.
19. Ibid.

texts were designed to be offered as comprehensive scientific theories is manifestly absurd.[20] Nevertheless, these religious texts still contain invaluable truths within them, as, amongst other things, they provide us with a map of how we ought to comport ourselves within the natural world. Or, as Dr. Jordan Peterson explains it:

> When we say, for example, that religion tells how we should act, we are saying the following: Genuine religion proposes that we live in a manner that is not only good for ourselves, but for our family and loved ones as well. However, this is

---

20. "Usually, even a non-Christian knows something about the earth, the heavens, and the other elements of this world, about the motion and orbit of the stars and even their size and relative positions, about the predictable eclipses of the sun and moon, the cycles of the years and the seasons, about the kinds of animals, shrubs, stones, and so forth, and this knowledge he holds to as being certain from reason and experience. Now, it is a disgraceful and dangerous thing for an infidel to hear a Christian, presumably giving the meaning of Holy Scripture, talking nonsense on these topics; and we should take all means to prevent such an embarrassing situation, in which people show up vast ignorance in a Christian and laugh it to scorn. The shame is not so much that an ignorant individual is derided, but that people outside the household of the faith think our sacred writers held such opinions, and, to the great loss of those for whose salvation we toil, the writers of our Scripture are criticized and rejected as unlearned men. If they find a Christian mistaken in a field which they themselves know well and hear him maintaining his foolish opinions about our books, how are they going to believe those books in matters concerning the resurrection of the dead, the hope of eternal life, and the kingdom of heaven, when they think their pages are full of falsehoods on facts which they themselves have learnt from experience and the light of reason? Reckless and incompetent expounders of holy Scripture bring untold trouble and sorrow on their wiser brethren when they are caught in one of their mischievous false opinions and are taken to task by those who are not bound by the authority of our sacred books. For then, to defend their utterly foolish and obviously untrue statements, they will try to call upon Holy Scripture for proof and even recite from memory many passages which they think support their position, although they understand neither what they say nor the things about which they make assertion." (Saint Augustine, *The Literal Meaning of Genesis 1:19:39*, A.D. 415)

not wholly sufficient, in that we must also take into consideration what is good for the greater society, and perhaps even the environment if we can manage it. What's more, we must then continue to reflect upon each of these considerations, the next day, the next week, the next year, and for the entirety of our lives. Religion, therefore, teaches us about a harmonious balancing of multiple modes of being—a balancing so precise that it can be analogous to the harmony produced by the various instruments of an orchestra. Accordingly, just as we feel a sense of awe when hearing a beautiful composition of music, when we achieve this balanced state of being, our brains have adapted to signify to us that how we are living is meaningful. Subsequently, when we receive authentic and sustained intimations of meaning, we can be confident that we are moving in the right direction. [21]

Wherefore, theological truths are not true in the same sense that analytical science is true, but rather, they are true in the sense that they help us to comprehend the reality of God whilst providing us guidelines on how to properly live at multiple and overlapping levels of being. As such, whilst it would be difficult to overstate the proficiency of science within its own domain, it is also unable to reach certain depths of human existence, and we must be both aware of and honest about its limitations. [22]

---

21. Joe Rogan, "Joe Rogan Experience #877- Jordan Peterson," November 28, 2016, The Joe Rogan Experience Podcast, https://www.jrepodcast.com/episode/joe-rogan-experience-877-jordan-peterson/

22. Hence, Aquinas notes that knowledge, understood simply, is distinct from the gift of wisdom, by which a man is not only knowledgeable but possesses knowledge of divine things. Knowledge "is a distinct gift from the gift of wisdom, as the gift of knowledge is only about human or created things." (Saint Thomas Aquinas, *Summa Theologiae* II-II, Q.9, A.2, A.D. 1273)

IV. PHILOSOPHICAL ARGUMENTS FOR THE EXISTENCE OF GOD: THE ARGUMENT FROM CONTINGENCY

Let us now consider a classic philosophical argument for the existence of God, the argument from contingency. As one of the oldest philosophical arguments for the existence of God, the argument from contingency hinges upon the principle of sufficient reason; namely, that things which exist have explanations for their being, and as to why they are not found otherwise.[23] Or, in other words, the attribute of existence compels a sufficient explanation, either in an external cause or via necessity. As such, any proposed external cause must also be contingent upon a further external cause or else be sufficient to explain its own existence.[24]

Furthermore, the principle of sufficient reason is not just essential for the advancement of human knowledge—it is a bedrock principle of human rationality itself. In fact, it is the very principle

---

23. "No fact can hold or be real, and no proposition can be true, unless there is a sufficient reason why it is so and not otherwise." (Gottfried Leibniz, *Monadology*, §32:217, A.D. 1714)

24. Edward Feser, *Five Proofs for the Existence of God* (San Francisco, CA: Ignatius Press, 2017), 13

presupposed in all scientific inquiry, philosophical investigations, theological postulations, and the like. However, just as every link on a vertical chain requires support from a higher link, so too are causal explanations both intertwined and reinforced by higher explanatory realities. Likewise, in either case if we do not eventually arrive at a foundational base, the entire support system will come crashing down. Consequently, it would be absurd for us to consider an infinite chain of external causes/causal explanations, in that it would ultimately lead us to a state of incoherence. Case in point: just as an appeal to an infinite length chain would fail to explain its vertical suspension, so too would an appeal to an infinite causal series fail to explain why we or anything exists.[25] Subsequently, we must eventually arrive at an uncaused, causal explanation, whose existence is not contingent, but necessary.[26]

What is more, although a contingent-less cause may seem vague or obscure, one can further deduce that such an entity must possess certain identifiable characteristics. For example, any uncaused cause must be eternally immutable and unchanging, as any occurrence of change would suggest a contingency from a prior cause. Likewise, it could not be subject to time or space, in that any entity within time and space is both susceptible to and capable of change. Finally, by definition, that which is not contingent must be of an immaterial nature, as material objects are composed of composite parts, which can be altered and rearranged. Wherefore, the principle of sufficient reason and the existence of contingent objects seem to not only necessitate an uncaused, causal explanation, at the very foundation of reality, but one which is immutable, eternal, immaterial and incorporeal as well.[27]

We are thus remided of the beautiful paean to God as the immutable source of creation found in the Psalms:

---

25. Ibid., 162
26. Ibid., 157
27. Ibid., 160

PATREM OMNIPOTENTEM

Long ago you laid the foundation of the earth, and the heavens are the work of your hands. They perish, but you endure; they will all wear out like a garment. You change them like clothing, and they pass away; but you are the same, and your years have no end. (Psalm 102:25-27, NRSVCE)

V. PHILOSOPHICAL ARGUMENTS FOR THE EXISTENCE OF GOD: THE TELEOLOGICAL ARGUMENT

We find ourselves in an orderly universe which is intelligible and coherent; however, intelligibility and coherence ultimately rely upon the consistency of logic. Furthermore, logical consistency depends upon a set of foundational laws, which can be summarized accordingly: [28]

a) **The Law of Identity**[29] —objects that exist are true to their forms, and, as such, an object ultimately is what it is and not what it is not. For instance, a rock is manifestly a rock, and not a car.

---

28. The Aristotelian laws of logic have been summarized from: Matt Slick, "The Transcendental Argument for the Existence of God." Christian Apologetics and Research Ministry, December 9, 2008, https://carm.org/defending-the-faith/the-transcendental-argument-for-the-existence-of-god/
29. Aristotle, *Metaphysics, Book IV, Part 4*

b) **The Law of Non-Contradiction**[30]—a proposition cannot be both true and false, in the same sense, at the same time. Therefore, it would be a logical contradiction to say, "This tree is not a tree."

c) **The Law of the Excluded Middle**[31]—there is no middle ground between true and false statements; a proposition is either true or its negation is true—there is no tertiary or central position.

What is more, these foundational laws of logic are also inherently absolute, in that they are unchanging and independent of external variables, such as location, time, weather, temperature, and the like. Accordingly, although the rationality of our universe is ultimately dependent upon the existence of logical absolutes, they, in turn, exist independently from the material universe. Case in point: even if the universe ceased to exist, logical laws such as "A=B, B=C, therefore A=C," would still exist and be true.[32] As such, it would be fair to conclude that the laws of logic are transcendental by nature, as they transcend our material universe.

Yet, still, logical absolutes also provide the framework for rational thought, and are therefore conceptual by nature.[33] Moreover, logical laws are neither tactile, quantifiable, nor measurable: they cannot be seen, heard, smelled, tasted, or touched. Consequently, logical absolutes are demonstrably abstract, and, as such, apprehended by the mind. Nevertheless, logical absolutes cannot be the products of human minds, for they are fallible and inconsistent. Furthermore, if logical absolutes were the concepts of human minds, the coherence of the material universe would be

---

30. Ibid.
31. Aristotle, *Metaphysics, Book IV, Part 7*
32. Slick, "The Transcendental Argument for the Existence of God."
33. Ibid.

dependent upon human existence. However, the universe predates all human life by some 13 billion years.

Subsequently, logical absolutes necessitate the existence of an infallible intellect, which is transcendent of the material universe. Correspondingly, it must be one which exists outside the constraints of time, as time is a product of the universe. And yet, to what can we attribute an infallible, transcendental, and eternal intellect apart from an omniscient God?[34]

> In the beginning was the [Logos], and the [Logos] was with God, and the [Logos] was God. He was with God in the beginning. All things came into being through him, and without him not one thing came into being. (John 1:1-3, NRSVCE)

---

34. [Forms] must be thought to exist nowhere but in the very mind of the Creator. For it would be sacrilegious to suppose that he was looking at something placed outside himself, when he created in accord with it what he created. But if the [forms] of all things created, or to be created, are contained within the divine mind, and if there can be nothing within the divine mind except what is eternal and unchangeable... then not only are they [forms], but they are truth, because they are eternal and they remain ever the same unchangeable. It is by participation in these [forms] that everything exists, in whatever manner it exists. (Saint Augustine of Hippo, *De Diversis Quaestionibus XLVI*, A.D. 395)

VI. PHILOSOPHICAL ARGUMENTS FOR THE EXISTENCE OF GOD: THE ARGUMENT FROM OBJECTIVE MORAL TRUTHS

For a proposition to be considered objectively true, it must be able to withstand the inherent biases that exist within human perception; that is to say, it must remain unchanged despite our personal feelings, interpretations, and prejudices.

With this in mind, as a collective species, mankind has certainly seemed to have reached certain moral consensuses—consensuses which have evolved into a variety of international laws, and a standard for basic human rights. These laws then, once violated, have subsequently resulted in adequate and proportional punishments, to achieve justice, protect the innocent, and dissuade others from acting in a similar fashion. Case in point: mankind has seemingly arrived at the moral consensus that the taking of an innocent life, without sufficient cause, is evil and thus worthy of retribution. As such, throughout the civilized world, if a person is found guilty of such an offense, he is subsequently sentenced to a lengthy imprisonment or, in extreme cases, even capital punishment. Nevertheless, even as humanity has become increasingly habituated to the reality and validity of retributive justice, the severity, fallibility, and volatility of our judicial processes raise questions of objective moral duties. For instance, do we have an objective moral obligation to seek justice and enforce the law? If so, what is the objective moral standard for these laws, and where does it derive from? Similarly, are heinous crimes against a fellow man truly and objectively immoral, or are they simply counterintuitive to the flourishing of our species?

To be sure, theists maintain that to assert that the taking of an innocent life is truly and objectively immoral, we must first conclude that a human person possesses inherent value. However, in the absence of a providential design and our innate reflection of the highest good [God], why should our species be considered more valuable than anything else that exists? Moreover, why should individuals of varying prosperities, ages, genders, intellects, and physical capabilities ever be considered fundamentally equal? In fact, if inherent value wasn't inscribed into human corporeality by an omniscient and omnipotent creator, then it remains to be seen how humanity could possess innate dignity or equal worth. What's more, as Dr. William Lane Craig so astutely notes in his works on objective morality, if we are to deny the existence of an impeccable God or an equivalent entity of moral perfection, then there exists no competent moral authority to issue binding ethical commands:

> Duty arises in response to a command from a competent authority. For example, if some random person were to tell me to pull my car over, I would have absolutely no legal obligation to do so. But, if a policeman were to issue such a command, I'd have a legal obligation to obey. The difference in the two cases lies in the persons who issued the command; one is qualified to do so, while the other is not. Similarly, in the case of moral obligations, these arise as a result of imperatives issued by a competent authority. And

in virtue of being the source of all Good, God is uniquely qualified to issue such commands as expressions of His nature.[35]

An atheist, then, in rejecting the possibility of God, must instead make the claim that our sense of ethics is simply a result of the evolutionary process, or else formed via societal conditioning.[36] In fact, insofar as one denies the existence of a God and His divine imparting of human dignity and worth, morality is relegated to a natural development, which has allowed for the flourishing of life. However, if one accepts this Neo-Darwinian supposition and embraces a naturalistic worldview, then he must in turn consider morality to be both relative and illusory. Indeed, for if the human race is simply the improbable result of random variations, through natural selection, then our existence is rendered as objectively meaningless as a speck of dust or grain of sand. Likewise, if the human mind is merely the unlikely culmination of unguided adaptable mutations, then how could we possibly be morally culpable for what we think, or how we act?

Regrettably, many atheists seem to overlook the consequences of their world view and the fact that naturalism simply cannot give rise to coherent moral objections.[37] For example, how could an atheist coherently say that the genocide of the European Jewish population under Hitler's Nazi régime, was objectively more immoral than the extermination of a rodent infestation? Moreover, if the Nazis had managed to triumph in their series of military campaigns, they may very well have compelled compliance with their set of erroneous moral convictions. Consequently, in the

---

35. William Lane Craig, "Does Theistic Ethics Derive an "Ought" from an "Is"?" Reasonable Faith with William Lane Craig, June 14, 2010, *https://reasonablefaith.org/writings/question-answer/does-theistic-ethics-derive-an-ought-from-an-is.*
36. William Lane Craig, *Reasonable Faith: Christian Truth and Apologetics*, 3rd ed. (Wheaton, IL: Crossway, 2008), 75
37. Ibid.

absence of an objective standard of ethics, a horrific event like the Holocaust could potentially be made morally licit by way of forced societal conditioning. Nevertheless, even as the human conscience can become temporarily compromised by corrupt ideologies like Nazism, the sane person—both theist and atheist alike— intuitively rejects these repugnant beliefs and the notion of moral relativism. However, it remains unclear how the atheist can defend any form of objective ethics, in the absence of an impeccable moral authority for its ontological foundation.

In summation, the human species seems to have an intuitive sense of objective morals which cannot be procured from the natural world, thus evincing the necessity of a supreme moral authority. However, atheism rejects the idea that such an authority could ever exist. Consequently, it does not seem possible for an atheist to make coherent moral objections and at the same time maintain his world view. What is more, although it is certainly possible for atheists to live in a morally upright fashion, it would be naïve to think that this could possibly translate across society at large. For, if our sense of ethics is proven to be both relative and illusory, then civilization is almost certain to regress into a play of impulse and self-worship.[38]

> This is the covenant that I will make with the house of Israel after those days, declares the Lord: I will put my laws in their minds, and write them on their hearts, and I will be their God, and they shall be my people. (Hebrews 8:10, NRSVCE)

---

[38]. "What will become of men then...without God and immortal life? All things are lawful then, they can do whatever they like?" (Fyodor Dostoevsky, *The Brothers Karamazov*, trans. Constance Garnett (New York, NY: The Lowell Press, 2009), 763

VII. PHILOSOPHICAL ARGUMENTS FOR THE EXISTENCE OF GOD: THE ARGUMENT FROM HUMAN DESIRE

Before forming an argument for the existence of God in relation to human desire, one must first differentiate between innate desires, and those which have been artificially contrived. For instance, one must draw a distinction between natural desires (such as the desire for food, water, sleep, sex, oxygen, or warmth), and the desire to own a Lamborghini.[39] Indeed, for innate desires are ultimately derived from within and arise via human nature, while artificial desires have external influences, such as societal conditioning, advertising, and so forth.[40] Correspondingly, any desire which has been naturally derived will be common from person to person, while superficial desires are both malleable and fluid, and will therefore differ considerably.[41] Wherefore, if we are able to keep this distinction in mind, regarding the nature and source of human

---

39. Dr. Peter Kreeft, "20 Arguments for God's Existence," Strange Notions, Accessed July 10, 2020, https://strangenotions.com/god-exists/
40. Ibid.
41. Ibid.

desires, it is possible to form a persuasive argument for belief in the existence of God.

Case in point: every natural or innate desire that we possess corresponds to and is ultimately explained by an object of fulfillment. For example, the natural desire to eat is both explained and fulfilled by the existence of food, as is the natural desire to drink by water. In fact, the very existence of our natural desires suggests that there must be corresponding objects in existence which are ultimately capable of their fulfillment. Or, in other words, the very fact that we hunger and thirst at all presupposes the existence of food and water.

Yet, still, our innate desires cannot be confined to the material realm alone, in that we also seem to inherently desire certain transcendental realities. For example, throughout human history, regardless of circumstance or surrounding conditions, mankind has pursued specific abstract realities, such as truth, justice, and happiness. However, with regards to these transcendental desires, there is also a notable deficiency in that there appears to be nothing within the natural world which is ultimately capable of their fulfillment. In fact, on the contrary, the opposite is true, as it is precisely in moments of great joy, triumph, and discovery when it becomes most apparent that these transcendental desires have only increased. Indeed, for no matter how much happiness we have in our lives, it is always intermittent and incomplete. Likewise, discovering a great truth only leads to more inquiry and the mind is left wanting. Further still, try as we might to address issues of evil, inequity, abuse, and corruption, justice continues to be denied, and the innocent continue to suffer. As such, given that these desires are also intrinsic to our human nature, they must point to the existence of a metaphysical source which is finally capable of their fulfillment—one of absolute truth, ultimate justice, and an eternal, unceasing beatitude. In other words, our intrinsic desires for truth, justice, and happiness, point to the existence of God. [42]

> Come to me, all you who are weary and are carrying heavy burdens, and I will give you rest. Take my yoke upon you and learn from me; for I am gentle and humble in heart, and you will find rest for your souls. For my yoke is easy and my burden is light. (Matthew 11:28-30, NRSVCE)

---

[42]. "Thou hast formed us for Thyself, oh Lord. Therefore, our hearts are restless until they find their rest in Thee." (Saint Augustine of Hippo, *Confessions* *1:1:5*, A.D. 397)

VIII. THE COMPLEMENTARITY OF GOD AND SCIENCE

Although there are certainly limitations to the scientific method and the reach of the physical sciences, when it comes to the study of the material universe, scientific inquiry must be taken seriously. Nevertheless, this is not to suggest that we must abandon the supernatural or juxtapose science and theism, as it is entirely possible to accept the preponderance of scientific and theistic propositions. Indeed, for as Oxford mathematician Dr. John Lennox explains in his works on the potency science, not all of causality can be confined to the natural/material realms:

> In some quarters the very success of science has led to the idea that because we can understand the mechanisms of the universe without bringing in God, we can safely conclude that there was no God who designed and created the universe in the first place. However, such reasoning involves a common logical fallacy, which we can illustrate as follows. Take a Ford motor car. It is conceivable that

someone from a remote part of the world, who was seeing one for the first time and who knew nothing about modem engineering, might imagine that there is a god inside the engine, making it go. He might further imagine that when the engine ran sweetly it was because Mr. Ford inside the engine liked him, and when it refused to go it was because Mr. Ford did not like him. Of course, if he were subsequently to study engineering and take the engine to pieces, he would discover that there is no Mr. Ford inside it. Neither would it take much intelligence for him to see that he did not need to introduce Mr. Ford as an explanation for its working. His grasp of the impersonal principles of internal combustion would be altogether enough to explain how the engine works. So far, so good. But if he then decided that his understanding of the principles of how the Engine works made it impossible to believe in the existence of a Mr. Ford who designed the engine in the first place, this would be patently false—in philosophical terminology he would be committing a category mistake. Had there never been a Mr. Ford to design the mechanisms, none would exist for him to understand.[43]

Admittedly, it would be unfair to imply that the scientific community uniformly subscribes to a strict materialism; however, via the use of this simple analogy, Dr. Lennox exposes a presupposition that permeates science academia; namely, that material causes are often assumed to be the only viable option, and, as such, a plethora of evidence of both intelligence and design is willfully and obstinately neglected. Furthermore, he suggests that physical and metaphysical causal explanations are, in fact, complementary by nature and therefore should not be considered

---

43. John C. Lennox, *God's Undertaker: Has Science Buried God?* (Oxford: Lion books, 2009), 44-45

mutually exclusive. Case in point: just as Henry Ford is not a competing causal explanation for the material components of his Model-T car, neither would positing the existence of God be at odds with natural processes and events. Likewise, just as you will not directly discover Henry Ford by revving an engine or removing a radiator cap, neither will you directly discover God through physical exploration and analysis. Indeed, for each is the author of the entire show, the metaphysical intellect behind the physical composition, and the reason that there is something to be examined in the first place.

What is more, all scientific inquiry presupposes the fact that the universe is intelligible and coherent. However, if the universe is truly the improbable result of random and chaotic events, then why would we ever expect to find order and intelligibility within it? Moreover, why would we expect mankind to have evolved to this extent and to be able to grasp said intelligence? To be sure, the process of unlocking the vast mysteries of our universe has required some of the greatest minds that humanity has had to offer; yet, for many, it remains unreasonable to suppose that a mind was involved in its authorship. Nevertheless, all intelligibility is habitually indicative of a subjective intelligence behind it, and thus, the very fact that we can understand our surroundings lends credence to the concept of a cosmic designer. Wherefore, when clear and complex signs of intelligence are found scattered throughout the universe, it is completely legitimate to posit the possibility that we are merely discerning the concepts of a superior mind. In point of fact, as Joseph Ratzinger astutely notes in his book, *Introduction to Christianity*:

> The universal intelligibility of nature, which is the presupposition of all science, can only be explained through recourse to an infinite and creative mind, which has thought the world into being. No scientist could even begin to work

unless and until he assumed that the aspect of nature which he was investigating was knowable, intelligible, and marked by form. But this fundamentally mystical assumption rests upon the conviction that whatever he comes to know through his scientific work is simply an act of re-thinking or re-cognizing what a far greater mind has already conceived. (Joseph Ratzinger, *Introduction to Christianity*, tr. J.R Foster (New York, NY: Herder and Herder, 1970)) [44]

---

[44]. Summarized quotation from: Bishop Robert Barron, "Einstein and God," Word on Fire Catholic Ministries, July 18, 2008, https://www.wordonfire.org/articles/barron/einsten-and-god/

IX. SCIENTIFIC CONSIDERATIONS FOR THE EXISTENCE OF GOD: THE BIG BANG THEORY

The Big Bang theory is widely considered to be the preeminent scientific explanation for the origin of our universe, wherein it is hypothesized that matter, time, and space all came into existence, from a point of cosmological singularity,[45] some 13.8 billion years ago.[46] Furthermore, since its original proposal in 1927, the theory has continued to garner support from a wide range of subsequent scientific discoveries, such as the overabundance of light elements within the observable universe, the detection of galactic redshifts, and the identification of leftover cosmic microwave background radiation from an initial explosive event. Correspondingly, it has also been corroborated by many other widely accepted scientific theories and laws, such as Einstein's Theory of General Relativity, and Hubble's Law, amongst others. As such, even as scientific models are habitually subject to readjustment and reevaluation, the

---

45. William Lane Craig, *Reasonable Faith: Christian Truth and Apologetics*, 3rd ed. (Wheaton, IL: Crossway, 2008), 127

46. Recent studies have suggested that the age of the universe could be in excess of 26.7 billion years; however, the problem of a finite beginning remains unchanged.

evidentiary support for The Big Bang theory is of an exceedingly high degree.

Notwithstanding, given the implications that the universe does not extend infinitely into the past, it is also imperative to consider the philosophical consequences of the prevailing scientific data—and, in doing so, the following cosmological argument has been advanced: [47]

1. Whatever begins to exist has a cause.
2. The universe began to exist.
3. The universe has a cause.

What is more, one can also infer that material entities within the universe could not have been its cause, as that which exists within the universe is dependent upon its existent laws and properties. Subsequently, this may ultimately result in a causal agency that is beyond our capabilities of detection; however, one can nonetheless deduce that this mysterious entity possesses certain identifiable characteristics. For example: [48]

a) The cause of the universe must be immaterial, for neither matter nor space began to exist until the universe expanded from its initial cosmological singularity.

b) The cause of the universe must transcend space and time, as time itself is also contingent upon expansion from cosmological singularity.

---

47. The "Kalam" cosmological argument has been summarized from: William Lane Craig, *Reasonable Faith: Christian Truth and Apologetics*, 3rd ed. (Wheaton, IL: Crossway, 2008), 111
48. Ibid., 152

c) The cause of the universe must ultimately be both immutable and unchanging, as any occurrence of change requires the requisite time and space within which to occur.

d) Given that it produced an explosive event of cosmic proportion, without a material cause, the cause of the universe must possess unimaginable power.

Wherefore, the very attributes that theists have historically ascribed to the source of all creation, have been seemingly confirmed by the preeminent scientific theory for the origin of our universe; that is to say, that the Big Bang Theory has evinced the existence of a transcendental, immutable, and metaphysical entity, which in its infinite power can create *ex nihilo*.[49]

---

49. Ibid., 154

X. SCIENTIFIC CONSIDERATIONS FOR THE EXISTENCE OF GOD: THE FINE TUNING OF THE UNIVERSE [50]

From galaxies to solar systems, right down to the atom and subatomic particles, the structure of our universe is held together by a series of constants and quantities. Furthermore, through the process of scientific evaluation, we have discovered that each of these constants and quantities has been dialed into an astonishingly precise value, in an extremely narrow life-permitting range. In fact, so much so, that if any of these values were to be theoretically altered by even the slightest of margins, no physical or interactive life of any kind could exist anywhere within the cosmos.

Case in point: consider gravity—a force which is derived from the gravitational constant. If the gravitational constant were varied by more than a fraction of 1 in 10^{60}, our world, our universe, and

---

50. The fine tuning argument has been summarized from: William Lane Craig, "The Fine-Tuning of the Universe," Reasonable Faith with William Lane Craig, June 8, 2016, https://www.reasonablefaith.org/finetuning

everything within it, would immediately cease to exist. What is more, to help convey just how minute a fraction of 1 in 10^{60} is, contrast it to the number of cells in a human body (10^{14}), or the number of seconds which have passed since the beginning of time (10^{20}); if the gravitational constant were altered by just *one* of these infinitely miniscule points, the universe would have either expanded too rapidly for the creation of celestial objects or else collapsed upon itself, rendering a similar result. Further still, as if an accuracy of 1 in 10^{60} wasn't improbable enough, an even greater precision is required when referring to the cosmological constant, for it must remain unchanged to a fraction of 1 in 10^{120} parts. Correspondingly, there is also the quantity of the distribution of mass and energy of the early universe, which had to remain consistent to an incomprehensible 1 in $10^{\wedge}10^{123}$ parts. Thusly, for all intents and purposes, we are speaking of probabilities so low that they approximate to the level of practical impossibility.

Admittedly, many still consider our improbable existence as a mere product of chance over time. The simple fact of the matter, however, is that our universe could not permit life if these, and many other such quantities and constants had not been independently and exquisitely balanced on a razor's edge. In point of fact, so much is this the case, that the speed of light, Planck's constant, Planck's mass-energy constant, the mass constant of the proton, the mass constant of the electron, the mass constant of the neutron, the ratio of electron to proton mass, the mass constant of the up/down/strange quarks, the gravitational coupling constant, the cosmological constant, the distribution of mass energy of the early universe, and Hubble's constant all must remain unchanged to an equally absurd degree of perfection. Relatedly, it must also be noted that these specified constants and quantities pertain solely to the physical structure and mechanics of the universe; we have not even considered all of the "fine tuning" necessary to account for the emergence of biological life or intelligent life.

PATREM OMNIPOTENTEM

As such, just as one would become suspicious at the prospect of the same individual winning the lottery several thousand times in a row, so too is the probability of such a finely tuned, life-permitting, orderly universe so infinitesimally small that the possibility of a "chance over time" occurrence is well beyond reach.[51] The mere passage of time—even vast spans of time—does not render these incomprehensible probabilities any more believable.

---

51. Astrophysicist Hugh Ross enumerates as many as 140 universal constants and quantities that must be finely tuned for the allowance of conscious life. For a complete list, see: Hugh Ross, *Why the Universe Is The Way It Is* (Grand Rapids, MI: Baker Publishing, 2008), 213

XI. SCIENTIFIC CONSIDERATIONS: THE SIGNATURE IN THE CELL

From the time that Darwin published his work on *the Origin of Species*, right up until the end of the twentieth century, scientists had drastically underestimated the complexity of the cell. Once thought to be the simplest of all organisms, today's understanding of the layout of the cell is more akin to a modern-day factory, as within each structure one can expect to find an elaborate network of multiple and interlocking assembly lines.[52] Furthermore, much like the automated industrial equipment of today, these cellular assembly lines can be further broken down into individual sets of protein "machines"—each of which is also composed of highly coordinated moving parts.[53]

In truth, unbeknownst to Darwin and his contemporaries, these highly automated protein "machines" are, in fact, long chain-like molecules, which are comprised from a specific set of twenty different amino acids. Correspondingly, depending upon the precise

---

52. Stephen C. Meyer, *The Return of the God Hypothesis* (Journal of Interdisciplinary Studies 11, 1999), 14
53. Ibid.

arrangement of these amino acids, the protein structure then folds into a diversity of three-dimensional shapes, thereby permanently affixing its specified function within the system of the cell.[54] In fact, so specified is the sequencing and folding of these amino acids, that a protein, once completed, can no longer substitute for its counterparts. Subsequently, just as the meaning and function of a word are ultimately dependent upon the arrangement of its letters, so too is the function of a protein molecule reliant upon the sequence of its amino acids. Likewise, in either case, any adjustment or change in the sequence invariably results in a loss of functionality.[55]

Wherefore, it should come as no surprise that the discovery of this specified sequencing within the protein molecule would ultimately force scientists to reassess the accuracy of Darwin's presuppositions. For if Darwin was indeed correct, and the cell was the simplest of all organisms, then how did it manage to consistently construct the correct-sized protein in the correct sequence for the correct function? What is more, the problem of specified sequencing within the cell became even more exacerbated as chance-based explanatory models were quickly proven untenable. Case in point: simply consider a standard rotary lock with 4 individual dials—each of which is numbered sequentially from zero to nine; if we were to calculate the odds of arriving at the proper combination by either randomness or chance, we would arrive at a value of 1 in $10 \times 10 \times 10 \times 10$, or a 1 in 10,000 probability.[56] However, if we were to apply this same logic to the amino acid sequencing of even a simple 10-site protein structure (a calculation consisting of 10 host sites, each having 1 of a possible 20 different amino acids) then a resulting probability of 1 in 10.24 trillion promptly ensues. Given then, that

---

54. Ibid., 16
55. Ibid.
56. Stephen C. Meyer, *Signature in the Cell: DNA and the Evidence for Intelligent Design* (New York, NY: HyperOne, 2009), 165

even a modest length protein structure consists of over 150 amino acid sites, an obvious problem began to arise for the "chance over time" hypotheses; namely, that to produce even a modest length protein structure, a correct sequence had to be derived from an inconceivable 10^{195} different combinations.[57]

Nevertheless, thoroughly determined to find a solution to the protein sequencing problem, a molecular biologist named Francis Crick eventually discovered that the sequencing of amino acids within the protein molecule could be directly linked to a prior specificity within the structure of the cell. Or, in other words, he had found that the specific arrangement of cytosine, adenine, guanine, and thymine along the spine of the DNA molecule functioned as a sort of written code for the process of protein construction.[58] To be sure, Dr. Crick's discovery would initially be hailed as a major scientific breakthrough. Over time, however, it proved to be a point of contention within the scientific community; indeed, for insofar as his findings accounted for the directed processes required for protein synthesis, they also invariably led to questions about the origins of this biological information. For instance, where did the information come from? How did the DNA molecule acquire the coded sequencing which allowed it to direct these mechanical operations? Was it a result of chance, necessity, or design? What's more, these questions then led to the ultimate question: the question of the origin of life itself.[59] In fact, given that life could simply not have begun in the absence of protein molecules, the problem of the origin of life was now essentially reducible to the origin of biological information.

And yet, what Cambridge philosopher of science Dr. Stephen Meyer suggests is that both necessity and chance-based models are

---

57. Ibid., 166
58. Stephen C. Meyer, *The Return of the God Hypothesis* (The Journal of Interdisciplinary Studies 11, 1999), 16-17
59. Ibid., 17

entirely inadequate to explain the enigma of specified sequencing within the cell, and that what we see at the very foundation of life bears a striking resemblance to a kind of biological engineering.[60] Or, in other words, prima facie, the structure and form at the very foundation of life denotes the work of an intelligent designer.

Accordingly, given that the discovery of information is habitually associated with conscious activity, Dr. Meyer further insists that when making an inference to the best explanation between multiple competing hypotheses, this lived experience must be taken into consideration.[61] Wherefore, when examining the phenomenon of protein synthesis, he ultimately summarizes his findings as such:

> After allowing considerations for all the possible combinations of functional proteins and genes, and for the maximum allowable sequencing attempts from the onset of space and time, chance-based models for chemical sequencing within the cell exceed the probabilistic resources of the universe. What is more, natural selection can only occur after an organism is able to copy itself to produce mutations, but here we are trying to explain the origin of the information that is required for a cell to copy itself. Consequently, we cannot invoke natural selection to explain the process required for natural selection, for this would be circular reasoning. Instead, the presence of specified information in DNA and protein molecules suggest a source extrinsic to physics and chemistry: when one seeks the source of the information in this morning's newspaper, or in an ancient inscription, one ultimately comes to a writer or scribe. Likewise, when a computer user traces the information on his screen back to its source, he

---

60. Ibid., 14
61. Ibid., 17-19

invariably comes to the mind of a software engineer or programmer. This also seems to be the case with the information which is found at the cellular level.[62]

---

62. Ibid.

XII. SCIENTIFIC CONSIDERATIONS: THE CAMBRIAN EXPLOSION

The Cambrian explosion is one of the most puzzling events in the history of our planet; for it not only challenges previously held timelines for the development of biological life, but it appears to contradict Neo-Darwinian models for the origin of species as well.

Case in point: within geoscientific fields of study, strata are defined as specified layers of sedimentary rock and soil that differ in material thickness and extend over hundreds and thousands of miles. Furthermore, via natural processes, each of these layers has been vertically stacked by its geological age and possesses a set of consistent internal characteristics, that distinguish it from its counterparts.

Notwithstanding, in recent years scientists have discovered a sudden appearance of intricate fossils within the Cambrian geological stratum, which include the majority of complex animal types, whilst dating to the same geological timeframe.[63]

---

63. Stephen C. Meyer, "Evolution: Bacteria to Beethoven," Discovery Institute, October 21, 2019, https://www.discovery.org/v/evolution-bacteria-to-beethoven.

However, what has truly confounded evolutionary biologists is that these discoveries have been simultaneously accompanied by an inexplicable lack of fossils in the earlier Precambrian stratum, which could serve as viable ancestral precursors.[64] As such, the disparity in complexity between a simple Precambrian organism and a fully formed Cambrian trilobite presents a major obstacle to natural selection and Neo-Darwinian apologists. Indeed, for Charles Darwin had proposed that leaps in biological complexity were accomplished via the natural selection of advantageous mutations, over many small incremental steps, yet what the Cambrian fossil discoveries suggest is the occurrence of a biological Big Bang.[65]

What is more, research scientist Dr. Douglas Axe has since complicated matters even further by successfully altering the structure of an enzyme protein, by way of manual extraction. For, because of this achievement, Dr. Axe was able to accurately predict the efficiency of the natural selection process and determine the percentage of possible mutations that could form a viable new protein molecule. However, what he would ultimately discover is that the probability of arriving at a functional new protein—the very molecule needed to accomplish the evolutionary incremental step process— was an astonishing 1 in 10^{77}.[66] As such, the probability of arriving at a functional new protein by way of unguided processes was as implausible as locating a single marked atom in a trillion Milky Way galaxies.[67] Wherefore, Dr. Axe would ultimately be forced to conclude that the number of coordinated genetic changes required to transform a simplistic Precambrian organism into a complex Cambrian trilobite could simply not have occurred in the required geological timeframe.

---

64. Ibid.
65. Ibid.
66. Ibid.
67. Ibid.

PATREM OMNIPOTENTEM

In summation, the Neo-Darwinian mechanism of natural selection is the best explanation we have for speciation and the detectable variances within the different classes of organisms. However, while it is sufficient to explain the survival of the fittest, significant questions have now been raised regarding the arrival of the fittest; [68] for, neither the sophisticated genetic code within the structure of the cell, nor the sudden appearance of biological complexity within the Cambrian geological stratum, can be suitably explained by any known natural process or event.

---

68. Stephen C. Meyer, "Dawkins's Dilemma," Stephen Meyer, Philosopher of Science, March 15, 2016, https://www.stephencmeyer.org/2016/03/25/dawkinss-dilemma/

XIII. CONCLUSION

William Shakespeare once described death as "the undiscovered country, from whose bourn no traveler has ever returned." [69] Indeed, the mystery and finality of our ultimate end has preoccupied man from the very onset of our existence. It is why we have continued to search for the purpose and consequence of our lives; why each new age has sought the supernatural, and a solution to human mortality. Admittedly, most would simply subscribe to the prevailing superstitions of their day. However, the philosophers of ancient Greece would be the first to take a markedly different approach; for they fundamentally rejected popular mythology and their surrounding culture of polytheism, to systematically address nature and existence by way of logic and reason. And yet, oddly enough, even as they had sought to thoroughly dispense with naivety and superstition, their natural philosophy would lead them nonetheless to a slew of theistic suppositions.

Take Plato, for instance; he would be among the first to posit the existence of an eternal human soul.[70] Influenced by the constancy

---

69. *Hamlet, Act 3, Scene 1*
70. Plato, *Phaedo (On the Soul)*, 100c-105d

and stability of mathematics, this founder of western philosophy would contrast the physical qualities of the natural world with metaphysical ideal forms. In fact, for Plato, reality was entirely dualistic, and, as such, was divisible into two divergent realms: a finite, volatile, transient realm, and one which was universal, immutable, and eternal.[71] However, insofar as items in the physical world were subject to change, transfiguration, defect, and death, for Plato they nevertheless participated in universal metaphysical forms, such as beauty, shape, color, cognizance, and the like.[72] For instance, the sky could be said to be participating in the ideal form of "blueness," a ball in the ideal form of "roundness," and an attractive woman in the ideal form of "beauty." Correspondingly, just as these ideal forms were abstract realities that could neither be destroyed, nor made to be "red," "square," or "unsightly," so too did Plato consider every universal metaphysical essence both permanent and congruent. Subsequently, it was within this dualistic worldview that he would ultimately contemplate the eternal fate of the human soul.

For Plato, the soul was what rendered the body living; what animated our physical makeup and what distinguished us from all insentient matter. Furthermore, given that the soul was what moved us to perceive, comprehend, and interact with the physical world at a level above all other creatures, Plato would further contend that it must be intimately connected with the ideal form of cognizance. However, if this assessment of the soul were indeed correct, and if all ideal forms were both eternally consistent and absolute, then how could the metaphysical essence that brought about the highest form of cognizant life ever be conquered by death? As such, Plato would ultimately conclude that the human soul was eternal.

---

71. Edward Feser, *Five Proofs for the Existence of God* (San Francisco, CA: Ignatius Press, 2017), 97

72. Ibid.

Then there was Aristotle, who was perhaps the greatest of all the classical philosophers; he would be the first to argue for the logical necessity of a foundational primary mover.[73] For Aristotle, all composite objects within the natural world had an innate potential to change. For example, although a cup of coffee might be warm to the touch, it was also potentially cooler.[74] However, Aristotle would also maintain that if this potential coolness was indeed to be actualized, it must be initiated by a previously actualized external force.[75] Subsequently, it would be the cooler air surrounding the cup that actualized the potential coolness of the water, not something intrinsic to the water itself.[76] Nevertheless, the cooler air surrounding the cup was also potentially otherwise, necessitating a further external actualized force. Consequently, fearing the logical implications of an infinite regress, Aristotle would ultimately conclude that the problem of potentiality demanded the solution of a fully actualized actualizer, which was, by definition, incapable of change.

Yet, still, for Aristotle, the actualization of a potential was not just a linear series of causes and effects: it was also hierarchical;[77] indeed, for how could an object have the potentiality to change if it did not first exist? In other words, although the water could be found in liquid form, it was not necessarily so; rather, the molecules, atoms, subatomic particles, and quarks which formed the water were themselves just further actualized potentials.[78] As such, Aristotle would not only propose that the potential of change was ultimately grounded by a fully actualized actualizer at the very

---

73. Aristotle, Physics, Book VIII, Part 2
74. Edward Feser, *Five Proofs for the Existence of God* (San Francisco, CA: Ignatius Press, 2017), 17
75. Ibid., 18-19
76. Ibid.
77. Ibid., 20-21
78. Ibid., 26-27

foundation of reality, but the very potential to exist, at each and every moment as well.

Furthermore, Aristotle not only saw the logical necessity for a foundational primary mover, but he also contended that natural entities were ingrained with an objective telos. For Aristotle, entities within the material realm had objective ends to which they were ultimately ordered, and, as such, they were not reducible to acts of randomness, necessity, or chance. In fact, in the end, he would go so far as to propose that one would never have complete knowledge of any item or entity, without first sufficiently identifying four "causal" agencies; namely: [79]

1. **The Material Cause**—the material composition or makeup of an entity.
2. **The Formal Cause**—an entity's recognizable shape, pattern, or form.
3. **The Efficient Cause**—the causal agency which explained how an entity came to be.
4. **The Final Cause**—the ultimate goal or end to which an entity was ordered.

What is more, even as determining, or distinguishing particular causes could be difficult in certain circumstances, Aristotle maintained nonetheless that his principles of causality were universally applicable. Indeed, for material and formal causal principles were readily identifiable, and without efficient causality, one would expect to find objects perpetually popping into and out of existence without cause or explanation.[80] Accordingly, if his principle of final causality was, in fact, illusory, then one would ultimately be unable to trust his own reasoning, as the human

---

[79]. Aristotle, *Physics, Book II, Part 3*
[80]. Edward Feser, *Five Proofs for the Existence of God* (San Francisco, CA: Ignatius Press, 2017), 42

intellect would not be ordered to the attainment of truth.[81] As such, for Aristotle, efficient and final causal principles were as equally applicable for the likes of biological organisms and inorganic matter as they were for obvious cases of human engineering and ingenuity. Case in point, in laying down routes for stability and water consumption, growing bark for protection, and accessing sunlight for the process of photosynthesis, Aristotle would contend that a sapling was attaining its end of becoming a tree.[82] Likewise, through the proper fetal development of the optic nerve, iris, retina, pupil, and lens, he would submit that the human eye was attaining its end of providing sight.[83] Further still, via the processes of erosion, weathering, drainage, and decomposition, he would assert that the earth was attaining its end of fertility, for the growth of vegetation. Consequently, as much as he rejected his surrounding culture of polytheism and superstition, via the use of natural philosophy, Aristotle concluded that the world was intelligible, marked by form, and goal driven.

Subsequently, in the 2,400 years following the philosophical revolution of ancient Greece, theists have continued to expound and expand on much of their reasoning and inference. In fact, so much so, that in the wake of historical revelation, Augustinian/Anselmian/Bonaventurian/Thomistic/Scotistic philosophy, and advances in modern science, many of these classical arguments have been both elevated and/or perfected. As such, for the modern-day theist, the existence of God is no longer a mere hypothesis—it is an all too obvious reality. For, invariably, we look around and find ourselves in a logically coherent, intelligible universe—one which had a finite beginning and whose laws and constants have been precisely tuned for the allowance of conscious life. We seem to possess an internal set of objective ethics which cannot be justified in the absence of a

---

81. Ibid., 150
82. Ibid., 217
83. Ibid., 219

supreme moral authority. Our intrinsic desires for truth, happiness, and justice transcend the capabilities of the natural world. We see marks of intelligence, engineering, and design at every level of nature and being—including unexplainable complexity within the fossil record and at the foundation of life itself. By way of natural philosophy, we arrive at the necessity of an immutable and unchanging foundational primary mover, or an eternal uncaused cause, whose characteristics reflect the traditional divine attributes.

Indeed, although many skeptics would have you believe otherwise, belief in the existence of God is much more than a nonsensical or naïve superstition—in fact, on the contrary, it appears that the opposite is true, for if one dares to utilize philosophy and theology alongside the physical sciences, a coherent and compelling case can be made for belief in the existence of God; one that is eminently rational, in accord with mankind's best deductions about the nature of the universe and observant of the principles of reason.

So, perhaps there is a reason for hope; perhaps there is a resolution to our human condition after all.

> "A game is being played at the extremity of this infinite distance where heads or tails will turn up. What will you wager?...you must wager. It is not optional. You are embarked. Which will you choose then? Let us see. Since you must choose, let us see which interests you least. You have two things to lose, the true and the good; and two things to stake, your reason and your will, your knowledge, and your happiness; and your nature has two things to shun, error and misery. Your reason is no more shocked in choosing one rather than the other since you must of necessity choose. This is one point settled. But your happiness? Let us weigh the gain and the loss in wagering that God is. Let us estimate these two chances. If you gain,

you gain all; if you lose, you lose nothing. Wager, then, without hesitation that He is." (Blaise Pascal, *Pensées 233,* A.D. 1670)

BOOK I BIBLIOGRAPHY

Christian Apologetics and Research Ministry, https://carm.org

Craig, William Lane. *Reasonable Faith: Christian Truth and Apologetics*, 3rd ed. Wheaton, IL: Crossway, 2008.

Discovery Institute, https://www.discovery.org

Feser, Edward. *Five Proofs for the Existence of God.* San Francisco, CA: Ignatius Press, 2017.

———. *The Last Superstition: A Refutation of the New Atheism.* South Bend, IN: St. Augustine's Press, 2008.

Dostoevsky, Fyodor. *The Brothers Karamazov.* Translated by Constance Garnett. New York, NY: The Lowell Press, 2009.

Lennox, John C. *God's Undertaker: Has Science Buried God?* Oxford: Lion books, 2009.

Meyer, Stephen C. *Darwin's Doubt: The Explosive Origin of Animal Life, and the Case for Intelligent Design.* New York, NY: HyperOne, 2014.

———. *The Return of the God Hypothesis.* Journal of Interdisciplinary Studies 11, 1999.

———. *Signature in the Cell: DNA and the Evidence for Intelligent Design.* New York, NY: HyperOne, 2009.

Reasonable Faith with William Lane, https://www.reasonablefaith.org

Ratzinger, Joseph. *Introduction to Christianity.* Edited by J.R. Foster. New York, NY: Herder and Herder, 1970.

Ross, Hugh. *Why The Universe Is the Way It Is.* Grand Rapids, MI: Baker Publishing, 2008.

Stephen C. Meyer, https://stephencmeyer.org

Strange Notions, https://strangenotions.com/god-exists/

Word on Fire Catholic Ministries, https://www.wordonfire.org

BOOK II:
FILIUM DEI UNIGENITUM
(THE ONLY BEGOTTEN SON OF GOD)

I. RELIGIOUS PLURALISM

If a compelling case can indeed be made for belief in the existence of God—if we can demonstrate that a fully actualized actualizer is requisite for grounding finite reality—then, as a result, obvious questions begin to arise. For instance, which, if any, of the religions today has the correct understanding of who, or what, this primary mover is? Or is it possible that they could all be correct? Aren't all religions essentially saying the same thing anyway?

In truth, as modern societies have continued to diversify, it is undeniable that they have in turn become more pluralistic in nature. So much so, that in most of the Western world, people of different creeds and cultures are now able to peacefully coexist, exchange ideas and insights, and express their personal beliefs freely. Nevertheless, because exposure to different interests, convictions, and lifestyles has been beneficial in many regards, societal pluralism has also unfortunately given rise to an erroneous perspective on religion; namely, that all religions contain a piece of the truth, yet none have a monopoly on it— for, at the end of the day, each religion is simply a different route to an identical destination. However, insofar as it is possible for differing religions to possess general commonalities or to agree upon specific doctrinal teachings, religious pluralism is an untenable concept for a variety of reasons:

1. Each of the major world religions makes an absolute claim to the truth—all of which are irreconcilable with the absolute claims of the others. In fact, so much is this the case, that these religions completely contradict one another on fundamental issues such as the existence of God, the nature of God, the number of gods, the will of God, the role of God within finite reality, the reality and authenticity of divine revelations, the destiny and final destination of mankind, morality and moral obligations, the existence of free will, and the path to eternal salvation. Subsequently, any attempt to either harmonize or synergize such distinct and contrasting claims would be entirely illogical, as it would violate the law of non-contradiction.

2. Christianity, Judaism, and Islam all simultaneously teach that a singular God, of moral perfection both created and sustains our universe. As such, it must necessarily follow that such a God, in His omnibenevolent and omniscient nature, could not actively will the existence of a religion that was fallacious or objectively false. Given, then, that each of these religions lays claim to distinct and contradictory divine revelations, it is logically impossible that they could all be correct; indeed, for how could an all-knowing and impeccable God produce three antithetical revelations? Wherefore, when considering the claims of the major monotheistic religions, there are only two possible outcomes: A) One of the monotheistic religions is true, or B) All are false.

3. Religious pluralism inherently implies that the adherents of individual religions are simply ignorant of the claims of their counterparts, and, as such, the decision to follow the teachings

of a specific religious tradition ultimately derives from a lack of exposure to, or understanding of, the truth found within all others. Nevertheless, access to information has never been more readily available than it is in today's world, as exposure to a diversity of religious claims is made possible via global internet access, streaming services, cable television, films and documentaries, public education, municipal libraries, widespread recreational travel, missionary work, and by way of natural migration/immigration. What is more, as much as individual upbringings, historical backdrops, and geographical locations can certainly influence religious affiliation, religious claims are not reducible to the motives for one's personal belief. Subsequently, just as it would be a logical fallacy to disregard religious pluralism as the erroneous byproduct of 21st century, western, heterogeneous societies, so to would it be a fallacy to reduce a religion and its claims to a mere product of birthdate, birthplace, upbringing, etc.[1]

4. In attempting to synthesize dissimilar claims, the religious pluralist unwittingly creates a unique and novel religion. Or in other words, because they profess to see the larger picture or the commonality between contrasting belief systems, religious pluralism unwittingly puts forth another absolute claim to the truth. Consequently, religious pluralism should not be seen as a compromise or an accommodation, but rather, as an additional and competing religious claim.

In summation, the proof of any pudding is in the eating. Wherefore, if any religion is to be trusted, it must produce sufficient evidence to support its supernatural claims. However, each religion must accomplish this task on its own individual merit, for religious

---

1. I.e., *The Genetic Fallacy,* which is the acceptance or rejection of argument based upon its origin rather than its content.

pluralism simply cannot exist between fundamentally opposed belief systems. Religious pluralism, therefore, is not a viable solution to the quest for truth—at least if we hope to remain within the boundaries which reason imposes upon us. Indeed, either one of the world's religions is true, or else they all are false. [2]

---

[2]. "Comparative religion has indeed allowed us to compare religions—and to contrast them. Fifty years ago, it set out to prove that all religions were much the same; generally proving, alternately, that they were all equally worthy and that they were all equally worthless." (G.K Chesterton, *Saint Thomas Aquinas* (Mineola, NY: Dover Publications, 2009), 70

II. SPIRITUAL, BUT NOT RELIGIOUS

After religious pluralism, perhaps the most common substitute for organized religion is the embrace of a detached spirituality, wherein a person simply claims to be "spiritual," without capitulating to an overbearing religious institutionalism. Admittedly, at face value, the notion of a personalized spirituality can be extremely attractive, in that it presents itself as an empowering and transformative anti-establishment alternative to conventional religious affiliation. However, the idea that one need only look within himself to negotiate the lasting consequences of eternity, is far more superficial and ostentatious than it is a serious substitution.

Case in point: a personalized spirituality implicitly rejects the notion of a higher or ultimate authority outside the individual self; thousands of years of theological speculation, philosophical postulations, and extractions from natural teleology are simply discounted, and instead, all spiritual convictions and metaphysical truths are established via one's subjective feelings and sentiments. What's more, when one projects his own fallible and subjective belief system onto God, he also renders the need for personal conversion and growth completely obsolete. Or, in other words, by rejecting the validity and credibility of conventional religious affiliation, one essentially becomes his own god and, thereby, is held accountable only to himself. Thusly, no matter how one considers it, a personalized spirituality ultimately devolves into equating truth and morality with one's own preferences.

In short, the phrase "spiritual but not religious" is rather hollow, as it simply allows one to say that he believes in a transcendental power without having to take any action or responsibility for his convictions. To be sure, if in an authentic pursuit of the truth (where one is truly seeking comprehensive answers to life's most pertinent questions) it would be an absurd course of action to revert within oneself wholly and unreservedly to try and solve the preeminent mysteries that exist within finite reality. [3]

---

3. "Of all the conceivable forms of enlightenment, the worst is what these people call the Inner Light. Of all the horrible religions, the most horrible is the worship of the God within." (G.K Chesterton, *Orthodoxy* (Mineola, NY: Dover Publications, 2020), 68

III. THE NECESSITY OF GRACE

Whereas each of the major world religions makes distinct and contrasting claims, all seemingly subscribe to a single core tenet of either merit or gratuitous grace. To be sure, belief systems of either category can contain wisdom, natural insight, and virtue; however, one must nevertheless be cognizant of these underlying precepts, as they have significant ramifications. So much so, that if creation, relation, reconciliation, or justification are even remotely divorced from the unmerited gift of divine grace, it invariably results in an irreparable defect or an irredeemable deficiency.

Case in point: consider both Buddhism and Hinduism. As each religion has continued to flourish over the course of several millennia, the precepts of Karma have been subsequently spread throughout India, China, and a majority of Southeast Asia. As such, within these regions, there is widespread belief in a cosmic law of equity, wherein acts of virtue are ultimately rewarded, whilst acts of evil are ultimately punished.[4] However, these rewards and punishments are not believed to come to complete fruition within

---

4. Wendy D. O'Flaherty, *Karma, and Rebirth in Classical Indian Traditions* (Los Angeles, CA: University of California Press, 1980), XI-XXV

this life, but rather, they are realized through a process of rebirth and reincarnation until a state of enlightenment is achieved.[5] Wherefore, even as the repercussions of one's actions may not be fully evident in this life, Karmic retribution will never fail to materialize in the next. Admittedly, at face value, the concept of inescapable Karma is extremely powerful, in that it satisfies our innate sense of justice, whilst appearing to be both impartial and fair. Nevertheless, if the doctrines of rebirth and reincarnation are, in fact, correct, then the concept of human dignity will have also lost its ontological foundation. Indeed, for if individual consciousness is truly transferable between all forms of sentient life, then how could distinctions of value exist between humanity and all other creatures?[6] Likewise, if pain and suffering are truly reducible to the just consequences of offenses committed in a current or previous life, then why should acts of charity and compassion be lauded and/or incentivized?

Furthermore, this form of meritocratic system is not confined to religions of the East, for even as Islam incorporates elements of grace, it is ultimately structured upon the merits of obedience. In fact, so much so, that for those who subscribe to the Islamic faith, one is believed to be either rewarded or punished in direct accordance with his submission to the will of Allah, as laid down by the prophet Muhammad. For example, consider the following passages from the Quran:

---

5. Ibid.

6. "For what is so marvelous as to believe that men could have been changed into the forms of beasts? How much more marvelous, however, would it be that the soul which rules man should take on itself the nature of a beast so opposed to that of man, and being capable of reason should be able to pass over to an irrational animal, than that the form of the body should have been changed? You yourselves, who teach these things, destroy what you teach. For you have given up the production of these portentous conversions by means of magic incantations." (Saint Ambrose of Milan, On the Death of Satyrus 2:127, A.D. 379)

> Nay, whoever submits himself completely to Allah, and is the doer of good, shall have his reward with his Lord. No fear shall come upon such, neither shall they grieve.
>
> ...anyone who accepts a way other than submission as his religion, it will not be accepted from him, and in the Hereafter, he will be with the losers. (Quran 2:112-113, 3:85)

Wherefore, even as Islam professes belief in a gracious and merciful God, the Quranic writings bear witness to a master-slave relationship with Allah, which is paralleled within Sharia law and throughout Islamic theocracies at large. As such, insofar as they subscribe to monotheism and principles of clemency and compassion, Islamic theocracies have scarcely resembled the structure and practices of their Judeo-Christian counterparts. For instance, Sharia law has not only historically permitted practices such as sex slavery, child marriage, polygamy, and mandatory bodily veiling but it has advanced them as being in conformity with the customs and teachings of Muhammad himself.[7] Likewise, because of its precepts, Islam is a religion which has been instinctively militant, and which was historically spread by the sword.[8] Islam has also sanctioned the political subjugation and

---

7. Robert Spencer and Phyllis Chesler, *The Violent Oppression of Women in Islam* (Los Angeles, CA: David Horowitz Freedom Centre, 2007), 12-18

8. Those who founded sects committed to false doctrines proceeded in a way that is opposite to this. The point is clear in the case of Muhammad. He seduced the people by promises of carnal pleasure to which the concupiscence of the flesh goads us. His teaching also contained precepts that were in conformity with his promises, and he gave free rein to carnal pleasure. In all this, as is not unexpected, he was obeyed by carnal men... [Furthermore], he did not bring forth any signs produced in a supernatural way, which alone fittingly gives witness to divine inspiration; for a visible action that can be only divine reveals an invisibly inspired teacher of truth. On the contrary, Muhammad said that he was sent in the power of his arms—which are signs not lacking even to robbers and tyrants." (St. Thomas Aquinas, *Summa Contra Gentiles* 1:6:4, A.D. 1259)

taxation of religious minorities,[9] as well as subscribed to tenets of consequentialism (e.g., belief that the ends justify the means).[10]

What is more, despite their many dissimilarities or their contentious/hostile past, Judaism, much like Islam, has historically held that the path to salvation lies in a supernatural faith in Yahweh, and the strict observance of Mosaic Law. Correspondingly, in contrast to their Christian counterparts, who maintain that the Old Testament prophecies have been fulfilled in full, Judaism awaits the arrival of a messiah, to bring forth a period of peace, unity, and restoration. Notwithstanding, modern-day Rabbinic Judaism no longer has access to the system of blood atonement sacrifice which was laid down by Moses in the temple—nor has it for 1,950 years. As such, in the likely scenario that an observant Jew fails to perfectly fulfill some 613 Mosaic laws, then he has no recourse to a Passover means by which redemption can be found via the application of innocent blood.[11] Furthermore, century after century, millennia after millennia, before the time of Christ, prophets arose from amongst the Jewish faithful, foretelling of the Messiah to come. And yet, since the days of Malachi in 400 B.C., these warnings have mysteriously subsided.[12] Consequently, if modern Jewish authorities are indeed correct, and Israel's messiah is still yet to come, then we must reconcile the fact that God went from providing perpetual messianic prophecies via Abraham, Moses, David, Isaiah,

---

9. For example, the "Jizya tax," which was historically levied against all non-Muslim religious for permission to practice their faith and as material proof of their willing submission to the Islamic state.

10. For example, the Islamic ethical principle known as "Taqiya," which allows one to commit a sinful act if the aim is a pious outcome.

11. "The [Mosaic] law was therefore given in order that grace might be sought; grace was given, in order that the law might be fulfilled. Now it was not through any fault of its own that the law was not fulfilled, but by the fault of the carnal mind; and this fault was to be demonstrated by the law and healed by grace." (Saint Augustine of Hippo, On Spirit and the Epistle 34, A.D. 412)

12 This section only refers to the messianic prophesies within the protocanonical books of scripture, as they are the books which have been accepted within Rabbinic Judaism.

Jeremiah, Ezekiel, Daniel, Hosea, Amos, Micah, Joel, Zechariah, and Malachi to a staggering silence for more than 2,400 years.

To this we now contrast Christian beliefs, which have been formed through a system of grace. Within Christianity, all possess an inviolable dignity which was bestowed upon them by their maker, for the image of God was inscribed into human corporeality in anticipation of the Incarnation. Furthermore, eternal rewards or punishments are not held to be a product of obedience/submission alone, as all fall short of the divine standard of ethics and, as such, are unable to merit salvation. In fact, our human propensity towards sin indelibly hinders the will and the intellect from adequately restraining our vices, and thus, if left to be judged by our merits alone, we can be certain of a just condemnation. However, even as impropriety and the inclination to sin preclude us from perfectly fulfilling the moral law, God, in His mercy, has brought us redemption through the blood atonement sacrifice of His Son. As such, within Christianity alone has God become flesh and entered our human suffering, and within Christianity alone has divinity been crucified, that we might reside in His love forever. Wherefore, in contrast to religions of merit, where one receives the just punishment he deserves, in this religion of grace one is mercifully offered the unmerited reward he does not deserve:

> For no human being will be justified in his sight by deeds prescribed by the law, for through the law comes the knowledge of sin. But now, apart from law, the righteousness of God has been disclosed, and is attested by the law and the prophets, the righteousness of God through faith in Jesus Christ for all who believe. For there is no distinction, since all have sinned and fall short of the glory of God; they are now justified by his grace as a gift, through the redemption that is in Christ Jesus, whom God put forward as a sacrifice of atonement by his blood, effective

> through faith. He did this to show his righteousness, because in his divine forbearance he had passed over the sins previously committed; it was to prove at the present time that he himself is righteous and that he justifies the one who has faith in Jesus. (Romans 3:20-26, NRSVCE)

Yet, still, even as grace and sacrificial atonement have ultimately purchased our redemption, within Christianity it also comes with a caveat; namely, that we are compelled to become reflections of God's grace so all might repent and be saved. As such, the Christian faithful are called to forgiveness and mercy, as we ourselves have been forgiven by God. Likewise, we are called to reach out to the suffering with a charitable hand, as an unconditional love for others both reflects and glorifies His righteousness. To be sure, there have been many instances of perversion and corruption throughout two thousand years of continuance; however, Christianity, at its best, has uniquely demonstrated these fundamental precepts up through the centuries. In fact, so much so, that in striving to emulate the grace and sacrifices of Christ, the Christian faithful have provided more health care, education, shelter, food, and relief than any other non-governmental body in the world.[13] What is more, the precepts of Christianity have not only given rise to unprecedented care for the vulnerable and downtrodden, they have also formed the foundation for the most equitable civilizations in the history of human existence. Subsequently, even as Christianity, via its reliance on grace, can lay claim to cohesion and consistency, it is the fruits that this grace has in turn produced that truly distinguish it from all other religions.

---

13. Matthew Kelly, *Rediscover Catholicism: A Spiritual Guide to Living with Passion & Purpose* (New York, NY: Beacon Publishing, 2014), 304

IV. THE TRINITY [14]

In contrast to the doctrines of its monotheistic counterparts, Christianity's teaching on the nature of God is unique and comparatively confounding. Indeed, for where a follower of Judaism or Islam might claim that God's nature is to love, the Christian religion instead professes that God, Himself, IS love. Or, in other words, within Christianity, God not only actively wills the good of all mankind, but He is also believed to be the subsistent source of love and relation itself. As such, for the Christian faithful, love is not simply an individual characteristic within the broader nature of God; rather, it is the foundation of His subsistent being. Furthermore, although this distinction may appear to be inconsequential, it has profound theological ramifications, for as C.S. Lewis so astutely notes in his treatise on *Mere Christianity*, it is this sui generis Christian claim which lays the groundwork for the doctrine of the Trinity:

---

14. This chapter includes references to a 2006 homily given by Bishop Robert Barron. For a full treatment, see: Bishop Robert Barron, "God is Love," Word on Fire Catholic Ministries, June 11, 2006, https://.wordonfire.org/videos/sermons/god-is-love/

All sorts of people are fond of repeating the Christian statement that 'God is love'. But they seem not to notice that the words 'God is love' have no real meaning unless God contains at least two Persons, in that Love is something that one person has for another. As such, if God was just a single person, then before the world was made, He was not love. This is, perhaps, the most important difference between Christianity and all other religions: that in Christianity, God is not a static thing—not even a person—but a dynamic, pulsating activity, a life, almost a kind of drama. In fact, the union between God the Father and God the Son is such a living concrete thing that this union is itself a Person, and thus, that which grows out of the joint life of the Father and the Son is also the third of the three Persons who are God. Subsequently, the Christian God consists of a divine Spirit of love, which eternally flows between the Father and the Son. [15]

Notwithstanding, as much as the reality of an infinite Fatherly love flowing through the Spirit to His Son offers remarkable insight into the inner personhood of God, it even more so provides a stunning revelation about the genesis of all creation—in that long before the universe began, there was already relationship and love eternal. To be sure, this eternal love then manifested itself throughout the entirety of the cosmos, in all its complementarity, interrelation, pageantry, and wonder. Wherefore, by the very framework of our creation and via our unique reflection of the divine nature, mankind was predestined to love in imitation of the triune God. In fact, so great was the love of the triune God that He not only willed all

---

15. C.S Lewis, *Mere Christianity,* (New York, NY: MacMillan Publishing Company, 1986), 151-152

creation into being, but so great was His desire for eternal relation with us that He afforded us the capacity to love:

> Beloved, let us love one another, because love is from God; everyone who loves is born of God and knows God. Whoever does not love does not know God, for God is love. God's love was revealed among us in this way: God sent his only Son into the world so that we might live through him. In this is love, not that we loved God but that he loved us and sent his Son to be the atoning sacrifice for our sins. Beloved, since God loved us so much, we also ought to love one another. No one has ever seen God; if we love one another, God lives in us, and his love is perfected in us. By this we know that we abide in him and he in us, because he has given us of his Spirit. (1 John 4:7-13, NRSVCE)

Further still, as Saint John so eloquently notes, whereas we ultimately fall short in our imitation of the divine love, through the salvific sacrifice of God, the Son, we can be reunited with Him, for God, the Father, was so on fire with the Spirit, that He sent the Son to suffer to gather us back into the divine love. Consequently, for the sake of our salvation and through the Incarnation of Jesus Christ, God has revealed Himself to be a triune play of three persons, in one essence: God from God, light from light, and consubstantial with one another.

In summation, the Holy Trinity is much more than a far-reaching abstraction; it is not some inconsequential doctrinal concept, or a matter of relevance only to prominent theologians. Rather, Trinitarian doctrine reveals the very grounds of reality, the motive and means for all creation, and how God has ultimately chosen to redeem the human race. Surreptitiously, it also explains to us who God is, as opposed to what He is, which is of fundamental importance if we hope to understand, let alone love Him.

Admittedly, the Christian concept of a triune God can be both intimidating and confounding. However, perhaps it is expectedly so; for, insofar as He has graciously afforded us the capacity to reason, how presumptuous it would be for us to assume that we could fully grasp the divine? [16]

---

16. "The true objects of enjoyment, then, are the Father and the Son and the Holy Spirit, who are at the same time the Trinity, one Being, supreme above all, and common to all who enjoy Him— that is, if He were an object, and not rather the cause of all objects, or indeed even if He is the cause of all. For it is not easy to find a name that will suitably express so great excellence, unless it is better to speak in this way: The Trinity, one God, of whom are all things, through whom are all things, in whom are all things. Thus, the Father and the Son and the Holy Spirit, and each of these by Himself, is God, and at the same time they are all one God; and each of them by Himself is a complete substance, and yet they are all one substance. The Father is not the Son nor the Holy Spirit; the Son is not the Father nor the Holy Spirit; the Holy Spirit is not the Father nor the Son: but the Father is only Father, the Son is only Son, and the Holy Spirit is only Holy Spirit. To all three belong the same eternity, the same unchangeableness, the same majesty, the same power. In the Father is unity, in the Son equality, in the Holy Spirit the harmony of unity and equality; and these three attributes are all one because of the Father, all equal because of the Son, and all harmonious because of the Holy Spirit." (Saint Augustine of Hippo, *On Christian Doctrine* 1:5, A.D. 397)

V. THE PROBLEM OF EVIL AND INNOCENT SUFFERING [17]

Inasmuch as Christianity lays claim to a God of love, the difficult realities of evil and innocent suffering present a theological problem which has troubled Christian apologists for millennia; for, admittedly, with the presence of such horror and agony in our world it would be easy for one to assume, that an omniscient and omnipotent God is either the cause of said suffering, or at the very least, indifferent to it. In fact, even the great Saint Thomas Aquinas would submit:

> It seems that God cannot exist; because if one of two contraries be infinite, the other would be altogether destroyed. But the name God means that He is infinite goodness. If, therefore, God existed, there would be no evil

---

17. This chapter includes references to a 2011 commentary by Bishop Robert Barron. For a full treatment, see: Bishop Robert Barron, "God, Tsunamis, and the Problem of Evil," Word on Fire Catholic Ministries, March 21, 2011, https://www.wordonfire.org/videos/bishop-barrons-commentaries/god-tsunamis-and-the-problem-of-evil/

or suffering discoverable; but there is evil and suffering in the world. Therefore, God cannot exist. [18]

Subsequently, how are we to reconcile these two seemingly contradictory realities, in the face of such a forceful objection?

In truth, at first glance, the reality of omnibenevolence certainly seems to be at odds with a fallen creation. Nevertheless, if we juxtapose the nature of God and evil, we soon find resolutions to these apparent tensions. For instance, if God truly is a fully actualized actualizer, then He cannot be the source of evil, in that evil itself, in the strict metaphysical sense, is simply a privation of the good. Or, in other words, just as a cavity exists as a defect in the tooth, so too is evil a lack of an integrity of being that ought to have existed. As such, it would not be possible for God—who is subsistent being and goodness itself— to either directly cause or actively will any lack thereof. Accordingly, it is also necessary to draw a firm distinction between the active will of God and the permissive will of God, in that God, in His providence, could permit certain evils to bring about some greater good. [19] What is more, if we can keep these distinctions in mind, regarding the nature and will of God, it is possible to make several additional observations about the realities of evil and innocent suffering:

1. For authentic love to exist in the world, or for any genuine relationship to be had, God must grant us the freedom of choice and individual or personal agency.

---

18. Saint Thomas Aquinas, *Summa Theologiae* I, Q. 2, A. 3, A.D. 1266
19. "In this universe, even what is called evil, when it is rightly ordered and kept in its place, commends the good more eminently, since good things yield greater pleasure and praise when compared to the bad things. For the Omnipotent God, whom even the heathen acknowledges as the Supreme Power over all, would not allow any evil in His works, unless in His omnipotence and goodness, as the Supreme Good, he is able to bring forth good out of evil. What, after all, is anything we call evil except the privation of good?" (Saint Augustine, *Enchiridion on Faith, Hope, and Charity 3:11*, A.D. 420)

Indeed, for true love necessitates the possibility of rejection, self-reflection, and personal development, and, as such, the very concept of pre-programmed or mandated love is as irrational as a circular square, a married bachelor, or an elderly infant. Nevertheless, the capacity for free choice also comes at a cost, as personal agency allows one to choose evil over goodness. Wherefore, if God had chosen to create a world without evil, it would have been one which was incapable of love.

2. God, in His omniscience, could have chosen to create a world which was suitable for fallen creatures—one conducive to humility, remorse, and reconciliation. As such, natural evils, while appearing to be senseless sources of suffering, could in fact play an essential role within creation. For example, disasters and droughts, while admittedly tragic, also serve to demonstrate that we are not in control. Moreover, they force us to recognize our own fragility, and compel us to seek out a source of ultimate comfort. Furthermore, the existence of these natural evils also manifests that the concept of an earthly utopia is an unattainable fantasy, and that our desire to live in perfect serenity is inescapably contingent upon the existence of an omnipotent God. In fact, how could one yearn for utopia in the first place, if he had not experienced an imperfect creation?

3. What might appear to us to be finite events of misfortune or injustice can oftentimes serve as a route of access to a deeper and more meaningful life. For instance, moments of suffering are frequently followed

by periods of achievement and growth. Likewise, times of despair bring forth courage and compassion and afford us the opportunity to reevaluate what is most important in our lives. Furthermore, what we, in our limited capacity, may regard as a loss might be seen as a gain from a different or later perspective. In fact, any suggestion that we could fully comprehend the weight and consequences of the acts and events in our lives would be, prima facie, a preposterous assertion. Indeed, for in the eyes of eternity, our brief existence is but one paragraph of one chapter of a near infinite catalog of books. And thus, whatever we experience in our day-to-day lives must be understood in the context of an infinitely wider and more complex bigger picture.

4. To accept the existence of the Christian God is to acknowledge a life beyond this one, wherein one embraces the possibility of an everlasting state of joy on the far side of the eschaton. Subsequently, within Christianity, there is a hope of a final deliverance, wherein nothing we experience in this life—not even the most agonizing suffering imaginable— is ultimately beyond redemption. Case in point: the day that Christ was betrayed, abandoned, unjustly condemned, scourged, and then mercilessly crucified, is a day that Christians refer to as Good Friday—a designation that could only make sense considering the resurrection. As such, when one accepts Christianity, he not only places his faith in a God who willingly takes part in the very worst of human suffering, but in a God who is ultimately capable of the redemption of all things as well.

FILIUM DEI UNIGENITUM

In summation, the realities of evil and innocent suffering seem to present a substantial objection to the Christian concept of God, in that they are seemingly needless and unjust. However, considering the prior observations, perhaps the ultimate question isn't why we are permitted to suffer, but rather, to whom should we turn amid our suffering? [20]

---

20. "Would that men come at last to see that it is quite impossible to reach the thicket of the riches and wisdom of God except by first entering the thicket of much suffering, wherein the soul finds its consolation and desire. The soul that longs for divine wisdom chooses first, and in truth, to enter the thicket of the cross." (Saint John of the Cross, *A Spiritual Canticle of the Soul and the Bridegroom Christ,* Stanza XXVI: 13)

VI. THE HISTORICITY OF JESUS CHRIST

Notwithstanding the prominence of the gospel accounts, details of the life of Jesus Christ are not confined to the biblical texts; indeed, a variety of ancient documents make claims about both Christ and Christianity. As such, not only are there a host of ancient sources which attest to the historicity of Jesus Christ, but they arise from authors of varying backgrounds, standings, and beliefs, as well. Furthermore, as much as various prejudices and partialities would predictably give rise to conflicting testimony, we are able to extrapolate probable historical facts from the sum of these independent accounts. However, to view each source in its proper historical context, and account for any such predisposition, we must first divide the aforementioned authors into three distinct categories:

Hostile Sources—Sources consisting of authors who are openly opposed to Christianity.

Impartial Sources—Sources consisting of authors who wrote of Jesus for the purposes of historical documentation; they are neither for nor against Christianity.

Associated Sources—Sources consisting of authors who are staunch defenders of the Christian faith.

Hostile Sources and Examples of their Claims [21]

Celsus of Greece—a second-century Greek philosopher and stark opponent of the Christian faith; Celsus would write a discourse criticizing Christianity, which he entitled *The True Word*. Within said discourse, Celsus would claim, that Jesus had been an illegitimate son of adultery, and that He had learned sorcery from the Egyptians.[22]

Cornelius Tacitus—a prominent Roman senator and historian from the late first century A.D; Tacitus would author a historical biography of the Roman empire, which he entitled *The Annals*. Although ultimately critical of Christianity, Tacitus would nonetheless recount that Jesus had been called the Christ and that He was put to death under the Roman prelate, Pontius Pilate.[23]

Second Century Rabbinic Authorities—the varying authors of a lengthy document of Jewish religious law, which was entitled *The Talmud* and completed around 200 A.D. Although a central text for Rabbinic Judaism, this document would nonetheless specify that Jesus was born in the town of Nazareth and was executed as an adult.[24]

Claudius Galenus—a second-century Greek physician and prominent critic of Christianity; Galenus reflects upon Jesus and his followers in several of his writings. Predictably, most of his claims

---

21. Hostile source examples cited from: Josh McDowell, *A Ready Defense: The Best of Josh McDowell*, comp. Bill Wilson (Nashville, TN: Thomas Nelson Inc., 2021), 191-203.
22. Celsus of Greece, *The True Word [Quoted in Origen of Alexandria, Against Celsus 1:28]*, C. A.D. 175
23. Cornelius Tacitus, *The Annals 15:44*, A.D. 116
24. Babylonian Talmud, *Tractate Sanhedrin 43a*, C. A.D. 200

would be derogatory and disparaging; however, Claudius would nonetheless note that Jesus was a teacher like Moses and that His followers believed in "undemonstrated" laws.[25]

Impartial Sources and Examples of their Claims [26]

Flavius Josephus—a distinguished Romano-Jewish historian from the late first century A.D; Josephus would author a historical commentary entitled *The Antiquities of the Jews*. Within said commentary, Josephus would specify that Jesus had been called the Christ and that he had a brother named James.[27]

Gaius Suetonius—a notable Roman scholar and historian from the early second century A.D; Suetonius would compose a biography of Roman Caesars, which he entitled *The 12 Caesars*. Although his biography would concentrate on the Roman emperors, Suetonius would also record that Jesus was called the Christ and that He had a sizeable Jewish following in Rome.[28]

Phlegon of Tralles—a second-century Greek biographer who was notably freed by emperor Hadrian; Phlegon would write a series of historical chronicles which included details about the life of Christ. Amongst other things, Phlegon would document that Jesus had a following of core disciples and that He had been able to predict the future.[29]

---

25. Claudius Galenus, *On the Pulse 2:4*, C. A.D. 176
26. Impartial source examples cited from: Josh McDowell, *A Ready Defense: The Best of Josh McDowell*, comp. Bill Wilson (Nashville, TN: Thomas Nelson Inc., 2021), 191-203
27. Flavius Josephus, *The Antiquity of the Jews 20:9:1*, A.D. 94
28. Gaius Suetonius, *The 12 Caesars 16;25*, A.D. 121
29. Phlegon of Tralles, *Chronicles* 14, *[Quoted in Origen of Alexandria, Against Celsus 2:14]*, C. A.D. 140

Mara Bar Serapion—an obscure stoic philosopher who hailed from the Roman province of Syria; Serapion would draft a letter to his son in 73 A.D. Within said letter, Serapion would mention that Jesus had been called a wise king and that He was executed unjustly.[30]

Associated Sources and Examples of their Claims

The Didache—an anonymous Christian treatise composed in the mid-first century A.D; the Didache is the oldest surviving catechism on Christian ethics, baptism, communion, and Church organization. Amongst other things, the Didache would note that Jesus was the eternal servant of God, that He was to return on the last day, and that He instituted the baptismal act.[31]

Clement of Rome—a preeminent first-century Bishop of Rome and a disciple of the Apostle Peter; Clement would author an epistle to the church of Corinth in 95 A.D. In said letter, Clement would record that Jesus Christ was the Son of God, that His blood was shed for the salvation of the world, and that His Apostles proclaim His message.[32]

Ignatius of Antioch—a prominent first-century bishop of Antioch and a learned disciple of the Apostles; Ignatius would draft a series of instructional epistles in the early second century A.D. In said letters, Ignatius would claim that Jesus Christ was the divine savior, that He was born of the Virgin Mary, and that He established a universal Church.[33]

---

30. Mara Bar Serapion, *Epistle to Serapion*, A.D. 93
31. Didache 1-16, A.D. 70
32. Clement of Rome, *Epistle to the Corinthians 1-65*, A.D. 95
33. Ignatius of Antioch, *Epistle to the Ephesians 1-20*, A.D. 110

Polycarp of Smyrna—a distinguished first-century bishop of Smyrna and a disciple of the Apostle John; Polycarp would author an epistle to the church of Philippi in the early second century A.D. In said epistle, Polycarp would note that Jesus was the Lord of heaven and earth, that He suffered crucifixion for our sins, and that He was raised from the dead in accordance with the Scriptures.[34]

In truth, the antecedent summary of these ancient documents is far from an exhaustive synopsis; however, even this cursory overview is sufficient to demonstrate an assortment of disparate claims. Nevertheless, in spite of these obvious discrepancies and dissimilarities, it is also necessary to note that there was one detail which was uniformly accepted as a verifiable historical fact; namely, that the historical person, Jesus of Nazareth, did indeed exist. As such, in accordance with this unanimous testimony, nearly all historians of antiquity agree that the historicity of Jesus Christ is, in effect, a historical certainty.[35] Wherefore, it is no longer historically viable to suggest that Jesus Christ did not exist. The man Jesus certainly existed; the only questions concern the details of His life and ministry.

Fortunately, there are several additional details of His life that are attested to by multiple unaffiliated ancient sources, which lends credence to the historical authenticity of the Gospels and the accuracy of the scriptural accounts. In fact, so much so, that many historians have reached a consensus of sorts, on a basic outline of Jesus's life, which parallels eight separate biblical claims about the person and ministry of Christ. These claims include: [36]

---

34. Polycarp of Smyrna, *Epistle to the Philippians 1-14*, C. A.D. 135
35. Bart D. Ehrman, *Forged: Writing the Name of God— Why the Bible's Authors Are Not Who We Think They Are* (New York, NY: HyperOne, 2011), 285
36. Bruce Chilton and Craig A. Evans, *Authenticating the Activities of Jesus* (Boston, MA: Brill Academia Publishers Inc, 2002), 3

1. That He was a Galilean who preached and healed.
2. That His activities were confined to Galilee and Judea.
3. That He was baptized by John the Baptist.
4. That He had a following of core disciples.
5. That He had a controversy in the Jewish temple.
6. That He was crucified by the Roman prelate, Pontius Pilate.
7. That after His death, his disciples continued His teachings.
8. That some of His disciples were also persecuted and/or martyred.

VII. CHRIST IN THE GOSPEL ACCOUNTS [37]

In modern times it has become increasingly fashionable to reduce the person of Jesus Christ to a great teacher, prophet, or guru. Nevertheless, whereas He admittedly assumed a finite nature, and entered human suffering, Christ also distinguished himself from all other religious founders, with His radical claims of divinity. Indeed, via persistent proclamations and miraculous demonstrations throughout His earthly life, Jesus unequivocally revealed Himself as fully divine, as well as fully human. Subsequently, similar to the plurality of persons within the unity of the Trinity, there is a mystery that comes with the union of God and man, in the person of Jesus Christ: "The more you think about it, the more staggering it gets. Nothing in fiction is so fantastic, as is this truth of the Incarnation."[38]

---

37. This chapter includes references to a 2009 commentary given by Bishop Robert Barron. For a full treatment, see: Bishop Robert Barron, *"Who is Jesus?,"* Word on Fire Catholic Ministries, July 10, 2001, https://www.wordonfire.org/videos/bishop-barrons-commentaries/who-is-jesus/

38. J.I. Packer, *Knowing God* (Downers Grove, IL: Intervarsity Press, 1973), 53

To be sure, the breathtaking claims of the Incarnation are repeatedly pronounced throughout the gospel accounts, wherein they are both implicitly and explicitly advanced by Christ and by His closest confidants as well. For example, at the onset of his Gospel account, John notably commences with the famous enunciation, "In the beginning, was the word" [John 1:1]. As such, in referencing the "word," John astutely parallels the creation story of Genesis, wherein the "word" was representative of the logos, or that which grounds the intelligibility of the universe. Furthermore, according to John, this very same "word," which was both "with God, and was God," then proceeded to become flesh in the person of Jesus Christ:

> In the beginning was the Word, and the Word was with God, and the Word was God. He was in the beginning with God. All things came into being through him, and without him not one thing came into being. What has come into being in him was life, and the life was the light of all people. The light shines in the darkness, and the darkness did not overcome it...The Word became flesh and made His dwelling among us. We have seen His glory, the glory of the one and only Son, who came from the Father, full of grace and truth. (John 1:1-5, 14, NRSVCE)

What is more, John then continues to depict the direct parity between Jesus and the God of the Old Testament, as he further recounts of Christ's striking proclamation, "Truly, Truly, I say to you, before Abraham [the Jewish Patriarch] was, I am" [John 8:58]. Indeed, for with such a declaration Jesus not only implicitly reveals His eternal coexistence with the Father, but in referring to Himself as "I am," He deliberately echoes God's curious response to Moses, in the Old Testament Exodus account:

But Moses said to God, "If I come to the Israelites and say to them, 'The God of your ancestors has sent me to you,' and they ask me, 'What is his name?' what shall I say to them?" God said to Moses, "I AM WHO I AM." He said further, "Thus you shall say to the Israelites, 'I AM has sent me to you.'" (Exodus 3:13-14, NRSVCE)

And yet, despite this testimony bespeaking of the divinity of Jesus Christ, perhaps the most explicit claim within the entirety of John's gospel stems from a series of misapprehensions by the disciples Phillip and Thomas; for, because of their continued confusion concerning His messianic identity, Jesus expressly reveals to His followers what they ought to have already known:

Do not let your hearts be troubled. Believe in God, believe also in me. In my Father's house there are many dwelling places. If it were not so, would I have told you that I go to prepare a place for you? And if I go and prepare a place for you, I will come again and will take you to myself, so that where I am, there you may be also. And you know the way to the place where I am going." Thomas said to him, "Lord, we do not know where you are going. How can we know the way?" Jesus said to him, "I am the way, and the truth, and the life. No one comes to the Father except through me. If you know me, you will know my Father also. From now on you do know him and have seen him." Philip said to him, "Lord, show us the Father, and we will be satisfied." Jesus said to him, "Have I been with you all this time, Philip, and you still do not know me? Whoever has seen me has seen the Father. How can you say, 'Show us the Father'? Do you not believe that I am in the Father and the Father is in me? The words that I say to you I do not speak on my own; but the Father who dwells in me does his works. Believe me that

I am in the Father and the Father is in me; but if you do not, then believe me because of the works themselves. Very truly, I tell you, the one who believes in me will also do the works that I do and, in fact, will do greater works than these, because I am going to the Father. I will do whatever you ask in my name, so that the Father may be glorified in the Son. If in my name you ask me for anything, I will do it." (John 14:1-14, NRSVCE)

In truth, the reality and immensity of the Incarnation are plainly laid out by the Apostle John. However, the claims of Jesus's divinity are not exclusive to his gospel account. Case in point: Mark would document a public affair wherein Christ elects to manifest His divine jurisdiction, and, as such, He forgives the sins of a paralyzed man prior to miraculously healing him. Predictably, the Pharisees nearby were bewildered by His boldness and His presumption to possess such authority, for He was publicly performing an act that was presumed to be reserved for God alone:

Then some people came, bringing to him a paralyzed man, carried by four of them. And when they could not bring him to Jesus because of the crowd, they removed the roof above him; and after having dug through it, they let down the mat on which the paralytic lay. When Jesus saw their faith, he said to the paralytic, "Son, your sins are forgiven." Now some of the scribes were sitting there, questioning in their hearts, "Why does this fellow speak in this way? It is blasphemy! Who can forgive sins but God alone?" At once Jesus perceived in his spirit that they were discussing these questions among themselves; and he said to them, "Why do you raise such questions in your hearts? Which is easier, to say to the paralytic, 'Your sins are forgiven,' or to say, 'Stand up and take your mat and walk'? But so that you may know that the Son of Man has authority on earth to forgive sins"—he said to the paralytic— "I say to you, stand up, take your mat and go to your home." (Mark 2:3-11, NRSVCE)

Accordingly, for a first-century Jew, there was no higher authority than the ancient Hebrew Scriptures, yet in the Gospel of Matthew, Jesus claims authority even over the Pentateuch:

You have heard that it was said to the people long ago, 'You shall not murder, and anyone who murders will be subject to judgment.' But I tell you that anyone who is angry with a brother or sister will be subject to judgment...You have heard that it was said, 'You shall not commit adultery.' But I tell you that anyone who looks at a woman lustfully has already committed adultery with her in his heart...It has been said, 'Anyone who divorces his wife must give her a certificate of divorce.' But I tell you that anyone who divorces his wife, except for sexual immorality, makes her the victim of adultery, and anyone who marries a divorced woman commits adultery...Again, you have heard that it was said to the people long ago, 'Do not break your oath, but fulfill to the Lord the vows you have made.' But I tell you, do not swear an oath at all: either by heaven, for it is God's throne; or by the earth, for it is his footstool; or by Jerusalem, for it is the city of the Great King... You have heard that it was said, 'Eye for eye, and tooth for tooth.' But I tell you, do not resist an evil person. If anyone slaps you on the right cheek, turn to them the other cheek also... You have heard that it was said, 'Love your neighbor and hate your enemy.' But I tell you, love your enemies and pray for those who persecute you, that you may be children of your Father in heaven. (Matthew 5:21-45, NRSVCE)

Further still, within the Gospel of Luke, we witness Christ supersede both the ancient prophets and Jewish authorities of His day, as He explicated the extensive costs of discipleship and the various sacrifices it entailed. To be sure, His forebears preached devotion to God and a strict fidelity to the Mosaic law; however, Jesus was asserting that HE was to be loved—more than family and even life itself. And yet, how could He possibly say such a thing if He was not, Himself, the highest good:

> Now large crowds were traveling with him; and he turned and said to them, "Whoever comes to me and does not hate father and mother, wife and children, brothers and sisters, yes, and even life itself, cannot be my disciple. Whoever does not carry the cross and follow me cannot be my disciple." (Luke 14:25-27, NRSVCE)

Wherefore, up and down the gospel accounts, Jesus not only proclaims to be a faithful servant of the Father, He claims to be God incarnate—so much so, that the entire impetus and motivation for His scourging and crucifixion was that the Pharisees had recognized this reality. [39] As such, this is why Christ ultimately compels a choice unlike any other religious figure or founder, for although many have claimed to have received revelation, they never went to His extremes. For example, Muhammad asserted to be an authoritative messenger, yet he never proclaimed to be God. Likewise, Moses professed to have received the moral law; however, he never implied he was divine. In fact, even Gautama Buddha, for all his wisdom, merely claimed to have found a path to enlightenment. To this now contrast the professions of Christ, which are comparatively and historically unparalleled: "I am the

---

39. Mark 14:61-65

way, the truth, and the life. No one comes to the Father, except through me." (John 14:6, NRSVCE)

Subsequently, where Muhammad professed to know the ways of Allah, Jesus proclaimed boldly, "I am the way." Where Moses claimed to have received the truth, Christ asserted that He was "the truth." Where the Buddha purported to have discovered the proper way of life, Christ declared that He was "the life." These are the claims which distinguish Christianity, for Christ alone has professed to be God. [40] As such, either the word became flesh in the person of Jesus Christ, or Christianity is a sham and Jesus is a fraud—to be sure, the gospels leave no room for compromise.

---

40. "A man who was merely a man, yet said the sort of things Jesus said, would not be a great moral teacher. He would either be a lunatic—on the level with the man who says he is a poached egg— or else he would be the Devil of Hell. You must make your choice. Either this man was, and is, the Son of God, or else a madman, or something worse. You can shut him up for a fool, you can spit at him and kill him as a demon, or you can fall at his feet and call him Lord and God. However, let us not come with any patronizing nonsense about his being a great human teacher. He has not left that open to us. He did not intend to." (C.S Lewis, *Mere Christianity* (London: Collins, 1952), 54-55.

VIII. THE HISTORICAL RELIABILITY OF THE GOSPEL ACCOUNTS

With the rise of naturalism in today's society, we have unfortunately seen a parallel rise of uncritical biblical skepticism. In fact, as secular culture has grown increasingly hostile to traditional Christian doctrine, flippant allegations of scriptural errancy have become, progressively, more and more common. Furthermore, given that the veracity of the Christian faith is intimately intertwined with the reliability of its Scriptures, if they are characterized as erroneous or unreliable depictions, then the totality of Christianity will inevitably be considered equally spurious. As such, an honest examination of the biblical texts—of their origins, accuracy, and consistency—is not only profitable for the defense of Christianity; it is, in fact, entirely necessary. However, to legitimately accomplish this task and defend the reliability of Scripture, one must first address several popular misconceptions about the biblical corpus and its exegesis.

For instance, anyone wishing to discredit the Bible must first overcome the misconception that it is a singular or homogenous book. Instead, the Bible is a collection of seventy-three individual books, written by a minimum of 40 different authors, in different genres, languages, locations, and eras, all over the span of some fifteen hundred years. As such, the Bible is more akin to a miniature library than a singular piece of literature.[41] Furthermore, much like the literary works of today, before attempting to interpret a passage of Scripture, one must first be aware of what section of the "biblical library" he is in, as any overly simplistic, literal reading of the biblical texts disregards the possibility that one may not be reading a historical or biographical piece of literature.[42] To be sure, many sections of the biblical catalog are meant to be historically and biographically factual; however, there are also writings which are instead poetic, allegorical, periphrastic, or hyperbolic. What's more, one must also consider the extensive period over which the Scriptures were written and the considerable timeframe they cover, as there are significant stylistic changes in writing from one era to the next. Indeed, two thousand years of exegetical quarrels, translational controversies, and contextual disputes, serve to demonstrate just how difficult biblical interpretation, classification, and translation can be. Subsequently, before claiming to know the significance of a passage found within the canon of Scripture, one must first consider original translations, traditional interpretations, historical backdrops, intended audiences, ancient literary practices, and the context of the entire revelation. In short, one simply cannot assert to have found a fatal error or contradiction within a scriptural text, without first having done a substantial amount of research, followed by a comprehensive evaluation.

Yet, still, notwithstanding the misconceptions regarding the nature and genre of Scripture, some legitimate questions have indeed been raised because of advances in textual criticism, and in light of recent archeological excavations. For instance, do the

---

41. Bishop Robert Barron, "Bill Maher and Not Understanding Either Faith or the Bible," June 13, 2014, Word on Fire Catholic Ministries, https://www.wordonfire.org/articles/barron/bill-maher-and-not-understanding-either-faith-or-the-bible

42. Ibid.

Scriptures that we possess today coincide with what the authors originally wrote, or have these writings been drastically altered? Likewise, what criteria were used to decide which books would be included within the canon of Scripture, and when was it established? Correspondingly, are there any external sources that can substantiate its numerous historical and geographical claims?

In truth, at the end of the day, it is paramount for Christian apologists to address reasonable questions and concerns, for the Scriptures simply cannot be trusted, nor can the claims of Christianity be taken seriously if they cannot stand up to scrutiny.

The Historical Preservation of the New Testament Texts

If we are to faithfully evaluate the historical reliability of the various New Testament accounts, it is first imperative to know if our modern translations coincide with the original texts. As such, to verify the continuity of these ancient documents and assess the accuracy of their claims, it is essential to scrutinize the Bible of today with the available manuscripts and fragments from antiquity. Furthermore, if we are to truly regard the canonical texts as infallible or inspired Scripture, then it is also necessary to review the operative methodology that determined their authenticity.

Notwithstanding, first and foremost, from the outset, it is also imperative to bear in mind that, when it comes to the biblical corpus, the body of available ancient documentation which can be used for comparative scrutiny is completely unparalleled, as the sheer volume of well-preserved ancient biblical manuscripts and fragments far exceeds any other literary work from classical antiquity. In fact, so much so, that the New Testament alone remarkably lays claim to over 24,000 ancient manuscripts [43] and fragments—the earliest of which [*The St. John's Fragment*] has been

---

43. Josh McDowell, *A Ready Defense: The Best of Josh McDowell*, comp. Bill Wilson (Nashville, TN: Thomas Nelson Inc., 2021), 43

dated to only decades from its original.[44] What's more, a complete manuscript of the fully established New Testament canon [*the Codex Sinaiticus*] has been dated to less than three centuries from the original texts. Now contrast this to Homer's *The Iliad*, which is widely considered to be one of the best preserved ancient literary works; *The Iliad* lays claim to only 643 manuscripts—the earliest of which has been dated to more than five hundred years from the original.[45] Likewise, the Aristotelian works, *Nicomachean Ethics, Politics, Metaphysics, Poetics,* and *Prior Analytics,* have only 49 available manuscripts—the oldest of which has been dated to over 1,400 years from the original documents.[46] As such, when one compares the conservation of New Testament writings to their contemporaneous counterparts, it is evident that the preservation of these ancient texts is nothing short of extraordinary.

Furthermore, given that the original documents of virtually all ancient texts have been irreparably damaged, lost, or destroyed, textual critics must utilize this available manuscript evidence to account for any errors or irregularities. Subsequently, it is through a process of comparing all ancient manuscripts and fragments and documenting each substantive change that anomalies can be adequately identified and an accurate original reconstructed. By way of example, several reviews of the New Testament manuscript record have documented upwards of 200,000 textual variances.[47] Notwithstanding, most of these discrepancies can be attributed to common scribal errors, such as spelling mistakes, grammatical flaws, missing sentences, and the like. In truth, less than one percent of the reported 200,000 variances have any effect on the meaning of the text within which they were found, and only a fraction of the remaining percentage is unresolved by the process of textual

---

44. Ibid., 45
45. Ibid.
46. Ibid.
47. Ibid., 46

criticism. As such, the complete collection of New Testament documents is regarded as having only 40 lines of textual corruption—a figure that corresponds to an overall consistency of over 99.5%.[48] What is more, even apart from this extraordinary textual continuity within the New Testament manuscript record, accurate originals could still be reproduced via the countless scriptural quotations in the writings of the early Church Fathers.[49] Wherefore, inasmuch as the New Testament manuscript record spans hundreds of years, and includes numerous translations, in multiple languages, not a single Christian teaching or belief is either based on, or has been changed by, any textual variance.[50]

The Establishment of the New Testament Canon

Historically speaking, the establishment of the New Testament canon is a process that began almost immediately, as, following the ascension of Christ, the Apostles and their disciples soon began to compose biographical accounts of His life and author numerous instructional epistles to the prominent churches in Christendom. Accordingly, the successors of the Apostles then began to establish a collection of verifiable writings that were uniform with oral apostolic teaching and consistent with the Old Testament revelation. What's more, having previously combatted the heretical writings of the Marcionites and Gnostics, early Christians were resolute in identifying counterfeit documents and defending authentic Scripture.

Admittedly, a New Testament canon was not authoritatively established until the council of Rome in 382 A.D;[51] however, both

---

48. Ibid., 45
49. Ibid., 47-48
50. Ibid., 46
51. *Decretum Gelasianum* 2, A.D. 520

Origen of Alexandria [52] and Athanasius the Confessor [53] had previously adopted identical canons. Furthermore, there is also record of a near uniform canon within the *Muratorian Fragment*—a document that predates the council of Rome by some 227 years.[54] As such, inasmuch as the process of establishing a New Testament canon involved rigorous discourse and debate, there is simply no credible reason to presume that we are in possession of a fraudulent, untraceable, or corrupted catalog of Scripture, when all evidence points to the contrary; namely, that we appear to possess the precisely documented words of the Apostles, and with an impressive degree of traceability.

The Historical Preservation of the Old Testament Texts

As was the case with the New Testament texts, the Jewish scribes who were entrusted with copying and preserving the Hebrew Scriptures were notoriously careful and meticulous. In fact, so much so, that they developed an intricate system in which they counted and compared the lines, letters, and words on every page of each new document to ensure its accuracy and precision.[55] As such, it should come as no surprise that the reliability of this scrupulous process continued to be revalidated with each new manuscript recovery. However, it was a recent discovery, in 1947, which truly cemented it beyond all doubt.[56]

Indeed, for in Qumran, Judea, while innocently exploring a system of caves, two shepherd boys would happen upon a collection of ancient pottery. Nevertheless, what would initially appear to be

---

52. Origen of Alexandria, *Homilies on Joshua 7:1* [cited in Eusebius's *Ecclesiastical History 6:25*], A.D. 250

53. Saint Athanasius of Alexandria, *Festival Letter 39:5*, A.D. 367

54. Gary Michuta, *Why Catholic Bibles Are Bigger*, 2nd ed. (San Diego, CA: Catholic Answer Press, 2017), 73

55. Josh McDowell, *A Ready Defense: The Best of Josh McDowell*, comp. Bill Wilson (Nashville, TN: Thomas Nelson Inc., 2021), 30

56. Ibid., 106

nothing more than a mundane archeological discovery would initiate the most pivotal biblical manuscript recovery in all of modern history, as within that system of desert caves were eventually discovered over nine hundred ancient Essene scrolls—the majority of which had been precisely cataloged and exquisitely preserved. What is more, after an extensive period of recovery and analysis, historians would proceed to confirm that these "dead sea scrolls" contained fragments from nearly every book in the Old Testament canon and dated to as far back as the second century B.C.[57] And yet, perhaps most impressive of all, is that in several instances, the Essene scrolls were found to have a 95% word-for-word accuracy rate [58] with the existent Masoretic manuscripts—portions of which had been transcribed up to a thousand years thereafter.[59] Wherefore, in light of the discoveries in Qumran, Judea, it would be more than fair to submit that the burden of proof has now been met by those who defend the Old Testament Scriptures as accurate preservations of the writings of ancient Israel.

The Establishment of the Old Testament Canon

Well before the Apostolic age, a translation and assembly of the ancient Jewish Scriptures was undertaken by the Alexandrian Jews, and completed by the mid second century B.C.[60] Nicknamed *the Septuagint*, this Greek translation of the Old Testament texts was in common use both at the time of Christ and in the early Apostolic era.[61] In fact, so much so, that not only are the vast majority of the scriptural references in the New Testament drawn directly from the

---

57. Ibid.
58. Ibid., 49
59. Ibid., 106
60. Achille Vander Heeren "Septuagint Version," in the *Catholic Encyclopedia* (New York, NY: Robert Appleton Company, 1912) Accessed May 15, 2022, from New Advent. https://www.newadvent.org/cathen/13722a.htm
61. Ibid.

Septuagint, but it was a primary source for the early Apostolic Fathers and later Patristic Fathers as well.[62] What is more, prominent first century Jewish scholars such as Philo of Alexandria and Flavius Josephus regularly utilized the Greek translation of the Hebrew Scriptures.[63] Likewise, Septuagint manuscripts were among those discovered in the Essene Dead Sea Scroll collection, and are believed to have been in regular circulation among numerous Jewish sects at that time.[64] As such, whilst the Old Testament canon was being affixed and vernacularized, in 382 A.D., it was judicious and sound to predicate it upon the traditional Septuagintal catalog of Scripture.[65]

Extra-Biblical Historical and Archeological Evidence

Although the biblical texts are primarily recognized for their supernatural claims, they also mention specific people, places, tribes, events, and dates—the majority of which are historically verifiable and/or falsifiable. As such, it should come as no surprise that a host of extrinsic historical evidence, which is pertinent to these biblical claims, has been located within ancient contemporaneous writings and in recent archeological excavations.

Case in point: extra-biblical sources have not only affirmed the historicity of Jesus Christ; they have also authenticated the historical existence of a further 101 biblical figures.[66] Accordingly, there are varying degrees of ancillary support for additional

---

62. Ibid.
63. Ibid.
64. Gary Michuta, "God Inspires Only In Hebrew," Hands On Apologetics, 2004, http://www.handsonapologetics.com/Articles/16-Was%20There%20An%20Alexandrian%20Canon.pdf
65. Gary Michuta, *Why Catholic Bibles Are Bigger*, 2nd ed. (San Diego, CA: Catholic Answer Press, 2017), 259
66. Dr. Titus Kennedy (Field Archaeologist), "Biblical Figures Found Through Archaeology," Drive Through History, July 13, 2020, https://drivethruhistory.com/biblical-figures-found-through-archaeology/

individuals as well. Furthermore, as much as the extra-biblical attestations of these ancient figures may seem relatively inconsequential, one must consider the fact that the scriptural texts chronicle individuals from different eras, cultures, countries, continents, social classes, and the like. Wherefore, when such a sizeable volume of confirmation is achieved despite considerable impediments, it ought not be rashly disregarded or dismissed as insignificant. What is more, although the historical validation of these biblical figures is itself substantive confirmation, additional affirmations have come via a host of recent archaeological excavations, which have authenticated many other meaningful scriptural details and events. For example:

1. *The existence of a Canaanite civilization, circa 1500 B.C.*—via the discovery of the *Statue of Idrimi* in 1939.

2. *The existence of an ancient tribe of Israel, as far back as 1207 B.C.*—via the discovery of the *Merneptah Stele Monolith* in 1896.

3. *The existence of a house of David in the kingdom of ancient Israel*—via the discovery of the *Tel Dan Stele* in 1993.

4. *The substantiation of the ancient Israeli battle against the Moabite tribe, in 830 B.C.*—via the discovery of the *Moabite Stone* in 1870.

5. *The confirmation of the Assyrian siege of Lachish, in 701 B.C.*—via the discovery of the *Lachish Reliefs* in 1847.

6. *The verification of an Assyrian campaign against King Hezekiah of Judah*—via the discovery of the *Azekah Inscription* in 1974.

7. *The verification of King Nebuchadnezzar's conquest of Israel, in 597 B.C.* —via the discovery of the *Nebuchadnezzar Chronicle* in 1896.

8. *The existence of Leprosy, in the first century A.D.*—via the discovery of ancient human remains, in Hinnom Valley in 2001.

9. *The existence of a Roman prefect of Judah (in particular Pontius Pilate)*—via the discovery of *the Pilate Stone* in 1961.

10. *The substantiation of the New Testament description of a Roman crucifixion*—via the discovery of the *Yehohanan Tomb* in 1968.

In short, there is a host of extraneous historical evidence that has vindicated the accuracy of the biblical accounts. However, this is not to imply that this is sufficient to substantiate their respective supernatural claims. Nevertheless, if the principal geographical and historical details in Scripture are proven to be credible and accurate, then they can provide supplemental support for their more profound assertions and force us to take them seriously—and this appears to be precisely the case with the existing body of evidence. Indeed, for insofar as certain biblical details and descriptions are undoubtedly periphrastic or hyperbolic, the Bible, at large, is typically considered a reliable historical authority. So much so, that many secular institutions utilize biblical texts as a primary source for archeological excavations and for general historical reference:

> Much of the Bible, in particular the historical books of the Old Testament, are as accurate of historical documents as any that we have from antiquity; they are, in fact, more accurate than many of the Egyptian, Mesopotamian, or

Greek histories. These biblical records can be and are used—as are other ancient documents— in archeological work. For the most part, the historical events described took place, and the peoples cited really existed. However, this is not to say that names of all peoples and places mentioned can be identified today, or that every event as reported in the historical books happened exactly as stated. (Smithsonian Department of Anthropology, *Statement on the Historical Accuracy of the Bible*, 1996) [67]

---

67. Christian Satellite Network, "The Smithsonian Department of Anthropology Statement," CSN Radio, December 1, 2019, https://csnradio.com/wp-content/uploads/2019/12/SmithsonianLetter-o.pdf.

IX. THE FITTINGNESS OF THE CROSS [68]

There is, perhaps, no religious claim more essential, more radical, or more confounding than that of the death and resurrection of Jesus Christ. Indeed, it is the claim upon which the entire Christian faith rests, the source of all hope for her faithful, and an event which unsettles the unsuspecting mind, when first reading the gospel accounts. For, in reality, if Christ truly was a divine messiah, then what was He doing on a cross? Moreover, why was such a brutal death necessary? What could possibly have been the point of all this hardship, suffering, pain, and sorrow?

To be sure, there is much to consider with respect to Christ's death on the cross. However, one cannot begin to comprehend the significance of this sacrificial act without first being cognizant of our fallen human nature. Wherefore, to suitably comprehend the magnitude of the Incarnation, crucifixion, and resurrection, it is necessary to expound upon the Christian concept of original sin prior to addressing the reality of substitutionary atonement.

---

68. This chapter includes references to a 2015 commentary by Bishop Robert Barron. For a full treatment, see: Bishop Robert Barron, "Why did Jesus Have to Die the Way he Did?" Word on Fire Catholic Ministries, April 3, 2015, https://www.wordonfire.org/articles/why-did-jesus-have-to-die-the-way-he-did/

Case in point: it is a fact of life that each of our descendants will either benefit or suffer from our actions.[69] However, this does not imply that they are personally rewarded or punished for our choices, but rather that they simply inherit the natural consequences of them.[70] Correspondingly, biblical sources submit that by using the gifts of the will and the intellect and then freely choosing sin, our first parents corrupted their initial state of holiness and then passed down this absence of original sanctity. In truth, we are not personally responsible for this inherited deprivation, or the choices of our ancient forbearers; however, we possess nonetheless the contingent effects of a propensity towards disorder and sin.[71] And thus, the sheer magnitude and gravity of human dysfunction would ultimately compel a divine solution, as only an offering of immeasurable goodness would suffice to redeem such perversion and depravity. Wherefore, it was fitting that a being of true divinity and humanity would reconcile the chasm between God and man, and it was fitting that the impeccable offering of Christ would reconcile God's infinite mercy with His infinite justice.

In fact, to this very day, contemporary theologians continue to reflect upon this mystifying reality, as it is impossible to comprehend the crucifixion of Christ without understanding the context of His Incarnation. As such, if we are to truly grasp the meaning and consequence of the cross, it is fitting that we first come to realize that the word became flesh to do battle with sin in the form of a spiritual warrior. What is more, if we recognize this reality, it should come as no surprise that when we read the gospel accounts, we see that all forms of human deviance and corruption come to do battle with Christ in His passion.

---

69. Trent Horn, "Is Original Sin Stupid?" Catholic Answers, July 10, 2018, https://www.catholic.com/magazine/online-edition/is-oringinal-sin-stupid
70. Ibid.
71. Ibid.

For instance, we see His inner circle sleep soundly while He agonizes over the suffering to come and the deception of a companion and disciple who would betray Him for thirty pieces of silver. We see Him denied and abandoned by His followers in His moment of greatest need and the injustice of His Jewish countrymen, who would conspire to bring false allegations against Him. We see the cowardice of a Roman prefect, who would order the merciless lashing of an innocent man, and the roars of a bloodthirsty mob, who would stop at nothing to see Him crucified. Indeed, we see Him beaten, betrayed, deserted, slandered, tortured, and unjustly sentenced, and then continuously and remorselessly mocked as He is stripped of his garments and nailed to the cross. To be sure, He had come to deliver the human race and combat the forces of sin, yet Jesus Christ breathed His last breath, having been crushed by the iniquity of the world.

However, this was not to be the final chapter, as the single most important event in human history was about to occur, in that the love of God would conquer all worldly evil when Jesus Christ was resurrected from the dead. Wherefore, in one singular act of compassion, we witness the true power of the love of God, in that the limitless love of our heavenly creator can swallow up the depravity and injustice of the world. Subsequently, all the human sin and dysfunction that had opposed Christ in the cruelty of His passion were brought to their knees as He arose victorious in the glory of His resurrection. [72] Thusly, the resurrection of Christ represents the ultimate victory of love over hatred, truth over falsehood, and life over death.

---

72. "The Cross had asked the questions, and the Resurrection has answered them; The Cross had asked: "Why does God permit evil and sin to nail Justice to a tree?" The Resurrection answered: "That sin, having done its worst, might exhaust itself and be overcome by a Love that is stronger than either sin or death." (Venerable Archbishop Fulton Sheen, *The Crisis in Christendom* (Washington, DC: National Council of Catholic Men, 1952), 100-101)

In summation, only infinite love could redeem the cumulative sin and hatred of the world. Therefore, to defeat iniquity and evil itself, the subsistent source of mercy and love came and battled it down to its very core—even to the point of excruciating death on a Roman instrument of torture. [73]

---

[73]. "He was pierced for our transgressions, he was crushed for our iniquities; the punishment that brought us peace was on him, and by his wounds we are healed." (Isaiah 53:5, NRSVCE)

X. THE HISTORICAL CASE FOR THE RESURRECTION

Although it is certainly vital to demonstrate why the willing sacrifice of Jesus Christ was essential for the redemption of mankind, an extraordinary claim, like the resurrection, is destined to be met with skepticism. Consequently, if Christians wish to engage the secular realm, and adequately defend their convictions, then it is incumbent on them to supply evidence for such a miraculous and revolutionary event. Notwithstanding, anecdotes of private revelation and supernatural experiences are unlikely to be persuasive, for as much as spiritual encounters are unquestionably invaluable for the development of personal faith, one cannot expect a cynic to be satisfied by unverifiable testimony. As such, prudence dictates that a rational, factual, and empirical case be made for the resurrection—a case based on the historical record of Christianity, the validity and credibility of New Testament eyewitness accounts, and the fulfillment of biblical prophecy. Indeed, for if the foundational claim of the Christian faith can be shown to be genuine and credible, then the burden of proof will have been met by those who affirm its authenticity.

ETERNALLY ONE, ETERNALLY THREE

The Origins of the Gospel Accounts

To accurately assess the reliability of the testimony within the New Testament gospel accounts, it is necessary to review the origins of these documents and their various authorship ascriptions. For to properly evaluate the credibility of these texts and the events described therein, one must be cognizant of when these alleged biographies were written and whom they were written by. Accordingly, if the gospels are proven to be later creations or to depend upon unreliable or tertiary testimony, then it would be difficult to justify belief in their contents and the miracles they profess to have observed.

Notwithstanding, as much as the foundations and formations of the gospel accounts are, admittedly, ongoing, and impassioned debates, when it comes to their origins and compositions, nearly all New Testament scholars acknowledge the following two realities:

a) That all four gospels can be confidently dated to within the first century A.D.[74]
b) That every authorship accreditation within the ancient manuscript record consistently ascribes the same four authors, to the same four gospel accounts.[75]

Furthermore, many New Testament scholars also view the universal consensus amongst early Christian ecclesiastical authorities as significant supplemental evidence, in that the authorship ascriptions of early anonymous Christian texts were frequently subject to disputations; however, there were no such disagreements or competing theories surrounding the origins of the gospel accounts.[76] Similarly, no apocryphal or counterfeit "gospels" were

---

74. William Lane Craig, *Reasonable Faith: Christian Truth and Apologetics*, 3rd ed. (Wheaton, IL: Crossway, 2008), 334
75. Ibid., 335
76. Ibid., 336

ever granted the same status as Scripture: they were not quoted by Church fathers, read within Christian assemblies, collected into volumes, or listed in catalogs; they were not noted by Christian adversaries, appealed to by heretics, the subject of extensive commentaries, or included in early canons. [77] In fact, on the contrary, precisely the opposite is true, as they were nearly universally rejected by the relevant Christian authorities in the eras succeeding their composition.[78] Yet, still, inasmuch as the historical, testimonial, and manuscript evidence certainly seem to evince the authenticity of the canonical gospels, questions pertaining to their factual reliability undoubtedly still remain. For instance, who exactly were these gospel authors? What was their relationship to Christ? And why should we consider their testimony trustworthy?

In truth, it would be impossible to speak with absolute certainty regarding documents from classical antiquity. That does not mean, however, that nothing can be gleaned from the evidence, as both the internal and extra-biblical testimonies strongly suggests the following: [79]

1. The first gospel account was written by Matthew—a first century tax collector and disciple of Jesus Christ.

2. The second gospel account was written by Mark—an associate of the Apostle Paul and a scribe to the disciple Peter.

3. The third gospel account was written by Luke—a first century physician, and companion of the Apostle Paul.

---

77. Ibid.
78. Ibid.
79. Ibid., 334-336

4. The fourth gospel account was written by John—a brother of the disciple James, and a member of Christ's most inner circle.

As such, prima facie, any notion that the canonical gospels were hearsay, fabrications, or fiction should immediately be dismissed, as two of the presumptive gospel authors were themselves Disciples of Christ, while the remaining two were highly educated first-century evangelists with direct access to eyewitnesses of the events they would record. Furthermore, the inconspicuous authorship ascriptions of two of the gospel accounts lend additional credence to their authenticity in that a first-century forger who was genuinely seeking to advance a counterfeit gospel would have scarcely ascribed an obscure evangelist as the author of his spurious account. Comparatively, the idiomatic expressions that mark the gospels also align with traditional ascriptions, as do the numerous names, dates, cultural details, events, and customs described therein.[80] What is more, given the scholarly consensus that the gospel accounts are in the genre of ancient biography, the fact that we possess four consistent narratives without suspicious harmonization is even further indicative of credibility.[81] For instance, when multiple eyewitness accounts produce insignificant variations and are in complete accordance with consequential details and an overall summary of an event, it is highly suggestive of reliability and atypical of conspiracy or collusion. In fact, within the first four verses of his gospel account, Luke explicitly states his forthright intentions:

> Inasmuch as many have undertaken to compile a narrative of the things which have been accomplished among us, just as they were delivered to us by those who from the beginning were eyewitnesses and ministers of the word, it

---

80. Ibid., 334
81. Ibid.

seemed good to me also, having followed all things closely for some time past, to write an orderly account for you, most excellent Theoph'ilus, that you may know the truth concerning the things of which you have been informed. (Luke 1:1-4, NRSVCE)

Further still, the presence of numerous unflattering and embarrassing details within the gospel accounts also suggests that they should not be viewed as hyperbolic or allegorical. [82] For example, they record that the son of God was raised by a modest carpenter in the simple town of Nazareth and that His genealogy included both reprobates and courtesans, amongst various other nefarious individuals. Similarly, the portrayal of the disciples is equally unflattering in that they are predominantly depicted as unlearned men—in fact, they are even described as erratic, unreliable, and lacking comprehension and conviction. Case in point: whilst the disciples would flee in fear for their lives, a group of women are documented as having stood firm alongside Christ throughout His passion. In fact, they are even chronicled as the first eyewitnesses of the resurrection, despite female testimony being regarded as unreliable at that time. As such, the very men who were attempting to evangelize the world via their written and verbal testimony were openly admitting to details which undermined their credibility and the persuasiveness of the gospel message. To be sure, an unassuming God and His errant disciples is hardly an awe-inspiring story; [83] consequently, it is difficult to imagine a motivation for including such details, apart from a concerted effort to report the truth.

---

82. Ibid.
83. Ibid.

ETERNALLY ONE, ETERNALLY THREE

Additional Biblical Testimony

Inasmuch as the internal, testimonial, and historical evidence evinces the credibility of the gospels, perhaps the most powerful witness for the resurrection is found within the Pauline epistles. Indeed, for with Paul, we witness a former Jewish Pharisee and fanatical persecutor of Christians who then unexpectedly encounters the risen Christ and, thereon, sustains a radical transformation:

> For I delivered to you as of first importance what I also received, that Christ died for our sins in accordance with the scriptures, that he was buried, that he was raised on the third day in accordance with the scriptures, and that he appeared to Cephas, then to the twelve. Then he appeared to more than five hundred brethren at one time, most of whom are still alive, though some have fallen asleep. Then he appeared to James, then to all the apostles. Last of all, as to one untimely born, he appeared also to me. For I am the least of the apostles, unfit to be called an apostle, because I persecuted the church of God. But by the grace of God, I am what I am, and his grace toward me was not in vain. (1 Corinthians 15:3-10, NRSVCE)

In truth, Paul unabashedly proclaims the resurrection throughout his numerous epistles. However, his writings are not limited to supernatural claims; rather, they cover an assortment of details. In fact, significant portions of his letters are reserved for personal recollections and memoirs, wherein he freely confesses his past transgressions and recounts numerous trials and tribulations:

> I repeat, let no one think me foolish; but even if you do, accept me as a fool, so that I too may boast a little. (What I am saying I say not with the Lord's authority but as a fool,

in this boastful confidence; since many boast of worldly things, I too will boast.) For you gladly bear with fools, being wise yourselves! For you bear it if a man makes slaves of you, or preys upon you, or takes advantage of you, or puts on airs, or strikes you in the face. To my shame, I must say, we were too weak for that!

But whatever anyone dares to boast of—I am speaking as a fool—I also dare to boast of that. Are they Hebrews? So am I. Are they Israelites? So am I. Are they descendants of Abraham? So am I. Are they servants of Christ? I am a better one—I am talking like a madman—with far greater labors, far more imprisonments, with countless beatings, and often near death. Five times I have received at the hands of the Jews the forty lashes less one. Three times I have been beaten with rods, once I was stoned. Three times I have been shipwrecked; a night and a day I have been adrift at sea; on frequent journeys, in danger from rivers, danger from robbers, danger from my own people, danger from Gentiles, danger in the city, danger in the wilderness, danger at sea, danger from false brethren; in toil and hardship, through many a sleepless night, in hunger and thirst, often without food, in cold and exposure. And, apart from other things, there is the daily pressure upon me of my anxiety for all the churches. Who is weak, and I am not weak?

Who is made to fall, and I am not indignant? If I must boast, I will boast of the things that show my weakness. The God and Father of the Lord Jesus, he who is blessed forever, knows that I do not lie. At Damascus, the governor under King Aretas guarded the city of Damascus in order to seize me, but I was let down in a basket through a window in the wall and escaped his hands. (2 Corinthians 11:16-33, NRSVCE)

Subsequently, throughout his years of evangelization, Paul would be victimized by nature and man, king and slave, Jew, and gentile alike; he would be persecuted, ridiculed, robbed, and starved— all for his newfound faith. As such, the testimony of Paul, perhaps more so than any other Apostle, ultimately raises a question: to what can we credit his radical transformation and sudden zeal for Christianity, apart from divine intervention? Indeed, for if he were a liar, then why would he cite a host of other witnesses who could affirm the risen Christ? Moreover, what was he to gain from manufacturing falsehoods and pursuing a life of evangelization? He left his religion, his kingdom, his country, and his jurisdiction, only to endure continuous labor and hardship; he exchanged comfort for oppression, prominence for imprisonment, and religious authority for an unjust execution. What is more, even a cursory reading of his epistles reveals that Paul was neither an extremist nor a simpleton. On the contrary, the artistic language he employs throughout his various letters reflects a man of eloquence, sobriety, and great intellect. Thusly, his willingness to suffer rules out the possibility of a deliberate lie or fraud, and likewise, his eloquence and intellectual acuity rule out any kind of delusion or insanity. Consequently, in the absence of further alternatives, one must consider the possibility that Paul's earnest testimony is ultimately worthy of belief—that perhaps the only thing that is able to sufficiently explain his radical conversion and willingness to endure a life of suffering is a supernatural encounter with the risen Christ, whilst en route to Damascus.[84]

---

84. "Would men in such circumstances pretend to have seen what they never saw; assert facts which they had no knowledge of, go about lying to teach virtue; and, though not only convinced of Christ's being an imposter, but having seen the success of his imposture in his crucifixion, yet persist in carrying on; and so persist, as to bring upon themselves, for nothing, and with full knowledge of the consequence, enmity and hatred, danger and death?" (William Paley, *A View of the Evidence of Christianity*, 2 vols., New ed. (Edinburgh: George Ramsay & Co., 1811), 1:310

FILIUM DEI UNIGENITUM

The Fulfillment of Scriptural Prophecy

Scattered throughout the Old Testament Scriptures is a litany of foreshadowing and prophetic passages—many of which predict the arrival of a future Jewish messiah. Furthermore, although these texts were written by independent authors, each of whom significantly predated Christ, they nevertheless managed to accurately foretell specific details and events in His life. In fact, many of these passages would be explicitly referenced by both Jesus and the Apostles, as they sought to convey that the prophecies of old had finally been fulfilled. Likewise, they were also avowed within the early Church and by early Christian evangelists, who believed the fulfillment of prophecy bore witness to the veracity of the gospel claims. Nevertheless, of all the Old Testament prophetic texts which are believed to have been fulfilled by the life of Christ, undoubtedly the most confounding are found within Daniel, who envisions the detailed chronology of the Incarnation.

What is more, these predictive passages are not confined to the Old Testament Scriptures, as Christ regularly prophesies of future events throughout the four gospels as well. For instance, Matthew would recount a public affair wherein Jesus admonishes the Pharisees, implicitly projecting an imminent global rise of Christianity. To be sure, the magnitude of such a forecast, some twenty centuries removed, can be difficult to fully appreciate; however, within the confines of a totalitarian Roman occupation, this was laughable conjecture at best. So much so, that numerous early Christian evangelists would go so far as to proclaim that the successful rise of Christianity in face of such formidable opposition was, itself, proof of its supernatural origins.

In summation, credible eyewitness testimony and a reliable historical record lend credence to the Christian faith; however, the existence of precursory and prophetic texts provides an additional evidentiary avenue. Indeed, for the successive fulfillment of these predictive passages, at times centuries after their composition, bears witness to both the inspiration of Scripture and the divinity of Jesus Christ.

Messianic Prophesies within the Book of Daniel

Whereas the Old Testament book of Daniel carefully chronicles the epoch of Jewish exile in Babylon, it is generally dated to somewhere between the second and sixth centuries B.C. To be sure, from the earliest times, both Christian and Jewish historians have consistently defended a contemporaneous sixth century B.C. dating;[85] however, many contemporary liberal scholars now advocate for the second century B.C. due to stated difficulties with historical content, language, and genre. Nevertheless, even as the origins and composition of the book Daniel remain the subject of scholarly debate, all parties acknowledge that it considerably predates both the establishment of the Roman Empire and the subsequent arrival of Christ.

Wherefore, if we can keep this consensus in mind regarding the origins and composition of Daniel, it provides sufficient context within which to examine the second chapter, wherein we find an unsettled King Nebuchadnezzar:

> Therefore, Daniel went to Arioch, whom the king had appointed to destroy the wise men of Babylon, and said to him, "Do not destroy the wise men of Babylon; bring me in before the king, and I will give the king the interpretation." Then Arioch quickly brought Daniel before the king and said to him: "I have found among the exiles from Judah a man who can tell the king the interpretation." The king said to Daniel, whose name was Belteshazzar, "Are you able to

---

85. Saint Jerome, *Commentary on Daniel 1:1*, A.D. 420

tell me the dream that I have seen and its interpretation?" Daniel answered the king, "No wise men, enchanters, magicians, or diviners can show to the king the mystery that the king is asking, but there is a God in heaven who reveals mysteries, and he has disclosed to King Nebuchadnezzar what will happen at the end of days. Your dream and the visions of your head as you lay in bed were these:

To you, O king, as you lay in bed, came thoughts of what would be hereafter, and the revealer of mysteries disclosed to you what is to be. But as for me, this mystery has not been revealed to me because of any wisdom that I have more than any other living being, but in order that the interpretation may be known to the king and that you may understand the thoughts of your mind. You were looking, O king, and lo! there was a great statue. This statue was huge, its brilliance extraordinary; it was standing before you, and its appearance was frightening. The head of that statue was of fine gold, its chest and arms of silver, its middle and thighs of bronze, its legs of iron, its feet partly of iron and partly of clay. As you looked on, a stone was cut out, not by human hands, and it struck the statue on its feet of iron and clay and broke them in pieces. Then the iron, the clay, the bronze, the silver, and the gold, were all broken in pieces and became like the chaff of the summer threshing floors; and the wind carried them away, so that not a trace of them could be found. But the stone that struck the statue became a great mountain and filled the whole earth.

This was the dream; now we will tell the king its interpretation. You, O king, the king of kings—to whom the God of heaven has given the kingdom, the power, the might, and the glory, into whose hand he has given human beings, wherever they live, the wild animals of the field, and the birds of the air, and whom he has established as ruler over them all—you are the head of gold. After you shall arise another kingdom inferior to yours, and yet a third kingdom of bronze, which shall rule over the whole earth. And there shall be a fourth kingdom, strong as iron; just as iron crushes and smashes everything, it shall crush and shatter all these. As you saw the feet and toes partly of potter's clay and partly of iron, it shall be a divided kingdom; but some of the strength of iron shall be in it, as you saw the iron mixed with the clay. As the toes of the feet were part iron and part clay, so the kingdom shall be partly strong and partly brittle. As you saw the iron mixed with clay, so will they mix with one another in marriage, but they will not hold together, just as iron does not mix with clay. And in the days of those kings the God of heaven will set up a kingdom that shall never be destroyed, nor shall this kingdom be left to another people. It shall crush all these kingdoms and bring them to an end, and it shall stand forever; just as you saw that a stone was cut from the mountain not by hands, and that it crushed the iron, the bronze, the clay, the silver, and the gold. The great God has informed the king what shall be hereafter. The dream is certain, and its interpretation trustworthy." (Daniel 2:24-45, NRSVCE)

Subsequently, as Daniel would explain to the Babylonian king, a succession of four empires was destined for earth—a prophecy which would be set forth from the outset of his reign and then proceed to come to fruition over the next six centuries.[86] As such, this series of kingdoms would begin in the seventh century B.C. with the Babylonian empire in which Daniel resided—a kingdom

---

86. Brandt J. Pitre, *The Case for Jesus: The Biblical and Historical Evidence for Christ* (New York, NY: Image, 2016), 107

which was depicted as a head of gold and representative of King Nebuchadnezzar himself.[87] Furthermore, just as the vision foretold, the Babylonian empire would be conquered in the sixth century B.C. by the invading King Cyrus the Second—the Medo-Persians would then establish the Achaemenid Empire, which was portrayed as the chest and arms of silver.[88] Accordingly, the third kingdom would be spread by Alexander the Great via an unprecedented series of military campaigns—although ultimately depicted as the belly and thighs of bronze, this renowned Macedonian king would lay siege to the Achaemenid Empire in the early fourth century B.C.[89] Wherefore, last but not least, there arose a preeminent fourth kingdom—one as durable as iron itself; the Roman Empire would ascend to power in the first century B.C., thereon satisfying the account of King Nebuchadnezzar's vision.[90]

Notwithstanding, after the establishment of the kingdom of iron, a rock was to be formed via supernatural hands—a rock which would crush the great empires of the world and establish the everlasting kingdom of God. Subsequently, the Jewish messiah was seemingly set to arrive on scene amidst the reign of the great Roman Empire, whereon Christ would be seen, in the first century A.D., proclaiming the realization of His long-foretold advent:

> Jesus said to them, "Have you never read in the scriptures: 'The very stone which the builders rejected has become the head of the corner; this was the Lord's doing, and it is marvelous in our eyes'? Therefore, I tell you the kingdom of God will be taken away from you and given to a nation producing the fruits of it. And he who falls on this stone will

---

87. Ibid.
88. Ibid.
89. Ibid.
90. Ibid.

be broken to pieces; if it falls on anyone, it will crush him."
(Matthew 21:41-43, NRSVCE)

Remarkably, this would also not be the end of Daniel's prophetic encounters, as he proceeds to receive a second revelation; for, in response to a penitential petition to God, he is afforded the counsel of the angel Gabriel:

> In the first year of Darius the son of Ahasu-e′rus, by birth a Mede, who became king over the realm of the Chaldeans—in the first year of his reign, I, Daniel, perceived in the books the number of years which, according to the word of the LORD to Jeremiah the prophet, must pass before the end of the desolations of Jerusalem, namely, seventy years. Then I turned my face to the Lord God, seeking him by prayer and supplications with fasting and sackcloth and ashes. I prayed to the LORD my God and made confession, saying, "O Lord, the great and terrible God, who keeps covenant and steadfast love with those who love him and keep his commandments, we have sinned and done wrong and acted wickedly and rebelled, turning aside from thy commandments and ordinances; we have not listened to thy servants the prophets, who spoke in thy name to our kings, our princes, and our fathers, and to all the people of the land. To thee, O Lord, belongs righteousness, but to us confusion of face, as at this day, to the men of Judah, to the inhabitants of Jerusalem, and to all Israel, those that are near and those that are far away, in all the lands to which thou hast driven them, because of the treachery which they have committed against thee..."
> ...While I was speaking and praying, confessing my sin and the sin of my people Israel, and presenting my supplication before the LORD my God for the holy hill of my

God; while I was speaking in prayer, the man Gabriel, whom I had seen in the vision at the first, came to me in swift flight at the time of the evening sacrifice. He came and he said to me, "O Daniel, I have now come out to give you wisdom and understanding. At the beginning of your supplications a word went forth, and I have come to tell it to you, for you are greatly beloved; therefore, consider the word and understand the vision. Seventy [Sevens] are decreed concerning your people and your holy city, to finish the transgression, to put an end to sin, and to atone for iniquity, to bring in everlasting righteousness, to seal both vision and prophet, and to anoint a most holy place. Know therefore and understand that from the going forth of the word to restore and build Jerusalem to the coming of an anointed one, a prince, there shall be seven [sevens]. Then for sixty-two [sevens] it shall be built again with squares and moat, but in a troubled time. And after the sixty-two [sevens], an anointed one shall be cut off, and shall have nothing; and the people of the prince who is to come shall destroy the city." (Daniel 9:1-11, 20-27, NRSVCE) [91]

To be sure, an obvious question invariably arises when first reading of Daniel's encounter, as it can be difficult to decipher what Gabriel is inferring with an obscure phrase like "seventy, sevens." The expression itself is somewhat ambiguous; however, if placed in the proper context, its significance becomes clear. Indeed, for Gabriel's *"seventy, sevens"* decree is a direct response to Daniel's penitential petition for mercy—a petition wherein he refers to a specific 70-year period of Jewish subjugation under Babylonian rule. As such, it would be fair to conclude that in his decree, Gabriel is playing upon

---

91. Most Catholic translations use the word "weeks" instead of "sevens." However, in Hebrew, the original word signifies "a period of seven." As such, a more literal translation is warranted and has been added in brackets.

the 70 years of Jewish captivity which were alluded to in Daniel's prayer. And thus, via the use of *"seventy, sevens,"* Gabriel is foretelling of a period of 70 years—of seven—yet to come, or a period of 490 years.[92]

What is more, after divulging the specific actions that would be required to atone for the wickedness of the Jewish people, Gabriel then proceeds to explain what was to become of their future messiah; namely, that following the decree to rebuild Jerusalem, there would pass seven plus 62 of the seven-year periods—or 483 years— until the anointed one would be put to death. Notwithstanding, both the ancient Babylonians and the ancient Israelites also utilized a 360-day calendar, and, as such, it is necessary to consider a 476-year equivalent in our modern-day Gregorian system.[93] Wherefore, given that the official decree to rebuild Jerusalem was promulgated by emperor Artaxerxes Longimanus in 444 B.C., we should expect to have seen the messiah's death in approximately 33 A.D.[94]

Predictably, the Jewish population in the early first century was well aware of Daniel's prophetic accounts.[95] So much so, that their anticipation would cause them to initially confuse John the Baptist for their long-awaited messiah.[96] Nevertheless, the anointed one was set to arrive on scene shortly, thereafter, having been foreordained via an angelic pronouncement to the immaculate Virgin Mary. Subsequently, in his only other earthly appearance within the entirety of the biblical canon, Gabriel announces the coming of Christ, and the culmination of his "seventy, sevens" decree. Further still, as Jesus would reach the age of maturity, and

---

92. Brandt J. Pitre, *The Case for Jesus: The Biblical and Historical Evidence for Christ* (New York, NY: Image, 2016), 114-116

93. Chuck Smith and Mark Eastman, *The Search for the Messiah* (Fountain Valley, CA, Joy Publishing, 1996), 104

94. Josh McDowell, A Ready Defense: The Best of Josh McDowell, comp. Bill Wilson (Nashville, TN: Thomas Nelson Inc., 2021), 56-59

95. Ibid.

96. John 1:19-23; Luke 3:15

then commence His earthly ministry, He would explicitly confirm that His envisaged timeline had at long last been achieved:

> Now after John was arrested, Jesus came into Galilee, preaching the gospel of God, and saying, "The time is fulfilled, and the kingdom of God is at hand; repent, and believe in the gospel." (Mark 1:14-15, NRSVCE)

In summation, there are numerous predictions within the Old Testament canon regarding the arrival of a Jewish messiah; however, the book of Daniel, perhaps more so than any other text, poses a significant problem to those who would dismiss it as mere legend or bronze-age mythology. Indeed, for how does one account for these two precise prophecies, each of which significantly predates the arrival of Christ, accurately forecasting both the chronology of His birth and the subsequent year of His death?

The Gospel of Matthew and the Sign of Jonah

Throughout the duration of His public ministry in the early first century A.D., wherever He traveled, Christ would be met by a sizable group of onlookers. Predictably, the vast majority within these assemblies had earnestly come to observe Him; however, there was also a contingent who reviled His influence and avowed to turn public opinion against Him. For instance, Matthew would chronicle numerous occasions wherein the Jewish Pharisees sought to undermine Christ's ministry, whereon they deliberately distorted the meaning of His sermons and disparaged His miraculous works. However, their attempts to defame Him continued to fail, so they opted to alter their approach and, by contrast, insist that He provide a public sign if He was, in fact, their messiah. Nevertheless, fully aware of their deceitful intentions and their utter lack of sincerity,

Jesus refused them their demonstration and instead replied accordingly:

> An evil and adulterous generation seeks for a sign; but no sign shall be given to it except the sign of the prophet Jonah. For as Jonah was three days and three nights in the belly of the whale, so will the Son of man be three days and three nights in the heart of the earth. The men of Nineveh will arise at the judgment with this generation and condemn it; for they repented at the preaching of Jonah, and behold, something greater than Jonah is here. The queen of the South will arise at the judgment with this generation and condemn it; for she came from the ends of the earth to hear the wisdom of Solomon, and behold, something greater than Solomon is here. (Matthew 12:39-41, NRSVCE)

To be sure, His public rebuke of the contemptuous Pharisees was a forceful condemnation. However, at first glance, Christ's allusion to the prophet Jonah appears to be a curious comparison at best. In fact, one could readily point to a multitude of other Old Testament accounts, which would further attest to His identity and serve to silence His ardent critics. So why then would Jesus choose such an analogy? Why would He refer to a seemingly disparate prophet when the Pharisees were scholars of the Jewish Scriptures and thus aware of more powerful texts? Moreover, what exactly was He seeking to convey with His allusion to "the sign of Jonah?"

Admittedly, when considering the innermost intentions of Christ, we are ultimately forced to speculate. However, perhaps with a careful analysis of the story of Jonah, His reasoning and motivations will become clearer.

Case in point: the book of Jonah chronicles the story of a man who was called upon by God to deliver a message of warning, for the city of Nineveh had become a place of great wickedness, which demanded its repentance and conversion. However, fearing persecution, Jonah chose to defy God's instructions and flee instead to the nearby city of Joppa—once there, he would acquire a passage to Tarshish and therein evade the burden of his mission. Nevertheless, shortly after his ship's departure, the vessel would encounter a sizable storm—a storm which continued to grow and strength and threaten the lives of all on board. What's more, the ship's men soon began to castigate Jonah and inculpate him for the storm, as he had informed them of his misguided plot to escape his divine commission. Consequently, out of options and miles from shore, the desperate crew would finally resort to throwing Jonah overboard—to satisfy the wrath of God—and with that, the great storm finally subsided. However, Jonah's saga was just beginning:

And the Lord appointed a great fish to swallow up Jonah; and Jonah was in the belly of the fish three days and three nights.
    Then Jonah prayed to the LORD his God from the belly of the fish, saying, "I called to the LORD, out of my distress, and he answered me; out of the belly of Sheol I cried, and thou didst hear my voice. For thou didst cast me into the deep, into the heart of the seas, and the flood was round about me; all thy waves and thy billows passed over me. Then I said, 'I am cast out from thy presence; how shall I again look upon thy holy temple?' The waters closed in over me, the deep was round about me; weeds were wrapped about my head at the roots of the mountains. I went down to the land_whose bars closed upon me forever; yet thou didst bring up my life from the Pit, O LORD my God. When my soul fainted within me,_I remembered the LORD; and my prayer came to thee,_into thy holy temple. Those who pay regard to vain idols forsake their true loyalty. But I with the voice of thanksgiving will sacrifice to thee; what I have

vowed I will pay. Deliverance belongs to the LORD!" And the LORD spoke to the fish, and it vomited out Jonah upon the dry land." (Jonah 1:17, 2:1-10, NRSVCE)

In truth, the sudden arrival of a monstrous fish certainly warrants attention. However, it is Jonah's prayer to the Lord which is of the foremost significance in this passage. For, it recounts that Jonah cried out from the belly of "Sheol," which was a Jewish moniker for realm of the dead,[97] and that he went down to "the land whose bars closed on him forever," yet the Lord brought up his life from "the pit." Accordingly, that when his "soul had fainted within him," he had proceeded to remember the Lord, and that in doing so his petitions had reached on high, to the summit of God's holy temple. To be sure, the language that is used within these verses repeatedly makes reference to a spiritual death and afterlife, whereby it is forcefully and conclusively established that Jonah had succumbed to the depths of the sea.[98] Subsequently, after 3 days and 3 nights in the belly of the fish, it was Jonah's corpse which washed up on dry land—a sentiment affirmed in the subsequent verses, as the saga then continued:

Then the word of the LORD came to Jonah the second time, saying, "Arise, go to Nineveh, that great city, and proclaim to it the message that I tell you." So Jonah arose and went to Nin′eveh, according to the word of the LORD. Now Nin′eveh was an exceedingly great city, three days' journey in breadth. Jonah began to go into the city, going a day's journey. And he cried, "Yet forty days, and Nin′eveh shall be overthrown!" And the people of Nin′eveh believed God; they proclaimed a fast, and put on sackcloth, from the

---

97. Brandt J. Pitre, *The Case for Jesus: The Biblical and Historical Evidence for Christ* (New York, NY: Image, 2016), 187
98. Ibid.

greatest of them to the least of them. Then tidings reached the king of Nin'eveh, and he arose from his throne, removed his robe, and covered himself with sackcloth, and sat in ashes. And he made proclamation and published through Nin'eveh, "By the decree of the king and his nobles: Let neither man nor beast, herd nor flock, taste anything; let them not feed, or drink water, but let man and beast be covered with sackcloth, and let them cry mightily to God; yea, let everyone turn from his evil way and from the violence which is in his hands. Who knows, God may yet repent and turn from his fierce anger, so that we perish not?" When God saw what they did, how they turned from their evil way, God repented of the evil which he had said he would do to them; and he did not do it. (Jonah 3:1-10, NRSVCE)

Wherefore, having been vomited out by the monstrous fish and washing ashore on dry land, we read that the Lord tells Jonah's lifeless body to "Arise, and go to Nineveh." Furthermore, inasmuch this decree may seem commonplace or innocuous, in this case it is also imperative to note, that in the original translation of this passage, the Hebraic verb utilized is "Cum." [99] Indeed, for this divine command is distinct to neither Jonah nor his mission, but it is a charge which is notably repeated by Christ, within the Gospel of Mark, as well:

> When they came to the house of the ruler of the synagogue, he saw a tumult, and people weeping and wailing loudly. And when he had entered, he said to them, "Why do you make a tumult and weep? The child is not dead but sleeping." And they laughed at him. But he put them all

---

99. Ibid.

outside and took the child's father and mother and those who were with him and went in where the child was. Taking her by the hand he said to her, "Talitha cum"; which means, "Little girl, I say to you, arise." And immediately the girl got up and walked; for she was twelve years old. And immediately they were overcome with amazement. (Mark 5:38-43, NRSVCE)

Subsequently, as is made evident by Christ in the Gospel of Mark, one is ultimately forced to conclude that the story of Jonah is likewise a chronicle of a death and resurrection. As such, just as Jonah was eventually revived after three days and nights in the sea, so too was Jesus resurrected after three days in the heart of the earth. What is more, Jonah then goes on to the city of Nineveh, and proceeds to convert its inhabitants, whereon the entire populace miraculously repents "from the greatest of them, to the least of them." Consequently, in specifically referencing the "sign of Jonah," it is also fair to presume that Christ in turn is similarly foreshadowing a miraculous conversion to come. However, in contrast to the story of Jonah, where it is merely one city which repents, at the behest of Jesus, this conversion is to engulf the entirety of the world; indeed, for "something greater than Jonah" was truly within their midst.[100] To be sure, Christ then proceeds to publicly pronounce these precise intentions, as He precipitates a global evangelization effort, in His final commission to the disciples:

> And Jesus came and said to them, "All authority in heaven and on earth has been given to me. Go therefore and make disciples of all nations, baptizing them in the name of the Father and of the Son and of the Holy Spirit, teaching them to observe all that I have commanded you; and lo, I am with

---

100. Ibid, 188-189

you always, to the close of the age." (Matthew 28:18-20, NRSVCE)

As such, one by one, city by city, the disciples went forth and converted the masses—a feat accomplished by sacrifice and love and in the face of relentless persecution. And yet, by some miracle, after executing Christ some 350 years prior and then relentlessly oppressing His followers, Christianity would become the official religion of the Empire in 380 A.D.[101] Predictably, early Christian evangelists recognized the significance of Christ's prophecy and His subsequent commission to the disciples, which is why prominent bishops such as Eusebius of Caesarea would assert that a veritable miracle was occurring. Indeed, for all around them, pagan temples were collapsing into the proverbial dustbin of history, and the gentiles were beginning to convert in droves to the God of Christianity [102]—and how could events of such magnitude be explained apart from the divine providence of Christ?

In truth, the sign of Jonah continues to persevere to this very day, as millions are converted to the Christian faith with the passing of each new year.[103] Subsequently, although a reliable historical record and credible eyewitness testimony lend credence to Christianity, the inexplicable fulfillment of precursory biblical prophecies has afforded us appreciable ancillary testimony. As the Church historian Eusebius distinctly noted in the 4th century A.D.:

> He prophesied that His doctrine should be preached throughout the whole world inhabited by man for a testimony to all nations, and by divine foreknowledge declared that the Church, which was afterwards gathered

---

101. Emperor Theodosius I, *Edict of Thessalonica*, A.D. 380
102. Brandt J. Pitre, *The Case for Jesus: The Biblical and Historical Evidence for Christ* (New York, NY: Image, 2016), 188-189
103. Lewis R. Rambo and Charles E. Farhadian, *The Oxford Handbook of Religious Conversion* (Oxford: Oxford University Press, 2014), 58

by His own power out of all nations, though not yet seen nor established in the times when He was living as man amongst men, should be invincible and undismayed, and should never be conquered by death, but stands and abides unshaken, settled, and rooted upon His own power as upon a rock that cannot be shaken or broken—the fulfilment of this prophecy must in reason be more powerful than any word to stop every gaping mouth of those who are prepared to exhibit a shameless effrontery.

For whom would not acknowledge the truth of the prophecy, when the facts so manifestly all but cry out and say, that it was indeed the power of God, and not human nature, which before these things came to pass foresaw that they should happen in this way, and foretold them, and in deeds fulfilled them? Certainly, the fame of His Gospel has filled the whole world on which the sun looks down; and the proclamations concerning Him ran through all nations, and are now still increasing and advancing in a manner corresponding to His own words...

...And in addition to all this, there is no small proof of the truth which we hold in the testimony of the Hebrew Scriptures, in which so vast a number of years beforehand the Hebrew prophets proclaimed the promise of blessings to all mortal life, and mentioned expressly the name of the Christ, and foretold His advent among men, and announced the novel manner of His teaching, which in its course has reached unto all nations. They predicted also the future unbelief in Him, and the gainsaying of the Jewish nation, and the deeds they wrought against Him, and the dismal fate which thereupon immediately and without delay overtook them: I mean the final siege of their royal metropolis, and the entire overthrow of the kingdom, and their own dispersion among all nations, and their bondage in the land of their enemies and adversaries, things which they are seen to have suffered after our Saviour's advent in accordance with the prophecies.

All these circumstances then confirm the story of the facts of our religion, and show that it was not contrived from any human impulse, but divinely foreknown, and divinely announced beforehand by the written oracles, and yet far more divinely proffered to all men by our Saviour; afterwards also it received power from God, and was so established, that after these many years of persecution both by the invisible demons and by the visible rulers of each age it shines forth far more brightly, and daily becomes more conspicuous, and grows and multiplies more and more. Thus, it is plain to see that the help which comes down from the God of the universe supplies to the teaching and name of our Saviour its irresistible and invincible force, and its victorious power against its enemies.[104]

---

[104] Eusebius of Caesarea, *Evangelical Preparation* 3-4, A.D. 313.

XI. CONCLUSION

In an entirely unprecedented fashion, the creation account of Genesis would reveal that the human race had been consciously made in the image and likeness of God, wherein a spark of divinity was inscribed into human corporeality in anticipation of the Incarnation. Nevertheless, it was not until the arrival of Christ that we were fully made cognizant of this reality, whereupon the eternal logos entered human history and assumed the image of man. To be sure, it is this unique and unparalleled claim which has distinguished Christianity from all other religions, for it has revealed the reality of the triune God, the subsequent foundation for all creation, and the extraordinary manner in which He has reconciled our fallen nature to Himself. As such, Christianity bears witness to an eternal God of love, the Incarnation of His begotten Son, and a salvific sacrifice which has ultimately become the greatest story to have ever been told. And yet, is that all there is to the Christian faith? Is the Incarnation just another ancient allegorical fable? How can we have confidence in the New Testament accounts and their numerous supernatural claims?

In truth, inasmuch as the original documents of nearly all ancient texts have been irreparably damaged, lost, or destroyed, the sheer number of well-preserved early manuscripts and fragments allows the New Testament to be scrutinized at a level unparalleled by any other writing from classical antiquity. Wherefore, even as scholars have no recourse to unblemished first-century manuscripts, the process of textual criticism has evinced that authentic modern biblical translations are, in essence, uniform with the original texts. [105] Furthermore, the process of establishing authoritative collations began almost immediately after the death of Christ, whereon only verifiable documents that were consistent with oral apostolic teaching were ever permitted inclusion. Correspondingly, one must also acknowledge a host of historical writings and recent archeological discoveries, which have validated numerous biblical claims and manifested an overall historical reliability.

What is more, a detailed examination of the biblical manuscript record, alongside concurrent Christian sources, reveals both consistent and continuous authorship attributions for all four gospel accounts. Comparatively, both the internal and extra-biblical evidence is also commensurate with the traditional ascriptions and bears witness to four congruous resurrection accounts without suspicious harmonization. As such, it can be credibly asserted that the gospel authors were neither ignorant nor disconnected from the events they would record, as two of the professed authors were, themselves, Disciples of Christ, while the remaining two were highly educated companions of other such eyewitnesses. Further still, a cursory reading of the New Testament also evinces that its authors were intelligent and reasonable, in that many of the Apostles included intimate and embarrassing details throughout their scriptural accounts, which is typically indicative of testimonial credibility, and an overall commitment to accuracy. In fact, the

---

105. Gary Michuta, *Why Catholic Bibles Are Bigger,* 2nd ed. (San Diego, CA: Catholic Answer Press, 2017), 255

Apostles would have had little to gain from spreading exaggerations or falsehoods, as the vast majority endured relentless persecution and suffered martyrdom for their newfound faith.[106] And yet, inasmuch as the respective New Testament texts are demonstrably credible and congruent, there is also the inexplicable testimony that comes by way of precursory prophetic texts. For, in reality, neither the messianic timeline foretold within the book of Daniel, nor the rise of Christianity predicted by Christ can be rationalized as mere coincidental occurrences or an ancient, coordinated conspiracies.

In summation, Christianity is a religion that admittedly makes a host of extraordinary claims—claims can be difficult to initially accept given that they challenge many commonly held secular presuppositions. Nevertheless, when one is confronted with the scope of comprehensive evidence that lends credence to the Christian claims, it would be difficult to maintain that they are mythological, ahistorical, insubstantial, or unreasonable. Accordingly, when one views the fruits of the Christian faith and the civilizations/cultures it has produced, it would be difficult to deny that its foundational precepts seem to have transcended those of its religious and ideological counterparts. And yet, inasmuch as Christianity is a rational religion that vigorously defends its precepts and historical claims, there are certainly tenets that ultimately require an additional step of faith. However, this is not to suggest that we suspend our faculties or ignore legitimate scrutiny, for as bishop Robert Barron explains, authentic faith is not credulity:

> There is no way, strictly on the basis of analytical reasoning, that I could ever come to know certain truths about God— indeed, there are certain truths that can only be known by way of revelation. It is I who then must choose

---

106. William Lane Craig, *Reasonable Faith: Christian Truth and Apologetics*, 3rd ed. (Wheaton, IL: Crossway, 2008), 338-340

to accept this revealed truth, acknowledging that it is congruent with God's nature, or else reject it as false. The step of faith that we take as Christians, therefore, is not some wild leap into the dark or a surrendering of the human intellect, for we have already arrived at the summit/limits of analytical reasoning—a point from which we are able to accept credible divine revelations that are congruent with our prior analytical understanding of the nature of God.[107]

---

107. Bishop Robert Barron, "What Faith Is and What it Isn't," Word on Fire Catholic Ministries, October 20, 2011, https://www.wordonfire.org/articles/barron/what-faith-is-and-what-it-isn't/

BOOK II BIBLIOGRAPHY

Catholic Answer, https://www.catholic.com

Chesterton, G.K. *Orthodoxy.* Mineola, NY: Dover Publications, 2020.

———.*Saint Thomas Aquinas.* Mineola, NY: Dover Publications, 2009.

Chilton, Bruce and Evans, Craig A. *Authenticating the Activities of Jesus.* Boston, MA: Brill Academia Publishers Inc, 2002.

Craig, William Lane. *Reasonable Faith: Christian Truth and Apologetics.* 3rd ed. Wheaton, IL: Crossway, 2008.

Drive Thru History, https://drivethruhisty

Ehrman, Bart D. *Forged: Writing the Name of God—Why the Bible's Authors Are Not Who We Think They Are.* New York, NY: HyperOne, 2011.

Hands On Apologetics, http://www.handsonapologetics.com

Kelly, Matthew. *Rediscover Catholicism: A Spiritual Guide to Living with Passion & Purpose.* New York, NY: Beacon Publishing, 2014.

Lewis, C.S. *Mere Christianity.* New York, NY: MacMillan Publishing Company, 1986.

McDowell, Josh. *A Ready Defense: The Best of Josh McDowell.* Compiled by Bill Wilson. Nashville, TN: Thomas Nelson Inc., 2021.

Michuta, Gary. *Why Catholic Bibles Are Bigger.* 2nd ed. San Diego, CA: Catholic Answer Press, 2017.

New Advent, https://www.newadvent.org

O'Flaherty, Wendy D. *Karma, and Rebirth in Classical Indian Traditions.* Los Angeles, CA: University of California Press, 1980.

Packer, J.I. *Knowing God.* Downers Grove, IL: Intervarsity Press, 1973.

Paley, William. *A View of the Evidence of Christianity.* 2 vols., New ed. Edinburgh: George Ramsay & Co., 1811

Pitre, Brandt J. *The Case for Jesus: The Biblical and Historical Evidence for* Christ. New York, NY: Image, 2016.

Rambo, Lewis R. and Farhadian, Charles E. *The Oxford Handbook of Religious Conversion.* Oxford: Oxford University Press, 2014.

Reasonable Faith with William Lane, https://reasonablefaith.org

Sheen, Abp. Fulton. *The Crisis in Christendom.* Washington, DC: National Council of Catholic Men, 1952.

Smith, Chuck and Eastman, Mark. *The Search for the Messiah.* Fountain Valley, CA: Joy Publishing, 1996.

Spencer, Robert and Chesler, Phyllis. *The Violent Oppression of Women in Islam.* Los Angeles, CA: David Horowitz Freedom Centre, 2007.

Word on Fire Catholic Ministries, https://www.wordonfire.org

BOOK III:
SPIRITUM SANCTUM, DOMINUM
(THE HOLY SPIRIT, THE LORD)

I. THE ROLE OF THE HOLY SPIRIT [1]

When the work which the Father gave the Son to do on earth [John 17:4] was accomplished, the Holy Spirit was sent on the day of Pentecost in order that He might continually sanctify the Church, and thus, all those who believe would have access through Christ in one Spirit to the Father. [Ephesians 1:18] He is the Spirit of Life, a fountain of water springing up to life eternal. [John 4:14, 7: 38-39] To those dead in sin, the Father gives life through Him, until, in Christ, He brings to life their mortal bodies. [Romans 8:10-11] The Spirit dwells in the Church and in the hearts of the faithful, as in a temple. [1 Corinthians 3:16, 6:19] In them He prays on their behalf and bears witness to the fact that they are adopted sons and daughters.[Galatians 4:6, Romans 8:15-16, 26] The Church, which the Spirit guides in the way of all truth [John 16:13] and which He unified in communion and in works of ministry, He both equips and directs with hierarchical and charismatic gifts and adorns with His fruits.[Ephesians 1:11-12, 1 Corinthians 12:4, Galatians 5:22] By the power of the Gospel, He makes the Church keep the freshness of

---

1. The following excerpt has been quoted from: Second Vatican Council, Dogmatic Constitution on the Church, *Lumen Gentium,* (21, November 1964), No. 4

youth. Uninterruptedly, He renews it and leads it to perfect union with its Spouse. [S. Irenaeus, Against All Heresies 3:24:1] The Spirit and the Bride both say to Jesus, the Lord, "Come!" [Revelation 22:17]

Thus, the Church has been seen as "a people made one with the unity of the Father, the Son and the Holy Spirit." [S. Cyprian, *De Oratione Dominica* 23]

II. SCRIPTURE, TRADITION, AND THE MAGISTERIUM

Although Christ expressed His desire for a unified Church and prayed that His faithful be one [John 17:20-23], the modern-day landscape of Christianity is one of disorder and division. Indeed, with a seemingly endless array of autonomous denominations, each espousing distinct and contradictory convictions, it would be hard to deny that Christianity today has become both convoluted and divisive. As such, how are we to determine who is ultimately correct regarding doctrines of faith and morals? Moreover, who has the authority to resolve these disputes and dictate who has erred and is in schism? Further still, how is it that Christianity became so contentious in the first place?

In truth, as much as varying and compounding disputes between Eastern and Western ecclesial authorities led to an initial fracturing of Christendom, what truly precipitated a pervasive de-harmonization of Christian doctrines, rituals, and institutions were the protestations of a 16th-century Augustinian friar named Martin

Luther. For, amongst other things, he would avow that Scripture alone was sufficient to be the ultimate and final Christian authority and that all questions of dogma, doctrine, and discipline were to be subjected exclusively to it.[2] Moreover, that the plain sense of Scripture was perspicuous to its beholder, regardless of training or tuition, and, as such, biblical interpretation did not belong to some rigid ecclesiastical body but rather to the universal "priesthood" of all believers.[3] Nevertheless, the subsequent rise of some thirty thousand new denominations in only five hundred years appears to have refuted Luther's novel propositions.[4] What's more, his principal doctrines have not only proven to be calamitous in practice but also, scripturally, tenuous positions.

Case in point: consider that the Bible has no "sacred" table of contents, nor does it specify which writings are Scripture, and thus, from the very outset one must rely on an extra-biblical authority to discern which texts are inspired. Accordingly, there is no set formula which can be applied to reproduce either the New or Old Testament canons, for any criteria that can justify the exclusion of certain texts will inevitably cast doubt on the inclusion of others. For example, the vast majority of authentic first century Christian

---

2. "Scripture alone is the true over-lord and master of all writings and doctrines on earth. If not, what are the Scriptures good for? Let us reject them and be satisfied with the books of men and human teachers." (Martin Luther, *An Argument in Defense of All the Articles of Dr. Martin Luther Wrongly Condemned in the Roman Bull*, A.D. 1521)

3. "The Holy Scriptures must be clearer, easier of interpretation, and more certain than any other writings, for all teachers prove their statements by them, as by clearer and more stable writings, and wish their own writings to be confirmed and explained by them. But no one can ever prove a dark saying by one that is still darker; therefore, necessity compels us to run to the Bible with all the writings of the doctors, and thence to get our verdict and judgment upon them." (Martin Luther, *An Argument in Defense of All the Articles of Dr. Martin Luther Wrongly Condemned in the Roman Bull*, A.D. 1521)

4. Stephen Beale, "Just How Many Protestant Denominations are there?" National Catholic Register, October 31, 2017, http://www.ncregister.com/blog/just-how-many-protestant-denominations-are-there%3famp

writings were included, whilst others [*the Didache, the Shepherd of Hermas, Clement's First Epistle to the Corinthians*] were notably left out. Likewise, anonymous texts were, for the most part, rejected, yet *the Epistle to the Hebrews* was curiously accepted. Furthermore, an authoritative canon wasn't even officially established until the council of Rome in 382 A.D., and even then, there was a scarcity of Scripture and illiteracy en-masse until the invention of the printing press in the fifteenth century. As such, what are we to make of the first 1500 years of Christianity without widespread personal access to Scripture? Are we to believe that we were devoid of a supreme and final authority for three-quarters of Christian history? Moreover, are we to believe that God permitted a false ecclesiastical authority to spread error freely and near-universally for the better part of two millennia? Correspondingly, how are we to resolve matters of faith and morals that are ambiguous in, or absent from Scripture? How do we reconcile these issues?

What is more, as much as the widespread discord within certain Protestant sects certainly testifies to the complexity of Scripture, the New Testament itself explicitly refutes the notion that its writings are clear or perspicuous. For example, Peter alleges that portions of the Pauline epistles were difficult to comprehend, and that the ignorant and unstable often distorted their meanings, along with other scriptural texts:

> Regard the patience of our Lord as salvation. So also our beloved brother Paul wrote to you according to the wisdom given to him, speaking of this as he does in all his letters. There are some things in them hard to understand, which the ignorant and unstable twist to their own destruction, as they do the other scriptures. You, therefore, beloved, since you are forewarned, beware that you are not carried away with the error of the lawless and lose your own stability. (2 Peter 3:15-17, NRSVCE)

Accordingly, Luke puts forth a similar sentiment in his chronicles on the *Acts of the Apostles* by noting that even a prominent official required interpretive assistance, whilst reading the prophet Isaiah:

> Then an angel of the Lord said to Philip, "Get up and go toward the south to the road that goes down from Jerusalem to Gaza." (This is a wilderness road.) So, he got up and went. Now there was an Ethiopian eunuch, a court official of the Candace, queen of the Ethiopians, in charge of her entire treasury. He had come to Jerusalem to worship and was returning home; seated in his chariot, he was reading the prophet Isaiah. Then the Spirit said to Philip, "Go over to this chariot and join it." So, Philip ran up to it and heard him reading the prophet Isaiah. He asked, "Do you understand what you are reading?" He replied, "How can I, unless someone explains it to me?" And he invited Philip to get in and sit beside him. (Acts 8:26-31, NRSVCE)

In fact, simply imagine a novice scholar discerning Shakespeare or Dante without structured guidelines or systematic review—it is even more counterintuitive with Scripture. Indeed, for these elaborate classical works require historical/cultural context, proficiency in language, familiarity with relevant authoritative commentaries, and general exegetical competency in order to accurately grasp their author's intentions. Case in point: up through the centuries numerous unqualified sects attempted to independently interpret the Scriptures, whereupon groups like the Donatists, Novatians, Arians, Pelagians and Nestorians began to promote novelties which were at odds with traditional exegesis. As such, defenders of orthodoxy forcefully combated these movements, and their heretical explications of the Scriptures. However, curiously enough, they didn't do so via the Scriptures alone but rather in conjunction with Church authority and oral Apostolic Tradition.

Unsurprisingly, the Scriptures themselves repeatedly bespeak of these complimentary authorities, and likewise, they never proclaim to be wholly sufficient or the final arbiter of truth. For instance, John concedes that there were numerous events that were not recorded within Scripture and that it would have been impossible to document the entirety of Christ's life or the totality of His ministry:

> This is the disciple who is testifying to these things and has written them, and we know that his testimony is true. But there are also many other things that Jesus did; if every one of them were written down, I suppose that the world itself could not contain the books that would be written. (John 21:24-25, NRSVCE)

Correspondingly, Paul refers to inspired oral teaching in two separate epistles to the Thessalonians, wherein he equates apostolic orations with the word of God and implores them to safeguard spoken Tradition:

> We also constantly give thanks to God for this, that when you received the word of God that you heard from us, you accepted it not as a human word but as what it really is, God's word, which is also at work in you believers. (1 Thessalonians 2:13, NRSVCE)

> So then, brothers and sisters, stand firm and hold fast to the traditions that you were taught by us, either by word of mouth or by our letter. (2 Thessalonians 2:15, NRSVCE)

Furthermore, Scripture also attests to the authority of the Church and deems it the pillar and ground of the truth [1 Timothy 3:15]. However, it is one that is singular, hierarchical, sovereign, and successional, and, as such, it is irreconcilable with the concept of denominationalism. Case in point: Matthew recounts Christ commissioning a Church that is singular and juridical in nature—one with the authority to bind and loose and excommunicate obstinate sinners:

> And I tell you that you are Peter, and on this rock I will build my church, and the gates of Hades will not overcome it. (Matthew 16:18, NRSVCE)

> If another member of the church sins against you, go and point out the fault when the two of you are alone. If the member listens to you, you have regained that one. But if you are not listened to, take one or two others along with you, so that every word may be confirmed by the evidence of two or three witnesses. If the member refuses to listen to them, tell it to the church; and if the offender refuses to listen even to the church, let such a one be to you as a Gentile and a tax collector. Truly I tell you, whatever you bind on earth will be bound in heaven, and whatever you loose on earth will be loosed in heaven. (Matthew 18:15-18, NRSVCE)

Subsequently, Paul then depicts a synonymous Church throughout his numerous epistles [1 Corinthians 1:10, Galatians 2:1-2, Hebrews 13:7-17],[5] and bears witness to an incipient Christian parallel [Bishop, Priest, Deacon] of the Jewish three-fold hierarchy [High Priest, Priest, Levite] of clerical offices which were functionally distinct:

> The saying is sure: whoever aspires to the office of bishop [episkopos] desires a noble task. Now a bishop [episkopos]

---

5. The Epistle to the Hebrews is, in fact, an anonymous text; however, it is typically regarded as having a "Pauline" character.

must be above reproach, married only once, temperate, sensible, respectable, hospitable, an apt teacher, not a drunkard, not violent but gentle, not quarrelsome, and not a lover of money. He must manage his own household well, keeping his children submissive and respectful in every way— for if someone does not know how to manage his own household, how can he take care of God's church? He must not be a recent convert, or he may be puffed up with conceit and fall into the condemnation of the devil. Moreover, he must be well thought of by outsiders, so that he may not fall into disgrace and the snare of the devil. Deacons [*Diakonos*] likewise must be serious, not double-tongued, not indulging in much wine, not greedy for money; they must hold fast to the mystery of the faith with a clear conscience. And let them first be tested; then, if they prove themselves blameless, let them serve as deacons [*diakonos*]. (1 Timothy 3:1-10, NRSVCE)

Let the priests [*presbuteros*] that rule well, be esteemed worthy of double honor: especially they who labor in the word and doctrine: For the scripture saith: Thou shalt not muzzle the ox that treadeth out the corn: and the laborer is worthy of his reward. Against a priest [*presbuteros*] receive not an accusation, but under two or three witnesses. (1 Timothy 5:17-19, DRA)

What is more, in accordance with and in fulfillment of the Old Testament Magisterium, which was passed down from Moses to the Pharisees [Matthew 23:1-3], the pedigree and authority of the New Testament episcopacy were then handed down in successive fashion. For example, Acts would recount that Matthias was added to the apostolic [episkopos] ministry, to fill the vacancy that was left by Judas following his unfavorable demise:

ETERNALLY ONE, ETERNALLY THREE

> Then they prayed and said, "Lord, you know everyone's heart. Show us which one of these two you have chosen to take the place in this ministry and apostleship [episkopos] from which Judas turned aside to go to his own place." And they cast lots for them, and the lot fell on Matthias; and he was added to the eleven apostles. (Acts 1:24-26, NRSVCE)

Respectively, Paul and Barnabas were then called to join the ranks of the episcopacy, [S. Chrysostom, *Homily 27 on the Acts of the Apostles*] that they might preach with authority and fulfill the works for which they were foreordained:

> Now in the church at Antioch there were prophets and teachers: Barnabas, Simeon called Niger, Lucius of Cyrene, Manaen (who had been brought up with Herod the tetrarch) and Saul. While they were worshiping the Lord and fasting, the Holy Spirit said, "Set apart for me Barnabas and Saul for the work to which I have called them." So, after they had fasted and prayed, they placed their hands on them and sent them off. (Acts 13:1-3, NRSVCE)

Further still, as Moses and his successors had ordained chosen recipients via the laying on of hands, [Numbers 11:16–25, Numbers 27:15–23, Deuteronomy 34:9] Acts describes the Apostles conferring holy orders in an equivalent/synonymous fashion:

> What they said pleased the whole community, and they chose Stephen, a man full of faith and the Holy Spirit, together with Philip, Prochorus, Nicanor, Timon, Parmenas, and Nicolaus, a proselyte of Antioch. They had these men stand before the apostles, who prayed and laid their hands on them. (Acts 6:5-6, NRSVCE)

> Confirming the souls of the disciples and exhorting them to continue in the faith: and that through many tribulations we must enter into the kingdom of God. And when they had ordained to them priests [presbuteros] in every church, and had prayed with fasting, they commended them to the Lord, in whom they believed. And passing through Pisidia, they came into Pamphylia. (Acts 14:21-24, DRA)

Wherefore, the authority of this hierarchical and successional Church was then exercised immediately and recurrently, as numerous controversies arose that threatened orthodoxy and the greater unity of Christendom. For instance, Acts would recount the assembling of a council to address the Jewish ceremonial laws [Acts 15:1-30], wherein the Apostles would declare that they were no longer binding, despite having no scriptural precedent to do so. What's more, the Church then continued, when necessary, to both arbitrate and intervene up through the centuries and define dogmas like the Trinity, the Hypostatic Union, and even affix the biblical canon. Consequently, whereas Scripture is undoubtedly an authoritative source which is profitable for teaching and reproof [2 Timothy 3:16], it is neither self-defining, nor easily interpreted, nor does it contain every apostolic teaching. Subsequently, the Church draws from sacred Apostolic Tradition alongside sacred Scripture and inserts herself to settle disputes when there are any controversies, ambiguities, or perceived conflicts between the two.

In summation, if left to our own devices, or if each individual Christian or Christian denomination becomes the single arbiter of the truth, an inevitable state of moral and doctrinal confusion will soon be sure to follow. As such, perhaps this is why Christ left us a living Magisterium, under the guidance of the Holy Spirit, that He might preserve His teachings, provide a perpetual voice of clarity, and avoid mass confusion and error. [6]

---

6. "Martin, you have not sufficiently distinguished your works. The earlier were bad and the latter worse. Your plea to be heard from the Scripture is one which is consistently made by heretics. You do nothing but renew the errors of Wyclif and Hus. How will the Jews, how will the Turks, exult to hear Christians discussing whether they have been wrong for all these years! Martin, how can you assume that you are the only one to understand the sense of Scripture? Would you put your judgment above that of so many famous men, and claim that you know more than them all? You have no right to call into question the most holy orthodox faith, instituted by Christ the perfect lawgiver, proclaimed throughout the world by the Apostles, sealed by the red blood of martyrs, confirmed by the sacred councils, defined by the Church in which all our fathers believed until death, and then gave to us as an inheritance." (Archbishop Eck of Trier, Statement at the Trial of Martin Luther at the Diet of Worms, A.D. 1521)

Early Christian Witness [7]
(For Scripture, Tradition, and the Magisterium)

*Note: The preserved writings of Apostolic and Patristic era ecclesiastical authorities bear invaluable witness to the teachings of the Apostles in that they testify to what the earliest Christians received, maintained, and passed on in successive fashion. In fact, many such witnesses, such as Clement of Rome,[8] Ignatius of Antioch,[9] and Polycarp of Smyrna [10] were themselves students of the Apostles. Likewise, their disciples, in turn, such as Irenaeus of Lyons [11] and Clement of Alexandria,[12] were only one generation removed. As such, insofar as these historical witnesses are fallible

---

7. Early Christian quotations and dating have been obtained from: (a)Jimmy Akin, *The Fathers Know Best: Your Essential Guide to the Teachings Of The Early Church* (San Diego, CA: Catholic Answers Press, 2010) (b) Erick Ybarra, *The Papacy: Revisiting the Debate between Catholics and Orthodox* (Steubenville, OH: Emmaus Road Publishing, 2022) (c) Catholic Answers, http://www.catholic.com/ (d) New Advent, http://www.newadvent.org/fathers

8. Eusebius of Caesarea, Ecclesiastical *History 3:4:10*, A.D. 313

9. Saint John Chrysostom, *Homily on Ignatius*, A.D. 395

10. Saint Irenaeus of Lyons, *Against All Heresies 3:3:4*, A.D. 189

11. Saint Jerome, *Illustrious Men 35*, A.D. 392

12. Clement of Alexandria, *Stromata 1:1*, A.D. 198

authorities and are, occasionally, disparate in their judgements, they reliably attest to the apostolic deposit of faith [1 Timothy 6:20-21, Jude 1:3] and to what the early Church/Christians believed. *

Pope Saint Clement I

Our Apostles knew through our Lord Jesus Christ that there would be strife for the office of bishop. For this reason, therefore, having received perfect foreknowledge, they appointed those who have already been mentioned, and afterwards added the further provision that, if they should die, other approved men should succeed to their ministry... [Wherefore,] If any shall disobey the words spoken by [God] through us, let them know that they will involve themselves in transgression and serious danger... Joy and gladness will you afford us, if you become obedient to the words written by us, through the Holy Spirit, and root out the lawless wrath of your jealousy according to the intercession which we have made for peace and unity in this letter. (*Epistle to the Corinthians 44; 59; 63*, A.D. 95)

Saint Ignatius of Antioch

For as many are of God, and of Jesus Christ, are also with the bishop. And as many as shall, in the exercise of penance, return into the unity of the Church, these too shall belong to God, that they may live according to Jesus Christ. Do not err, my brethren. If any man follows him that makes a schism in the Church, he shall not inherit the kingdom of God. If anyone walks according to a strange opinion, he agrees not with the passion of Christ. (*Epistle to the Philadelphians 3*, A.D. 110)

In like manner, let all reverence the deacons as an appointment of Jesus Christ, and the bishop as Jesus Christ, who is the Son of the Father, and the priests as the

Sanhedrim of God, and assembly of the Apostles. Apart from these, there is no Church. (*Epistle to the Trallians 3*, A.D. 110)

Saint Irenaeus of Lyons

It is within the power of all, therefore, in every Church, who may wish to see the truth, to contemplate clearly the tradition of the Apostles manifested throughout the whole world; and we are in a position to reckon up those who were by the Apostles instituted bishops in the Churches, and [to be able to demonstrate] the succession of these men to our own times; those who neither taught nor knew of anything like what these [heretics] rave about. For if the Apostles had known hidden mysteries, which they were in the habit of imparting to the perfect apart and privily from the rest, they would have delivered them especially to those to whom they were also committing the Churches themselves. For they were desirous that these men should be very perfect and blameless in all things, whom also they were leaving behind as their successors, delivering up their own place of government to these men, which men, if they discharged their functions honestly, would be a great boon [to the Church]. (*Against All Heresies 3:3:1*, A.D. 189)

Tertullian of Carthage

[The Apostles] then in like manner founded churches in every city, from which all the other churches, one after another, derived the tradition of the faith, and the seeds of doctrine, and are every day deriving them, that they may become churches. Indeed, it is on this account only that they will be able to deem themselves Apostolic, as being the offspring of Apostolic churches. Every sort of thing must necessarily revert to its original for its classification. Therefore the churches, although they are so many and so great, comprise but the one primitive church, (founded) by the Apostles, from which they all (spring). In this way all are primitive, and all are Apostolic, while they are all proved to be one, in (unbroken) unity... let all the heresies, when challenged to these two tests by our Apostolic Church, offer their proof of how they deem themselves to be Apostolic. But in truth they neither are so, nor are they able to prove themselves to be what they are not. Nor are they admitted to peaceful relations and communion by such churches as are in any way connected with Apostles, because they are in no sense themselves Apostolic because of their diversity as to the mysteries of the faith. (*Against the Heresies 20*, A.D. 200)

Origen of Alexandria

There are many who think they hold the opinions of Christ, and yet some of these think differently from their predecessors, yet, as the teaching of the Church, transmitted in orderly succession from the Apostles, and remaining in the churches to the present day, is still preserved, that is alone to be accepted as truth that differs in no respect from the ecclesiastical and Apostolic Tradition. (*Fundamental Doctrines 2*, A.D. 225)

Saint Cyprian of Carthage

The Church is one, and as she is one, cannot be both within and without. For if she is with [the heretic] Novatian, she was not with Cornelius. But if she was with Cornelius, who succeeded the bishop, Fabian, by lawful ordination, and whom, beside the honor of the priesthood the Lord glorified also with martyrdom, Novatian is not in the Church; nor can he be reckoned as a bishop, who, succeeding to no one, and despising the evangelical and Apostolic Tradition, sprang from himself. For he who has not been ordained in the Church can neither have nor hold to the Church in any way. (*Epistle 75:3*, A.D. 254)

Eusebius of Caesarea

At that time there flourished in the Church Hegesippus, whom we know from what has gone before, and Dionysius, bishop of Corinth, and another bishop, Pinytus of Crete, and besides these, Philip, and Apolinarius, and Melito, and Musanus, and Modestus, and finally, Irenæus. From them has come down to us in writing, the sound and orthodox faith received from Apostolic tradition. (*Ecclesiastical History 4:21*, A.D. 312)

Saint Basil of Caesarea

Of the dogmas and messages preserved in the Church, some we possess from written teaching and others we receive from the Tradition of the Apostles, handed on to us in mystery. In respect to piety, both are of the same force. No one will contradict any of these, no one, at any rate, who is even moderately versed in matters ecclesiastical. Indeed, were we to try to reject unwritten customs as having no great authority, we would unwittingly injure the gospel in its vitals; or rather, we would reduce [Christian] message to a mere term. For instance, to take the first and most general example, who is there who has taught us in writing to sign with the sign of the cross those who have trusted in the name of our Lord Jesus Christ? What writing has taught us to turn to the East at prayer? Which of the saints has left us in writing the words of the invocation at the displaying of the bread of the Eucharist and the cup of blessing? For we are not, as is well known, content with what the Apostle or the Gospel has recorded, but both in preface and conclusion we add other words as being of great importance to the validity of the ministry, and these we derive from unwritten teaching. Moreover, we bless the water of baptism and the oil of the chrism, and besides this the catechumen who is being baptized. On what written authority do we do this? Is not our authority silent and mystical tradition? Nay, by what written word is the anointing of oil itself taught? And whence comes the custom of baptizing thrice? And as to the other customs of baptism from what Scripture do we derive the renunciation of Satan and his angels? Does this not come from that unpublished and secret teaching which our fathers guarded in a silence out of the reach of curious meddling and inquisitive investigation? Well had they learnt the lesson that the awful dignity of the mysteries is best preserved by silence. What the uninitiated are not even allowed to look at was hardly likely to be publicly paraded about in written documents. (*The Holy Spirit 27:66*, A.D. 375)

Saint Epiphanius of Salamis
It is needful to make use of tradition, for not everything can be gotten from Scripture. The holy Apostles handed down some things in Scripture and other things in tradition. (*Against Heresies 61:6*, A.D. 377)

Saint Augustine of Hippo
As to those other things which we hold on the authority, not of Scripture, but of tradition, and which are observed throughout the whole world, it may be understood that they are held as approved and instituted either by

the Apostles themselves, or by plenary Councils, whose authority in the Church is most useful, e.g. the annual commemoration, by special solemnities, of the Lord's passion, resurrection, and ascension, and of the descent of the Holy Spirit from heaven, and whatever else is in like manner observed by the whole Church wherever it has been established. (*Epistle 54:1:1*, A.D. 400)

Saint Vincent of Lerins

I have continually given the greatest pains and diligence to inquiring, from the greatest possible number of men outstanding in holiness and in doctrine, how I can secure a kind of fixed and, as it were, general and guiding principle for distinguishing the true Catholic Faith from the degraded falsehoods of heresy. And the answer that I receive is always to this effect; that if I wish, or indeed if anyone wishes, to detect the deceits of heretics that arise and to avoid their snares and to keep healthy and sound in a healthy faith, we ought, with the Lord's help, to fortify our faith in a twofold manner, firstly, that is, by the authority of God's Law, then by the tradition of the Catholic Church. Here, it may be, someone will ask, Since the canon of Scripture is complete, and is in itself abundantly sufficient, what need is there to join to it the interpretation of the Church? The answer is that because of the very depth of Scripture all men do not place one identical interpretation upon it. The statements of the same writer are explained by different men in different ways, so much so that it seems almost possible to extract from it as many opinions as there are men. Novatian expounds in one way, Sabellius in another, Donatus in another, Arius, Eunomius and Macedonia in another, Photinus, Apollinaris and Priscillian in another, Jovinian, Pelagius and Caelestius in another, and latterly Nestorius in another. Therefore, because of the intricacies of error, which is so multiform, there is great need for the laying down of a rule for the exposition of Prophets and Apostles in accordance with the standard of the interpretation of the Church Catholic. (*Commoratorium 4*, A.D. 434)

III. THE PAPACY

Regrettably, there are several prevalent misconceptions surrounding the office of the papacy, both in regard to who the pope is and what his primary function in the Church entails. Case in point: whilst the Church plainly asserts that the office of the pope has been divinely instituted, granted primacy, and receives protection from universally promulgating error, her correspondent doctrines of Papal supremacy and infallibility are often unduly misconstrued for impeccability and totalitarianism. Nevertheless, as Dr. Scott Hahn so astutely notes in his numerous works on the papacy:

> ...when Catholics look at the pope, we look at him not as some tyrant, not as some authoritarian "know-it-all," and not as some magician who can concoct new revelations out of whole cloth. Rather, we look to him as a father figure who has been established by Christ, over the family that He has purchased with His blood. [13]

---

[13]. Dr. Scott Hahn, *Answering Common Objections: Talk 1- The Pope* (Sycamore, IL: Saint Joseph Communications, 2004)

Subsequently, the Church does not teach, nor has it ever taught, that the pope is omnipotent, omniscient, free from sin, or infallible in all situations, but rather that he possesses supremacy to preserve unity and orthodoxy and is safeguarded from binding the Church faithful to error. In point of fact, not only are there a series of official avenues via which a pope can be questioned and/or filially corrected, but as a member of the Church, he is bound to attend sacramental confession, receive absolution, and perform acts of contrition.[14] Correspondingly, the Church has never maintained that the pope has the unbridled authority to declare new or unfounded revelation, but rather that all public revelation ceased with the death of the Apostles, wherein it was affixed as a deposit of faith [1 Timothy 6:20-21, Jude 1:3].[15] Conversely, the Church teaches that, in virtue of the promise of Christ to Saint Peter, and, by extension, his lawful successors:

> The pope is preserved from the possibility of error when, in the exercise of his office as shepherd and teacher of all Christians, and in virtue of his supreme Apostolic authority, he defines a doctrine concerning faith or morals, which is to be held by the entire Church.[16]

What is more, any "new" dogma which is defined by a pope, whether alone or in conjunction with the college of bishops, must not bring about a divergence of doctrine but rather one which conforms with both Scripture and Tradition.[17] Wherefore, the Church insists that her teachings on the office of the pope—in particular its primacy, successive nature, and infallibility— stand on

---

14. Ibid.
15. First Vatican Council, First Dogmatic Constitution on the Church of Christ, *Pastor Aeternus*, (18, July 1870), Ch. 4, No. 6
16. Ibid., Ch. 4, No. 9
17. Ibid., Ch. 4, No. 6

SPIRITUM SANCTUM DOMINUM

a foundation of Scripture and Tradition, which explicitly evince the following propositions:

1. That Simon Peter was given a unique primacy amongst all other disciples.
2. That he traveled to the city of Rome, and therein was martyred.
3. That his primacy was entrusted to an unbroken chain of successors.
4. That when a lawful successor of Saint Peter speaks in an official capacity on doctrines of faith and morals, he is preserved from the possibility of binding the Church to error via the intercession of the Holy Spirit.

IV. THE PRIMACY OF SIMON PETER

Whereas the primacy of Peter is admittedly a matter of contention within contemporary Christianity, there are a host of protestant scholars who have acknowledged the biblical foundations of Petrine supremacy. For example, R.T. France has conceded that the gospels evince Peter as chief of the disciples and that he is habitually depicted as a natural leader, spokesman, and overseer.[18] Likewise, W.F Albright has openly recognized Peter's supremacy in Scripture and has proposed that a denial of his preeminence is a misguided rejection of conclusive biblical evidence.[19] As such, how does one reconcile the willing testimony of these distinguished protestant scholars? Why were they able to affirm Petrine supremacy, whilst many others staunchly deny it? Moreover, why did they find the scriptural case for his preeminence so compelling?

In truth, to appreciate the force of the scriptural evidence one need only look to the testimony of Christ, for He repeatedly distinguishes Peter from all other disciples, throughout the four

---

18. R.T France, *The Gospel of Matthew* (Grand Rapids, MI: Wm. B. Publishing Co., 2007), 376-378

19. W.F Albright and C.S Mann, *The Anchor Bible: Matthew* (Garden City, NY: Doubleday, 1971), 196-197

gospel accounts. Case in point: Matthew would chronicle a significant exchange in the region of Caesarea Philippi, wherein Simon arises from amongst his brethren to proclaim the divinity of Jesus. Unsurprisingly, Christ then responds to Simon's profession in stereotypical fashion, via bestowing upon him a series of blessings, each accompanied by a two-fold elucidation:

> Now when Jesus came into the district of Caesarea Philippi, he asked his disciples, "Who do people say that the Son of Man is?" And they said, "Some say John the Baptist, but others Elijah, and still others Jeremiah or one of the prophets." He said to them, "But who do you say that I am?" Simon Peter answered, "You are the Messiah, the Son of the living God." And Jesus answered him, "Blessed are you, Simon son of Jonah! For flesh and blood has not revealed this to you, but my Father in heaven. And I tell you, you are Peter [Kepha/Cephas], and on this rock [Kepha/Cephas] I will build my church, and the gates of Hades will not prevail against it. I will give you the keys of the kingdom of heaven, and whatever you bind on earth will [have been] bound in heaven, and whatever you loose on earth will [have been] loosed in heaven." [20] (Matthew 16:13-19, NRSVCE)

To be sure, it would be difficult to discount the fact that the revelation of Christ's divinity was given to Simon alone or the fact that he was singularly blessed in front of the other disciples. Accordingly, given the context of Simon's antecedent declaration and the reality that Jesus changes his name to "rock" [Kepha/Cephas], it would be difficult to deny that Christ is flipping

---

20. Most Catholic translations use the phrases "will be bound in heaven," and "will be loosed in heaven." However, a more literal translation of the Greek uses a periphrastic future perfect passive.

the script and is recognizing Peter as the foundation of the Church. Admittedly, this does not discount the fact that there are other such scriptural metaphors for the grounding and foundation of the Church.[21] However, in a certain sense, via this exclusive imagery, it has been seen as uniquely founded on Peter.[22] What is more, Christ then proceeds to entrust to Peter the keys of the kingdom of heaven, which then remain in his sole possession throughout the entirety of the revelation of Scripture.

Notwithstanding, whereas Matthew explicitly witnesses to the unique prerogatives of Simon Peter, evidence of Petrine supremacy is not sequestered to his gospel account. For instance, Luke would document a dispute that arose from among the twelve disciples, wherein they debated who was to be considered the greatest and who would ultimately rise to ascendency. Foreseeably, Christ would intervene to admonish His disciples and their desire to laud a certain superiority. Nevertheless, He also dismissed the notion that they were to function as a classless or egalitarian authority. On the contrary, He professed that there was indeed a greatest amongst them, who was to ultimately serve the others, and then disclosed His petition for Simon's faith [individually], and implored that he strengthens his brothers:

> A dispute also arose among them as to which one of them was to be regarded as the greatest. But he said to them, "The kings of the Gentiles lord it over them; and those in authority over them are called benefactors. But not so with you; rather the greatest among you must become like the youngest, and the leader like one who serves. For who is greater, the one who is at the table or the one who serves?

---

21. Jimmy Aikin, *The Fathers Know Best: Your Essential Guide To The Teachings Of The Early Church* (San Diego, CA: Catholic Answers Press, 2010), 189
22. Ibid.

Is it not the one at the table? But I am among you as one who serves." "You are those who have stood by me in my trials; and I confer on you, just as my Father has conferred on me, a kingdom, so that you may eat and drink at my table in my kingdom, and you will sit on thrones judging the twelve tribes of Israel." "Simon, Simon, listen! Satan has demanded to sift all of you like wheat, but I have prayed for YOU that your own faith may not fail; and you, when once you have turned back, strengthen your brothers." (Luke 22:24-32, NRSVCE)

Accordingly, John then records a similar charge following the resurrection, wherein Jesus entrusts Peter [individually] with fostering His flock, prior to His heavenly ascension:

When they had finished breakfast, Jesus said to Simon Peter, "Simon son of John, do you love me more than these?" He said to him, "Yes, Lord; you know that I love you." Jesus said to him, "Feed my lambs." A second time he said to him, "Simon son of John, do you love me?" He said to him, "Yes, Lord; you know that I love you." Jesus said to him, "Tend my sheep." He said to him the third time, "Simon son of John, do you love me?" Peter felt hurt because he said to him the third time, "Do you love me?" And he said to him, "Lord, you know everything; you know that I love you." Jesus said to him, "Feed my sheep." (John 21:15-17, NRSVCE)

Furthermore, we then see Peter in the early Church exercising preeminent authority and he receives no challenge from his fellow Apostles regarding his unsolicited imperatives. For example, when the Apostles are faced with a vacant office following the death of Judas, it is Peter who arises from amongst his brethren and resolves that he is to be succeeded [Acts 1:15-26]. Likewise, when the disciples are openly ridiculed by pilgrims at the Jewish festival of Pentecost, it is Peter who denounces them for crucifying the Messiah and demands that they repent and be baptized [Acts 2:14-41]. What's more, Peter and John are then petitioned by a disabled man within the Jewish temple colonnade, and it is Peter who resolves to heal his paralysis and then preaches to the astonished onlookers [Acts 3:1-24]. As such, Peter and John are subsequently put on trial before the Jewish Sanhedrin. However, Peter condemns his would-be inquisitors and leaves his former superiors speechless [Acts 4:1-13].

Wherefore, within the first four chapters of Acts alone, Peter has exercised authority over his fellow Apostles, over the pilgrims at Pentecost, within the Jewish temple colonnade, and over the high priests of the Jewish Sanhedrin—all without a vocal challenge to his sovereignty and with complete confidence in his convictions. Further still, when Ananias and Sapphira were guilty of conspiracy, it would be Peter who delivered God's sentence of death [Acts 5:1-11], and it was he who passed judgment on Simon the sorcerer, who endeavored to purchase the power of the Holy Spirit [Acts 8:9-25]. Likewise, when gentiles were seeking full admittance into the Church, it was Peter who ensured they were baptized [Acts 11:1-18], and when a council was convoked to combat the Judaizer controversy, he arose and settled the dispute [Acts 15:6-12]. Indeed, he is the only disciple to walk on water [Matthew 14:22-33], the only disciple to have his name altered [Matthew 16:18], the only disciple to receive the keys to the kingdom of heaven [Matthew 16:19], and among the few chosen to witness Christ's agony and transfiguration [Mark 9:2-12, Mark 14:32-37]; he is named first in the scriptural litanies of disciples [Matthew 10:2-4, Mark 3:14-19, Luke 6:13-16, Acts 1:13], the first disciple to witness the resurrection [1 Corinthians 15:5, Luke 24:34], the principal healer in the early Church [Acts 3:6-10, Acts 9: 32-43, Acts 5:15-16], and primary disciplinarian [Acts 5:1-11, Acts 11:1-18]. As such, how are we to explain this unrivaled preeminence and Peter's exertion of supreme authority if he were not clearly and publicly inaugurated by Jesus Christ Himself?

Early Christian Witness
(For the Primacy of Simon Peter)

Saint Ignatius of Antioch

To the church also which holds the presidency, in the location of the country of the Romans, worthy of God, worthy of honor, worthy of the highest happiness, worthy of praise, worthy of obtaining her every desire, worthy of being deemed holy, and, because you hold the presidency in love, is named from Christ, and from the Father... You [the church at Rome] have envied no one, but others you have taught. I desire only that what you have enjoined in your instructions may remain in force. (*Epistle to the Romans [Introduction]*, A.D. 110)

Saint Irenaeus of Lyons

We do put to confusion all those who, in whatever manner, whether by an evil self-pleasing, by vainglory, or by blindness and perverse opinion, assemble in unauthorized meetings; [we do this, I say,] by indicating that tradition derived from the Apostles, of the very great, the very ancient, and universally known Church founded and organized at Rome by the two most glorious Apostles, Peter and Paul; as also [by pointing out] the faith preached to men, which comes down to our time by means of the successions of the bishops. For it is a matter of necessity that every Church should agree with this Church, on account of its preeminent authority. (*Against All Heresies 3:3:2*, A.D. 189)

Saint Clement of Alexandria

The blessed Peter, the chosen, the preeminent, the first among the disciples, for whom alone with himself the Savior paid the tribute [Matt. 17:27], quickly grasped and understood their meaning. And what does he say? 'Behold, we have left all and have followed you. (*Who Is the Rich Man That Is Saved 21,* A.D. 200)

Tertullian of Carthage

If, because the Lord has said to Peter, Upon this rock will I build My Church, to you have I given the keys of the heavenly kingdom; or, Whatsoever you shall have bound or loosed in earth, shall be bound or loosed in the heavens, you therefore presume that the power of binding and loosing has derived to you, that is, to every Church akin to Peter, what sort of man are you, subverting and wholly changing the manifest intention of the Lord, conferring (as that intention did) this (gift) personally upon Peter? On YOU, He says, will I build My Church; and, I will give to YOU the keys, not to the Church; and, Whatsoever YOU shall have loosed or bound, not what they shall have loosed or bound. For so withal the result teaches. In (Peter) himself the Church was reared; that is, through (Peter) himself; (Peter) himself essayed the key. (*On Modesty 21,* A.D. 220)

Origen of Alexandria

If we were to attend carefully to the Gospels, we should also find, in relation to those things which seem to be common to Peter . . . a great difference and a preeminence in the things [Jesus] said to Peter, compared with the second class [of Apostles]. For it is no small difference that Peter received the keys not of one heaven but of more, and in order that whatsoever things he binds on earth may be bound not in one heaven but in them all, as compared with the many who bind on earth and loose on earth, so that these things are bound and loosed not in [all] the heavens, as in the case of Peter, but in one only; for they do not reach so high a stage with power as Peter to bind and loose in all the heavens. (*Commentary on Matthew 13:31*, A.D. 249)

Saint Cyprian of Carthage

The Lord says to Peter: 'I say to you,' he says, 'that you are Peter, and upon this rock I will build my Church, and the gates of hell will not overcome it. And to you I will give the keys of the kingdom of heaven...' On him he builds the Church, and commands him to feed the sheep, and although he assigns a like power to all the Apostles, yet he founded a single chair [cathedra], and he established by his own authority a source and an intrinsic reason for that unity. Indeed, the others were also what Peter was [Apostles], but a primacy is given to Peter, by which it is made clear that there is one Church and one chair...If someone does not hold fast to this unity of Peter, can he think that he holds the faith? If he deserts the chair of Peter upon whom the Church was built, can he be confident that he is in the Church? (*Unity of the Catholic Church 4*, A.D. 251)

Council of Sardica

For this will seem to be best and most fitting indeed, if the priests from each province refer to the head, that is, to the chair of Peter the Apostle. (*Canon 3*, A.D. 343)

Saint Cyril of Jerusalem

The Lord is loving toward men, swift to pardon but slow to punish. Let no man despair of his own salvation. Peter, the first and foremost of the Apostles, denied the Lord three times before a little servant girl, but he repented and wept bitterly. (*Catechetical Lectures 2:19*, A.D. 350)

Saint Ephraim the Syrian

[Jesus said] Simon, My follower, I have made you the foundation of the holy Church. I betimes called you Peter [Kefa or Rock] because you will support all its buildings. You are the inspector of those who will build on earth a Church for Me. If they should wish to build what is false, you, the foundation will condemn them. You are the head of the fountain from which my teaching flows, you are the chief of My disciples. Through you I will give drink to all peoples. Yours is that life-giving sweetness which I dispense. I have chosen you to be, as it were, the first-born in My institution, and so that, as the heir, you may be executor of my treasures. I have given you the keys of my kingdom. Behold I have given you authority over all My treasures! (*Homily 4:1*, A.D. 353)

Saint Optatus of Milevis

You cannot then deny that you do know, that upon Peter first in the city of Rome was bestowed the episcopal Cathedra, on which sat Peter, the head of all the Apostles (for which reason he was called Cephas), that, in this one cathedra, unity should be preserved by all. (*The Schism of the Donatists 2:2*, A.D. 367)

Saint Jerome

Simon Peter, the son of John, from the village of Bethsaida in the province of Galilee, brother of Andrew the Apostle, and himself chief of the Apostles, after having been bishop of the church of Antioch and having preached to the Dispersion —the believers in in circumcision, in Pontus, Galatia, Cappadocia, Asia and Bithynia— pushed on to Rome in the second year of Claudius to overthrow Simon Magus, and held the sacerdotal chair there for twenty-five years until the last, that is the fourteenth, year of Nero. (*Illustrious Men 1*, A.D. 392)

Saint Augustine of Hippo

Among these [Apostles] Peter alone almost everywhere deserved to represent the whole Church. Because of that representation of the Church, which only he bore, he deserved to hear 'I will give to you the keys of the kingdom of heaven.' (*Sermon 295:2*, A.D. 411)

Phillip the legate [of Pope Celestine I]

There is no doubt, and in fact it has been known in all ages, that the holy and most blessed Peter, prince and head of the Apostles, pillar of the faith, and foundation of the Catholic Church, received the keys of the kingdom from our Lord Jesus Christ, the Savior and Redeemer of the human race, and that to him was given the power of binding and losing sins. (*Address to the Council of Ephesus [Session 3]*, A.D. 431)

Pope Saint Leo I

Our Lord Jesus Christ... has placed the principal charge on the blessed Peter, chief of all the Apostles... He wished him who had been received into partnership in his undivided unity to be named what he himself was, when he said: "You are Peter and on this rock I will build my Church," that the building of the eternal temple might rest on Peter's solid rock, strengthening his Church so surely that neither human rashness could assail it, nor the gates of hell prevail against it. (*Epistle 10:1,* A.D. 445)

V. PETER IN ROME

There is seemingly a lack of scriptural citations for Peter's presence in Rome; however, there are a host of reasons to maintain that he both resided and eventually died there. For instance, insofar as Peter would note, in his first epistle, that he was writing to Asia Minor from "Babylon" [1 Peter 5:13], "Babylon" is frequently employed in Scripture as a pseudonym for Rome, so as to highlight its idolatry and vices [Revelation 16:19, 17:5, 18:2].[23] Moreover, Peter also records that he was accompanied by Mark whilst writing his first epistle [1 Peter 5:13], and Mark would be summoned by the Apostle Paul, whilst in the midst of his Roman imprisonment [2 Timothy 4:11].[24]

Furthermore, the city of Babylon had been long destroyed prior to Peter's ministry, and was nowhere approximate to the provinces he was addressing in the equivalent of modern-day Western Turkey

---

[23]. Jimmy Aikin, *The Fathers Know Best: Your Essential Guide To The Teachings Of The Early Church* (San Diego, CA: Catholic Answers Press, 2010), 200

[24]. James Rochford, "Was Peter Really in Babylon," Evidence Unseen. Accessed October 15, 2021, https://evidenceunseen.com/bible-difficulties-2/nt-difficulties/1-2-timothy-titus-philemon-hebrews-james-1-2-peter/1-pet-513-was-peter-really-in-babylon/

[1 Peter 1:1].[25] In point of fact, Diodorus of Sicily would record, in the first century B.C., that Babylon had been left in ruin, and that the vast majority of the area within its walls had been taken over by agricultural growth.[26] Similarly, Strabo would note, mere decades before Christ, that Babylon was a barren city[27] and all evidence suggests that Christianity scarcely impacted Mesopotamia, until the several centuries thereafter.[28] As such, it is highly improbable that Peter would have ventured to Babylon when it had been left a desolate city, and when early Christian evangelists had yet to reach the Mesopotamian region, in any meaningful capacity.

Finally, Peter also states, in his second epistle, that he was anticipating his imminent death [2 Peter 1:14], and therefore, it is presumptive that he also died in Rome, after his final correspondence. Correspondingly, Scripture also stipulates that he was predestined to die in accordance with the prophecy of Christ [John 21:18-19], and, as such, seems to indicate that he was to be gloriously martyred, by way of a Roman crucifixion. Wherefore, as much as the See of Rome received a certain prestige on account of its imperial power, political prominence, and Pauline influence, it was ultimately the martyrdom of Peter and the divesting of his authority, which granted it an enduring primacy.

---

25. Craig Bloomberg, *From Pentecost to Patmos: an Introduction to Acts through Revelation* (Nashville, TN: B&H Academic, 2006), 443

26. Diodorus of Sicily, *Bibliotheca 2:9:9*, 30 B.C.

27. Strabo, *Geographica 16:1:5*, 7 B.C.

28. Craig Bloomberg, *From Pentecost to Patmos: an Introduction to Acts through Revelation* (Nashville, TN: B&H Academic, 2006), 443

Early Christian Witness
(For Peter in Rome)

Ignatius of Antioch

I do not, as Peter and Paul, issue commandments unto you [the Church of Rome]. They were Apostles; I am but a condemned man: they were free, while I am, even until now, a servant. But when I suffer, I shall be the freed man of Jesus, and shall rise again emancipated in Him. (*Epistle to the Romans 4,* A.D. 110)

Saint Dionysius of Corinth

You [Pope Soter] have thus by such an admonition bound together the planting of Peter and of Paul at Rome and Corinth. For both of them planted and likewise taught us in our Corinth. And they taught together in like manner in Italy and suffered martyrdom at the same time. (*Epistle to Pope Soter [From Eusebius's Ecclesiastical History 2:25:8],* A.D. 170)

Saint Irenaeus of Lyons

Matthew also issued among the Hebrews a written gospel in their own language, while Peter and Paul were evangelizing in Rome and laying the foundation of the Church. (*Against All Heresies 3:1:1,* A.D. 189)

Tertullian of Carthage

Since, moreover, you are close upon Italy, you have Rome, from which there comes even into our own hands the very authority (of Apostles themselves). How happy is its church on which the Apostles poured forth all their doctrine along with their blood! Where Peter endures a passion like his Lord's! Where Paul wins his crown in a death like John's! Where the Apostle John was first plunged, unhurt, into boiling oil, and thence remitted to his island-exile! (*Against the Heretics 36,* A.D. 200)

Caius of Rome

It is, therefore, recorded that Paul was beheaded in Rome itself, and that Peter likewise was crucified under Nero. This account of Peter and Paul is substantiated by the fact that their names are preserved in the cemeteries of that place even to the present day. It is confirmed likewise by Caius, a member of the Church, who arose under Zephyrinus, bishop of Rome. He, in a published disputation with Proclus, the leader of the Phrygian heresy, speaks as follows concerning the places where the sacred corpses of the aforesaid Apostles are laid: "But I can show the trophies of the Apostles. For if you will go to the Vatican or to the Ostian way, you will find the trophies of those who laid the foundations of this church. (*Disputation with Proclus [From Eusebius's Ecclesiastical History 2:25:5],* A.D. 210)

Saint Peter of Alexandria

Thus Peter, the first of the Apostles, having been often apprehended, and thrown into prison, and treated with ignominy, was last of all crucified in Rome. (*Penance, Canon 9,* A.D. 306)

Lactantius

And while Nero reigned, the Apostle Peter came to Rome, and, through the power of God committed unto him, wrought certain miracles, and, by turning many to the true religion, built up a faithful and steadfast temple unto the Lord. When Nero heard of those things, and observed that not only in Rome, but in every other place, a great multitude revolted daily from the worship of idols, and, condemning their old ways, went over to the new religion, he, an execrable and pernicious tyrant, sprung forward to raze the heavenly temple and destroy the true faith. He it was who first persecuted the servants of God; he crucified Peter and slew Paul. (*Deaths of the Persecutors 2,* A.D. 318)

Saint Cyril of Jerusalem

And he so deceived the City of Rome that Claudius set up his statue, and wrote beneath it, in the language of the Romans, Simoni Deo Sancto, which being interpreted signifies, To Simon the Holy God. As the delusion was extending, Peter and Paul, a noble pair, chief rulers of the Church, arrived and set the error right; and when the supposed god Simon wished to show himself off, they straightway showed him as a corpse. For Simon promised to rise aloft to heaven, and came riding in a dæmon.' chariot on the air; but the servants of God fell on their knees, and having shown that agreement of which Jesus spoke, that If two of you shall agree concerning anything that they shall ask, it shall be done unto them [Matthew 18:19], they launched the weapon of their concord in prayer against Magus, and struck him down to the earth. And marvelous though it was, yet no marvel. For Peter was there, who carries the keys of heaven: and nothing wonderful, for Paul was there, who was caught up to the third heaven, and into Paradise, and heard unspeakable words, which it is not lawful far a man to utter. (*Catechetical Lectures 6:14-15,* A.D. 350)

Pope Saint Damasus I

In addition to this, there is also the companionship of the vessel of election, the most blessed Apostle Paul, who contended and was crowned with a glorious death along with Peter in the city of Rome in the time of Caesar Nero... They equally consecrated the above-mentioned holy Roman Church to Christ the Lord... (*Decree of Damasus 3,* A.D. 382)

Saint Augustine of Hippo

However, if all men throughout all the world were of the character which you most vainly charge them with, what has the chair done to you of the Roman Church, in which Peter sat, and which Anastasius fills today; or the chair of the Church of Jerusalem, in which James once sat, and in which John sits today, with which we are united in catholic unity, and from which you have severed yourselves by your mad fury? (*Answer to the Epistles of Petilian the Donatist 2: 51,* A.D. 402)

VI. PAPAL SUCCESSION

With His third and final blessing to Peter in Matthew's gospel account, Christ entrusts Peter with the keys to the kingdom of heaven and affords him the definitive authority to bind and loose [Matthew 16:19]. To be sure, He would then subsequently afford the remaining disciples with a correspondent/ comparable power [Matthew 18:18]; however, He notably omits the entrustment of the keys, which remain affixed in Peter's sole possession. As such, even as Jesus elucidates that the Petrine keys denote the power to bind and loose, this cannot exhaust their symbolism or significance, as much as they are certainly intricately linked. Indeed, for the remaining disciples are then similarly endowed with a binding and loosing power [Matthew 18:18], yet the keys to the kingdom of heaven are entrusted to Simon Peter alone. Wherefore, if we are explicating the full significance of the keys, and the dynastic office they historically depict, it is necessary to return to the Old Testament Davidic Kingdom, wherein we see an emphatic typological parallel:

Thus says the Lord GOD of hosts: Come, go to this steward, to Shebna, who is master of the household, and say to him: What right do you have here? Who are your relatives here, that you have cut out a tomb here for yourself, cutting a tomb on the height, and carving a habitation for yourself in the rock? The LORD is about to hurl you away violently, my fellow. He will seize firm hold on you, whirl you round and round, and throw you like a ball into a wide land; there you shall die, and there your splendid chariots shall lie, O you disgrace to your master's house! I will thrust you from your office, and you will be pulled down from your post. On that day I will call my servant Eliakim son of Hilkiah and will clothe him with your robe and bind your sash on him. I will commit your authority to his hand, and he shall be a father to the inhabitants of Jerusalem and to the house of Judah. I will place on his shoulder the key to the house of David; what he shall open, no one shall shut; what he shall shut, no one shall open. I will fasten him like a peg in a secure place, and he will become a throne of honor to his ancestral house. And they will hang on him the whole weight of his ancestral house, the offspring and issue, every small vessel, from the cups to all the flagons. (Isaiah 22:15-23, NRSVCE)

In truth, the intertextual echoes between the Isaian and Matthean passages are apparent to even the most ardent detractors. However, some continue to maintain that they are inadvertent allusions, and, as such, deny the evident typological parallel. Nevertheless, there are a myriad of reasons to affirm that Christ was explicitly referencing Isaiah's Old Testament account, and that Peter was entrusted a priestly and successional prime ministerial office, synonymous to that of Eliakim. Case in point,[29] Matthew would go to extraordinary lengths at the beginning of his gospel account [Matthew 1:6-16], to meticulously catalog the lineage of Jesus and establish him as the new and eternal Davidic king [2 Samuel 7:8-16, Luke 1:32-33]. As such, both passages pertain to the removal of a corrupted leadership under a Davidic king, to one of purity and stability, so as to ensure a faithful governance [Matthew 21:43-46]. In fact, both Peter and Eliakim are even likened to analogous steadfast objects, and receive their offices prior to a siege of Jerusalem, in their respective times [Isaiah 36:1-22, 2 Kings 18:17-37, Luke 21:5]. Likewise, both Peter and Eliakim are also entrusted with the keys to their respective kingdoms, which afford them the authority to make definitive judgements in their particular communities. What is more, Christ's resolution to reference the book of Isaiah in response to Peter's profession, is also duplicated elsewhere in Scripture, whilst His messianic identity is being evinced [Luke 4:16-21]. Accordingly, just as Jesus elects to portray Peter as a royal steward via His reference to keys to the kingdom of heaven, He depicts the remaining disciples with Davidic royal imagery [1 Kings 4:1-7], via His reference to twelve thrones of judgment [Matthew 19:28].

Wherefore, when one views the verses in Matthew's account within the context set forth by the book of Isaiah, the typology between Peter and Eliakim becomes utterly unmistakable. Indeed, for where Eliakim was driven as a peg into a firm place and afforded a seat of honor, Peter was made a foundational rock and granted a seat of primacy. Likewise, where Eliakim wielded the lasting power to open doors that couldn't be shut, Peter maintained the ultimate authority to bind what couldn't be loosed. As such, given that

---

29. The subsequent typological examples have been summarized from: Suan Sonna, "The New Eliakim Typological Argument for the Papacy," Intellectual Conservatism, 2022, https://academia.edu/83386611/The_New_Eliakim_Typological_Argument_for_the_Papacy/

Eliakim was entrusted with a set of dynastic keys to the earthly Davidic Kingdom, it bespeaks of Peter's successional keys to its heavenly New Testament equivalent.

What's more, inasmuch as Peter was the preeminent figure among the twelve disciples, he was not alone in his holding of a dynastic seat of authority. For instance, the book of Acts recounts a preliminary occurrence of apostolic succession, wherein Matthias is added to Judas's seat, subsequent to his unfavorable passing [Acts 1:23-26]. Consequently, if it was deemed necessary to fill the vacancy of Judas—the lowest of all the disciples— how much more necessary would it have been to establish a successor for the office of the new Prime Minister? Correspondingly, insofar as the Magisterium of ancient Israel was passed down in successive fashion [Matthew 23:1-3], it is fitting for its New Testament equivalent to be handed on in a synonymous manner. Furthermore, we then witness the successors of Peter, up through the centuries, regularly wielding the keys to the kingdom of heaven, whilst guiding the new and eternal Israel under its heavenly Davidic king. For example: [30]

1. In A.D. 95, Pope Saint Clement I intercedes in an internal dispute in the church of Corinth subsequent to an unlawful deposition of legitimate ecclesiastical authorities—all while the Apostle John was still living, and in closer proximity, in Ephesus. [31]

---

30. The subsequent examples have been summarized from: Erick Ybarra, *The Papacy: Revisiting the Debate between Catholics and Orthodox* (Steubenville, OH: Emmaus Road Publishing, 2022).

31. Saint Irenaeus of Lyons, *Against All Heresies 3:3:3*, A.D. 189; Pope Saint Clement I, *Epistle to the Corinthians 1-65*, A.D. 95

2. In A.D. 140, Pope Saint Hyginus excommunicates Cerdon (The father of the Marcionite heresy) from the universal Church. [32]

3. In A.D. 193, Pope Saint Victor I elects to temporarily excommunicate the churches of Asia Minor over the Quartodeciman controversy. [33]

4. In A.D. 217, Pope Saint Callixtus I grants communion to repentant adulterers and fornicators via a universal edict. [34]

5. In A.D. 251, Pope Saint Cornelius excommunicates the arch heretic and antipope Novatus from the universal Church.[35]

6. In A.D. 256, Saint Cyprian appeals to Pope Saint Stephen I, requesting that he instruct the bishops of Gaul to condemn Marcianus of Arles. [36]

7. In A.D. 260, Pope Saint Stephen I issues an epistle to the bishops of North Africa, forbidding them to readminister valid baptisms, even valid baptisms performed by heretics.[37]

8. In A.D. 342, Pope Saint Julius I intervenes in the Arian controversy and subsequently revokes the unlawful deposition of Saint Athanasius of Alexandria. [38]

9. In A.D. 376, Saint Jerome appeals to Pope Saint Damasus I, requesting that he settle a dispute between three rival claimants to the Patriarchy of Antioch. [39]

---

32. Saint Irenaeus of Lyons, *Against All Heresies 3:4:3*, A.D 189
33. Eusebius of Caesarea, *Ecclesiastical History 5:24:9-11*, A.D. 312
34. Tertullian of Carthage, *On Modesty 1*, A.D. 220
35. Saint Cyprian of Carthage, *Epistle 51:1 (Epistle to Antonianus)*, A.D. 254; Eusebius of Caesarea, *Ecclesiastical History 6:43:1-3*, A.D. 312
36. Saint Cyprian of Carthage, *Epistle 66:2-3 (Epistle to Pope Stephen)*, A.D. 254
37. Saint Vincent of Lerins, *Commonitoriam 6:15-18*, A.D. 434
38. Pope Saint Julius I, *Epistle to Antioch 22-27*, A.D. 342
39. Saint Jerome, *Epistle 15:5 (Epistle to Pope Damasus)*, A.D. 376

10. In A.D. 385, Pope Saint Siricius issues an authoritative decree on baptism, Church discipline, and other such matters, in response to inquiries from Bishop Himerius of Tarragona. [40]

11. In A.D. 431, Pope Saint Celestine I addresses the First Council of Ephesus [via his legate Phillip] and declares that it had always been known that the Apostle Peter, prince and head of the Apostles, pillar of the faith, and foundation of the Catholic Church, lives and judges in his successors. [41]

12. In A.D. 449, Pope Saint Leo I intercedes against the heresies of Eutyches and Nestorius and the illegitimate Second Council of Ephesus by composing a tome which defended the two natures of Christ. The Council of Chalcedon then subsequently submits to his teaching and adopts it in its dogmatic definition. [42]

13. In A.D. 519, Pope Saint Hormisdas brings an end to the Acacian schism between Eastern and Western Churches by having the Patriarch of Constantinople and 2500 Eastern bishops and priests sign a libellus, which affirmed the Primacy and indefectibility of the Roman See, as well as the express acceptance of the Council of Chalcedon/Leo's Tome. [43]

---

40. Pope Saint Siricius, *Directa Decretal*, A.D. 385
41. Phillip the legate [of Pope Saint Celestine I], *Address to Council of Ephesus [Session 3]*, A.D. 431
42. Council of Chalcedon, *Acts of the Council of Chalcedon* (8 October- 1 November, 451), Session 2, Session 5
43. Pope Saint Hormisdas, *Confession of the Faith*, A.D. 519

Early Christian Witness
(For Papal Succession)

Pope Saint Clement I

Our Apostles knew through our Lord Jesus Christ that there would be strife for the office of bishop. For this reason, therefore, having received perfect foreknowledge, they appointed those who have already been mentioned, and afterwards added the further provision that, if they should die, other approved men should succeed to their ministry. (*Epistle to the Corinthians 44*, A.D. 95)

Saint Heggesipus

When I had come to Rome, I visited [Pope] Anicetus, whose deacon was Eleutherus. And after [Pope] Anicetus died, [Pope] Soter succeeded, and after him [Pope] Eleutherus. In each succession and in each city, there is a continuance of that which is proclaimed by the law, the prophets, and the Lord. (*Memoirs [From Eusebius's Ecclesiastical History 4:22]*, A.D. 175)

Saint Irenaeus of Lyons

The blessed Apostles, then, having founded and built up the Church, committed into the hands of Linus the office of the episcopate. Of this Linus, Paul makes mention in the Epistles to Timothy. To him succeeded Anacletus; and after him, in the third place from the Apostles, Clement was allotted the bishopric. This man, as he had seen the blessed Apostles, and had been conversant with them, might be said to have the preaching of the Apostles still echoing [in his ears], and their traditions before his eyes. Nor was he alone [in this], for there were many still remaining who had received instructions from the Apostles. In the time of this Clement, no small dissension having occurred among the brethren at Corinth, the Church in Rome dispatched a most powerful letter to the Corinthians... to this Clement there succeeded Evaristus. Alexander followed Evaristus; then, sixth from the Apostles, Sixtus was appointed; after him, Telephorus, who was gloriously martyred; then Hyginus; after him, Pius; then after him, Anicetus. Soter having succeeded Anicetus, Eleutherius does now, in the twelfth place from the Apostles, hold the inheritance of the episcopate. In this order, and by this succession, the ecclesiastical tradition from the Apostles, and the preaching of the truth, have come down to us. (*Against All Heresies 3:3:3*, A.D. 189)

Tertullian of Carthage

Let them produce the original records of their churches; let them unfold the roll of their bishops, running down in due succession from the beginning in such a manner that [their first] bishop shall be able to show for his ordainer and predecessor some one of the Apostles or of Apostolic men—

a man, moreover, who continued steadfast with the Apostles. For this is the manner in which the Apostolic churches transmit their registers: as the church of Smyrna, which records that Polycarp was placed therein by John; as also the church of Rome, which makes [Pope] Clement to have been ordained in like manner by Peter. (*Against the Heretics 32*, A.D. 200)

<u>Pseudo Tertullian (Likely Commodianus),</u>
In this chair in which he himself had sat, Peter in mighty Rome commanded Linus, the first elected, to sit down. After him, Cletus too accepted the flock of the fold. As his successor, Anacletus was elected by lot. Clement follows him, well-known to Apostolic men. After him Evaristus ruled the flock without crime. Alexander, sixth in succession, commends the fold to Sixtus. After his illustrious work was completed he passed it on the Telephorus. He was excellent, a faithful martyr. After him, learned of law and a sure teacher, Hyginus, in ninth place, now accepted the chair. Then Pius, after him, whose blood brother was Hermas... and Anicetus accepted his lot in pious succession. (*Poem Against the Marcionites*, A.D. 285)

<u>Eusebius of Caesarea</u>
Paul testifies that Crescens was sent to Gaul [2 Tim. 4:10], but Linus, whom he mentions in the Second Epistle to Timothy [2 Tim. 4:21] as his companion at Rome, was Peter's successor in the episcopate of the church there, as has already been shown. Clement also, who was appointed third bishop of the Church at Rome, was, as Paul testifies, his co-laborer and fellow soldier. (*Ecclesiastical History 3:4:9-10*, A.D. 312)

Saint Optatus of Milevis

On this one Cathedra, which is the first of the Endowments, Peter was the first to sit. To Peter succeeded Linus, to Linus succeeded Clement, to Clement Anacletus, to Anacletus Evaristus, to Evaristus Sixtus, to Sixtus Telesphorus, to Telesphorus Hyginus, to Hyginus Anicetus, to Anicetus Pius, to Pius Soter, to Soter Alexander, to Alexander Victor, to Victor Zephyrinus, to Zephyrinus Calixtus, to Calixtus Urban, to Urban Pontianus, to Pontianus Anterus, to Anterus Fabian, to Fabian Cornelius, to Cornelius Lucius, to Lucius Stephen, to Stephen Sixtus, to Sixtus Dionysius, to Dionysius Felix, to Felix Marcellinus, to Marcellinus Eusebius, to Eusebius Miltiades, to Miltiades Silvester, to Silvester Marcus, to Marcus Julius, to Julius Liberius, to Liberius Damasus, to Damasus Siricius, who to-day is our colleague, with whom 'the whole world,' through the intercourse of letters of peace agrees with us in one bond of communion. Now do you show the origin of your Cathedra, you who wish to claim the Holy Church for yourselves! (*The Schism of the Donatists 2:3*, A.D. 367)

Saint Ambrose of Milan

They [the Novatian heretics] have not the succession of Peter, who hold not the chair of Peter, which they rend by wicked schism; and this, too, they do, wickedly denying that sins can be forgiven [by the sacrament of confession] even in the Church, whereas it was said to Peter: 'I will give unto thee the keys of the kingdom of heaven, and whatsoever thou shalt bind on earth shall be bound also in heaven, and whatsoever thou shall loose on earth shall be loosed also in heaven.' (*Penance 1:7:33*, A.D. 388)

Saint Jerome

Clement, of whom the Apostle Paul writing to the Philippians says, 'With Clement and others of my fellow-workers whose names are written in the book of life,' the fourth bishop of Rome after Peter, if indeed the second was Linus and the third Anacletus, although most of the Latins think that Clement was second after the Apostle. (*Illustrious Men 15*, A.D. 392.)

Saint Augustine of Hippo

For if the lineal succession of bishops is to be taken into account, with how much more certainty and benefit to the Church do we reckon back till we reach Peter himself, to whom, as bearing in a figure the whole Church, the Lord said: Upon this rock will I build my Church, and the gates of hell shall not prevail against it! [Matthew 16:18] The successor of Peter was Linus, and his successors in unbroken continuity were these:—Clement, Anacletus, Evaristus, Alexander, Sixtus, Telesphorus, Iginus, Anicetus, Pius, Soter, Eleutherius, Victor, Zephirinus, Calixtus, Urbanus, Pontianus, Antherus, Fabianus, Cornelius, Lucius, Stephanus, Xystus, Dionysius, Felix, Eutychianus, Gaius, Marcellinus, Marcellus, Eusebius, Miltiades, Sylvester, Marcus, Julius, Liberius, Damasus, and Siricius, whose successor is the present Bishop Anastasius. In this order of succession, no Donatist bishop is found. (*Epistle 53 1:2*, A.D. 400)

Phillip the legate [of Pope Saint Celestine I]

There is no doubt, and in fact it has been known in all ages, that the holy and most blessed Peter, prince and head of the Apostles, pillar of the faith, and foundation of the Catholic Church, received the keys of the kingdom from our Lord

Jesus Christ, the Savior and Redeemer of the human race, and that to him was given the power of binding and losing sins: who down even to today and forever both lives and judges in his successors. The holy and most blessed Pope Celestine, according to due order, is his successor and holds his place, and us he sent to supply his place in this holy synod. (*Address to Council of Ephesus [Session 3]*, A.D. 431)

Pope Saint Sixtus III

From the outcome of this affair, you have learnt what it means to be in agreement with us. The blessed Apostle Peter, in his successors, has handed down what he received. Who would be willing to separate himself from the doctrine of him whom the Master himself instructed first among the Apostles? It was not hearsay or selected speech which taught him; he was trained with the others by the mouth of the teacher. He had not to search among writings and writers; he received the original and direct faith which can admit of no dispute, on which we must always meditate, and in which we must abide, so that following the Apostles with a pure affection, we may be counted Apostolical. (*Epistle 6 [to Bishop John of Antioch]*, A.D. 433)

VII. PAPAL INFALLIBILITY

Inasmuch as the New Testament writings are inspired by God and are profitable for teaching and reproof [2 Timothy 3:16], Christ did not explicitly leave us these texts but rather a singular, authoritative, hierarchical, and successional Church, which then produced and preserved said Scriptures. Likewise, whereas each of the Apostles was synonymously afforded the authority to bind and loose [Matthew 18:18], Christ uniquely entrusted Peter and his successors with the keys to the kingdom [Matthew 16:19], and, as such, ultimate and final jurisdiction. Subsequently, in view of the aforementioned structure of authority, which was laid down by Christ and the Apostles, how can we be afforded certainty in our convictions and assurances that we possess inerrant doctrines, dogmas, and Scriptures? Further still, how could Paul proclaim that the Church, itself, was the pillar and foundation of the truth [1 Timothy 3:15] or how could Jesus assert that the Church would be led into all truth until the consummation of the world [John 16:13, Matthew 28:20], if its foundational rock and visible head, was able to universally promulgate error?

Wherefore, in order that the gates of Hades might not prevail against His Church [Matthew 16:18], and so that His vicar might bind and loose on earth with divine backing [Matthew 16:19], the Holy Spirit intercedes on Christ's behalf, to prevent Peter's faith from failing [Luke 22:32]. Consequently, the infallibility of the pope is not a consequence of merit or incongruous with our fallible human nature, for it is God who protects the Petrine office from the possibility of error, whilst defining a doctrine to be held definitively and universally. Subsequently, when Jesus informs Peter that whatever he binds on earth WILL have been bound in heaven [Matthew 16:19], it should come as no surprise that He uses a periphrastic future perfect passive, which indicates that in spite of Peter's personal failures, his judgments would be reflective of what God had already determined.[44] As such, when Peter arises at the Council of Jerusalem and declares that gentiles could be saved apart from circumcision [Acts 15:6-11], we can be assured that his pronouncement was indicative of God's judgment, as much as he was certainly a fallible individual [Galatians 2:11-21]. What's more, the concept of an infallible teaching office also finds precedent in the Old Covenant Jewish priesthood, as Christ implies that the scriptural and disciplinary judgements of the Sanhedrin received an analogous divine backing in spite of their personal nonobservance [Matthew 23:1-4].[45] Likewise, John also insinuates that the high priest of Israel was beneficiary to a type of recurrent divine mediation, whereon even Caiaphas was afforded the capacity to prophesy whilst he was plotting to kill his Savior [John 11:49-53].[46] Further still, virtually every Christian denomination already accepts the fact that, via the intercession of the Holy Spirit, fallible men

---

44. Suan Sonna, "The Biblical Case for an Infallible Magisterium," Pints with Aquinas, 2021, https://academia.edu/49351757/The_Biblical_Case_For_An_Infallible_Magisterium
45. Ibid.
46. Ibid.

infallibly authored what would become the canonical Scriptures, and, as such, one must be willing to apply a continuation of this principle to the chair of Saint Peter, insofar as the scriptural and historical evidence compels it.

In summation, although the doctrine of infallibility was not officially defined until the First Vatican Council in 1869, the concept of an incorruptible Petrine See has been affirmed since the onset of the papacy. Accordingly, it is a doctrine that is rooted in both Holy Scripture and Holy Apostolic Tradition, and one which is philosophically and theologically fitting so as to ensure the inerrancy of our convictions. Indeed, for if not defined by an infallible authority, one could not be assured of the veracity of the most central aspects of Christianity, such as Trinitarian doctrine, the hypostatic union, or an inerrant biblical canon.

Early Christian Witness
(For Papal Infallibility)

Pope Saint Clement I

If, however, any shall disobey the words spoken by [God] through us, let them know that they will involve themselves in transgression and serious danger... Joy and gladness will you afford us, if you become obedient to the words written by us, through the Holy Spirit, and root out the lawless wrath of your jealousy according to the intercession which we have made for peace and unity in this letter. (*Epistle to the Corinthians 59;63*, A.D. 95)

Saint Ignatius of Antioch

You [the church at Rome] have envied no one, but others you have taught. I desire only that which you have enjoined in your instructions [on others] may remain in force. Only request in my behalf both inward and outward strength, that I may not only speak, but [truly] will; and that I may not merely be called a Christian, but really be found to be one. (*Epistle to the Romans 3*, A.D. 110)

Saint Irenaeus of Lyons

It behooves us to learn the truth from those who possess that succession of the Church [chiefly, the Church at Rome (III, Ch. 3, V. 2)] which is from the Apostles, and among whom exists that which is sound and blameless in conduct, as well as that which is unadulterated and incorrupt in speech. For these also preserve this faith of ours in one God who created all things; and they increase that love [which we have] for the Son of God, who accomplished such marvelous dispensations for our sake: and they expound the Scriptures to us without danger, neither blaspheming God, nor dishonoring the patriarchs, nor despising the prophets. (*Against All Heresies 4:26*, 189 A.D.)

Saint Cyprian of Carthage

After such things as these, moreover, they still dare—a false bishop having been appointed for them by heretics—to set sail and to bear letters from schismatic and profane persons to the throne of Peter, and to the chief church whence priestly unity takes its source; and not to consider that these were the Romans whose faith was praised in the preaching of the Apostle, and to whom heterodoxy has no access? (*Epistle 54:14*, A.D. 256)

Saint Gregory of Nazianzen

Regarding the faith which they uphold, the ancient Rome has kept a straight course from of old, and still does so, uniting the whole West by sound teaching, and is just, since she presides over all and guards the universal divine harmony. (*Carmen de Vita Sua 1*, A.D. 381)

Pope Saint Damasus I

Likewise, it is decreed... that it ought to be announced that... the holy Roman Church has been placed at the forefront not by the conciliar decisions of other churches, but has received the primacy by the evangelic voice of our Lord and Savior, who says: 'You are Peter, and upon this rock I will build my Church, and the gates of hell will not prevail against it; and I will give to you the keys of the kingdom of heaven...' [Matt. 16:18–19]. The first see, therefore, is that of Peter the Apostle, that of the Roman Church, which has neither stain nor blemish nor anything like it. (*Decree of Damasus 3*, A.D. 382)

Pope Saint Siricius I

For in view of our office there is no freedom for us, on whom a zeal for the Christian religion is incumbent greater than on all others, to dissimulate or to be silent. We bear the burdens of all who are oppressed, or rather the blessed Apostle Peter, who in all things protects and preserves us, the heirs, as we trust, of his administration, bears them in us... it is also inappropriate henceforth for you to deviate from that path, if you do not wish to be separated from our company by synodal sentence. (*Directa Decretal*, A.D. 385)

Saint Augustine of Hippo

My brothers, suffer with me. Where you find such things, do not hide them, may it not be a perverse mercy in you: by all means, if you find such things, do not hide them. Refute the contradictors and lead the resistant ones to us. For now, about this case, two councils were sent to the Apostolic See [of Rome]: whence also responses came. [As such,] the case is finished: if only the [Pelagian] errors were at some point finished! (*Sermon 131*, A.D. 415)

Pope Saint Zosimus

Although the tradition of the Fathers has attributed such great authority to the Apostolic See [of Rome] that no one would dare to disagree wholly with its judgment, and it has always preserved this [judgment] by canons and rules, and current ecclesiastical discipline up to this time by its laws pays the reverence which is due to the name of Peter, from whom it has itself descended...; since therefore Peter the head is of such great authority and he has confirmed the subsequent endeavors of all our ancestors, so that the Roman Church is fortified ... by human as well as by divine laws, and it does not escape you that we rule its place and also hold power of the name itself, nevertheless you know, dearest brethren, and as priests you ought to know, although we have such great authority that no one can dare to retract from our decision, yet we have done nothing which we have not voluntarily referred to your notice by letters. (*Epistle 12* [*To the Bishops of Africa*], A.D. 418)

Pope Saint Boniface I

We have dispatched such a writing, that the brethren one and all may understand, first that they ought not have met in council without your knowledge; secondly that there is to be no revision of our decision. For it has never been lawful to reconsider what has been settled by the Apostolic see [of Rome]. (*Epistle 13 [to Bishop Rufus of Thessalonica]*, A.D. 420)

Theodoret of Cyrus

Wherefore, I beseech your sanctity, persuade the very sacred and holy archbishop to bid me hasten to your council. For that holy see [of Rome] has precedence over all churches in the world, for many reasons; and above all for this, that it is free from all taint of heresy, and that no bishop of heterodox opinion has ever sat upon its throne, but it has kept the grace of the Apostles undefiled. (*Epistle 116 [To Presbyter Renatus]*, A.D. 440)

Pope Saint Hormisdas

The first means of safety is to guard the rule of strict faith and to deviate in no way from those things that have been laid down by the Fathers. For it is impossible that the words of Our Lord Jesus Christ: "Thou art Peter; and upon this rock I will build my church" [Matthew 16:18], should not be verified. And their truth has been proved by the course of history, for the Apostolic [Roman] see of the Catholic religion has always been kept unsullied. (*Confession of the Faith,* A.D. 519)

John [Patriarch of Jerusalem]

As for us, that is to say, the Holy Church, we have the word of the Lord, who said to Peter, chief of the Apostles, when giving him the primacy of the faith for the strengthening of the churches, "You are Peter, etc...". To this same Peter he has given the keys of heaven and earth; it is in following his faith that to this day his disciples and the doctors of the Catholic Church bind and loose; they bind the wicked and loose from their chains those who do penance. Such is, above all, the privilege of those who, on the first most holy and venerable see [of Rome], are the successors of Peter, sound in the faith, and according to the word of the Lord, infallible. (*Epistle to the Catholicos of the Gregorian Monks,* A.D. 590)

Pope Saint Agatho

For this is the rule of the true faith, which this spiritual mother of your most tranquil empire, the Apostolic Church of Christ, has both in prosperity and in adversity always held and defended with energy; which, it will be proved, by the grace of Almighty God, that she [the Roman Church] has never erred from the path of the Apostolic tradition, nor has she been depraved by yielding to heretical innovations, but from the beginning she has received the Christian faith from her founders, the princes of the Apostles of Christ, and remains undefiled unto the end, according to the divine promise of the Lord and Savior himself, which he uttered in the holy Gospels to the prince of his disciples: saying, 'Peter, Peter, behold, Satan has desired to have you, that he might sift you as wheat; but I have prayed for you, that (your) faith fail not. And when you are converted, strengthen your brethren.' Let your tranquil Clemency therefore consider, since it is the Lord and Savior of all, whose faith it is, that promised that Peter's faith should not fail and exhorted him to strengthen his brethren, how it is known to all that the Apostolic pontiffs, the predecessors of my littleness, have always confidently done this very thing. (*Address to the 3rd Council of Constantinople [Session 4],* A.D. 681)

VIII. THE SEVEN SACRAMENTS

The sacramental theology of the Catholic Church is rooted in the incarnational principle, whereby, via an infusion of grace into the material order, it becomes elevated to the divine. As such, the Church does not regard her sacraments as mere illustrative or customary practices; instead, they are the gifts of Christ, which have been entrusted to His Church so as to dispense the divine life to the faithful.[47] Correspondingly, the sacraments do not represent personal acts of piety or practices preformed apart from divine grace, but rather, they are the very channels of grace through which our Savior gathers His faithful to eternal salvation.[48]

Subsequently, following the ascension of Christ into heaven and the establishment of the New and Eternal Covenant [Hebrews 13:20], a transformation and restoration of Old Testament rituals and practices soon began to transpire. However, due to the unity and immutability of the Father and the Son and the prefiguration of the New Covenant in the Old, a certain degree of continuity was

---

47. Catechism of the Catholic Church (1992), Paragraph 1131
48. Ibid., Paragraph 1129

demanded in the sacramental practices that unfolded. As such, one should not be surprised to find preservations of the priesthood, sworn matrimony, and ritualistic anointing, for the same God who instructed the nation of Israel oversaw its Christian fulfillment. Similarly, if one grants that Christianity and the Church are the providential realizations of Judaism and ancient Israel, we expect to find a certain degree of liturgical continuity between them. And thus, when one views the incorporation of vestments, candles, bells, oils, incense, chants, psalms, servers, alters, and sacrificial oblations in the Catholic mass today, it has been fittingly seen as the restorative and transformative Old Testament liturgical consummation. Nevertheless, this is not to imply that any changes or adaptations were superfluous or lacking warrant, for in light of the cross and the imperatives of Christ, certain rituals were necessarily transfigured. Case in point: the penitential practices of ancient Israel were renewed in the sacrament of confession. Likewise, the once-mandatory custom of infant circumcision was perfected in the sacrament of baptism. Yet, still, this is also not to suggest that the sacraments are arbitrary or mere whimsical renewals of Old Testament practices, in that they are a set of indispensable and sanctifying tools that penetrate into all areas of the Christian lived experience. [49] Indeed, for via baptism, confirmation and the Eucharist we are born into the Christian life,[50] and via extreme unction and confession we are spiritually healed.[51] Accordingly, via matrimony and holy orders, we are called to lives of service, which are formed through the virtue of charity. [52] Wherefore, if we aspire to complete our Christian race and obtain our eternal reward [1 Corinthians 9:24-26], then it behooves us to

---

49. Ibid., Paragraph 1123
50. Ibid., Paragraph 1212
51. Ibid., Paragraph 1421
52. Ibid., Paragraph 1534

access these visible channels, which afford us reconciliation, renewal, and sustenance.

> The sacraments are efficacious signs of grace, instituted by Christ and entrusted to the Church, by which divine life is dispensed to us. The visible rites by which the sacraments are celebrated signify and make present the graces proper to each sacrament. They bear fruit in those who receive them with the required dispositions. (Catechism of the Catholic Church (1992), Paragraph 1131)

IX. THE SACRAMENT OF BAPTISIM

In accordance with the precedent set forth by Christ [Matthew 3:16-17] and the subsequent imperatives of His final commission [Matthew 28:18-20], the sacrament of baptism is nearly universally practiced throughout all of modern Christendom. However, when it comes to the process of its administration or its perceived significance and effects, there is a disparity of conviction in the Christian world and far from unanimity. Case in point: many protestant denominations consider baptism to be a mere public manifestation of one's conscious decision to follow Christ, and, as such, it is presumed to be unsuitable for children, who lack the faculty of reason. Accordingly, as the visual demonstration of one's personal conversion, or its metaphorical depiction, baptism is not believed to confer salvific properties on its willing recipient.[53] Wherefore, it would be fair to conclude that within the vast majority of Protestant denominations, baptism is viewed as an illustrative act as opposed to a necessity for salvation.

---

53. Jimmy Aikin, *The Fathers Know Best: Your Essential Guide To The Teachings Of The Early Church* (San Diego, CA: Catholic Answers Press, 2010), 261

Nevertheless, when one views the application of baptism in Scripture and the properties it purports to confer, it would be hard to maintain that it is a discretionary practice or a mere allegorical symbol. Case in point: Christ would declare, in the Gospel of Mark, that one must believe and be baptized to be saved and that those who willingly withheld belief was bound for condemnation [Mark 16:16]. Correspondingly, in the Gospel of John, Jesus echoes His warning regarding the necessity of baptismal grace, stating that no one could enter the kingdom of God unless they were born of water and the Spirit [John 3:5-8]. Furthermore, the Apostles also bear witness to the regenerative properties of baptism throughout their instructional epistles and equate it to a means of grace via which one receives an initial justification. For example, whilst testifying to a group of hostile pilgrims at the Jewish festival of Pentecost, Peter avowed that baptism eradicated sins and conferred the reception of the Holy Spirit [Acts 2:38]. Accordingly, whilst writing to the provinces of Asia Minor within his first epistle, Peter also affirmed that baptism was salvific and rendered one an heir to life eternal [1 Peter 3:21-22]. In point of fact, even whilst Paul was being healed by Ananias so as to begin his foreordained ministry, he was advised that baptism was required to eliminate his sins, and thus, he ought not to delay or tarry [Acts 22:15-16].

What is more, inasmuch as personal transgressions are demonstrably remitted via baptism throughout the New Testament Scriptures, one must further account for original sin, which is a predisposition present in even children. For instance, a child does not need to be taught how to lie; it is a natural effect of his fallen nature, and likewise, no amount of conditioning could prevent him from sinning; it is the inescapable consequence of an inherited deprivation. Subsequently, even as Christ explicitly expressed His desire for children to receive His kingdom [Luke 18:15–16], He would nonetheless maintain that in order to be saved, they must be born of water and the Spirit [John 3:5-8]. Wherefore, who are we to defy Christ and His desire to incorporate children into His kingdom? Are we to disregard His exhortations on the necessity of baptism or discount the gravitas of our inherited affliction? Further still, the book of Acts recounts Peter affirming that baptism was pertinent for children [Acts 2:39], and likewise, Paul is recorded throughout the New Testament as baptizing entire households [Acts 16:14-15, Acts 16:32-33, 1 Corinthians 1:14-16]. In fact, Paul goes so far as to equate baptism with circumcision whilst writing to the Church in Colossae [Colossians 2:11-15], and, as such, seems to imply that infants were obliged to be baptized in preparation for the faith within which they would be raised.

Notwithstanding, even as God has explicitly bound our salvation to the sacrament of baptism, He, Himself, is not bound by His sacraments.[54] As such, the Church has perennially maintained that those who die without having received water baptism MAY yet have recourse to His mercy. For instance, those who have willingly forfeited their lives for the Christian faith are assumed to have received a baptism by blood.[55] Similarly, those invincibly ignorant of their errors, who have genuinely followed their conscience and sought God MAY have recourse to a baptism of volition.[56] Nevertheless, the Church knows of no other means apart from sacramental baptism that assures the remission of sins, and, as such, she remains faithful to the commission that she has received and strives to ensure that all nations are baptized. [Matthew 28:18-20][57]

---

54. Ibid., Paragraph 1257
55. Tertullian of Carthage, *On Baptism 16*, A.D. 203; Saint Cyprian of Carthage, *Epistle 72:22*, A.D. 255; Saint Gregory of Nazianz, *Orations 39:17*, A.D. 381
56. Second Vatican Council, Dogmatic Constitution on the Church, *Lumen Gentium*, (21, November 1964), No. 16
57. Catechism of the Catholic Church (1992), Paragraph 1257

Early Christian Witness
(For the Sacrament of Baptism)

Hermas of Rome

And I said, I heard, sir, some teachers maintain that there is no other repentance than that which takes place when we descended into the water and received remission of our former sins. He said to me, That was sound doctrine which you heard; for that is really the case. (*The Shepard 4:3:1-2*, A.D. 80)

Saint Justin Martyr

As many as are persuaded and believe that what we teach and say is true, and undertake to be able to live accordingly, are instructed to pray and to entreat God with fasting, for the remission of their sins that are past, we are praying and fasting with them. Then they are brought by us where there is water and are regenerated in the same manner in which we were ourselves regenerated. For, in the name of God, the Father and Lord of the universe, and of our Savior Jesus Christ, and of the Holy Spirit, they then receive the washing with water. For Christ also said, Unless you be born again, you shall not enter into the kingdom of heaven. (*First Apology 61*, A.D. 151)

Saint Irenaeus of Lyons

He [Jesus] came to save all through Himself; all, I say, who through Him are reborn in God: infants, and children, and youths, and old men. (*Against All Heresies 2:22:4*, A.D. 189)

Tertullian of Carthage

The prescript is laid down that "without baptism, salvation is attainable by none" (chiefly on the ground of that declaration of the Lord, who says, 'Unless one be born of water, he has not life'). (*On Baptism 12*, A.D. 203)

Saint Hippolytus of Rome

Baptize first the children, and if they can speak for themselves let them do so. Otherwise, let their parents or other relatives speak for them. (*The Apostolic Tradition 21:16*, A.D. 215)

Origen of Alexandria

Every soul that is born into flesh is soiled by the filth of wickedness and sin. . . In the Church, baptism is given for the remission of sins, and, according to the usage of the Church, baptism is given even to infants. If there were nothing in infants which required the remission of sins and nothing in them pertinent to forgiveness, the grace of baptism would seem superfluous. (*Homilies on Leviticus 8:3*, A.D. 248)

Saint Cyprian of Carthage

As to what pertains to the case of infants: You [Fidus] said that they ought not to be baptized within the second or third day after their birth, that the old law of circumcision must be taken into consideration, and that you did not think that one should be baptized and sanctified within the eighth day after his birth. In our council it seemed to us far otherwise. No one agreed to the course which you thought should be taken. Rather, we all judge that the mercy and grace of God ought to be denied to no man born. (*Epistle 64:2*, A.D. 253)

Saint Athanasius of Alexandria

As we are all from earth and die in Adam, so being regenerated from above of water and Spirit, in Christ we are all quickened. (*Four Discourses Against the Arians 3:26* A.D. 360)

Saint Gregory of Nazianzus

Do you have an infant child? Allow sin no opportunity; rather, let the infant be sanctified from childhood. From his most tender age let him be consecrated by the Spirit. Do you fear the seal [of baptism] because of the weakness of nature? Oh, what a pusillanimous mother and of how little faith! (*On Holy Baptism 40:7*, A.D. 388)

Saint John Chrysostom

You see how many the benefits of baptism are, and some think its heavenly grace consists only in the remission of sins, but we have enumerated ten honors [it bestows]! For this reason, we baptize even infants, though they are not defiled by [personal] sins, so that there may be given to them holiness, righteousness, adoption, inheritance, brotherhood with Christ, and that they may be his [Christ's] members. (*Baptismal Catechesis 1:6:21*, A.D. 388)

<u>Saint Augustine of Hippo,</u>
The custom of Mother Church in baptizing infants is certainly not to be scorned, nor is it to be regarded in any way as superfluous, nor is it to be believed that its tradition is anything except Apostolic. (*The Literal Interpretation of Genesis 10:23:39*, A.D. 408)

X. THE SACRAMENT OF CONFIRMATION

Subsequent to the reception of baptismal grace, when one reaches an age of discretion, the Church enjoins us to receive the sacrament of confirmation, which both completes and seals our baptism.[58] Wherefore, whilst in infancy one is regenerated via water and Spirit and via affirmations made on their behalf, in adolescence these baptismal vows are confirmed by each individual recipient themselves.[59] Furthermore, this renewal of vows is then followed by an anointing of oil and an imposition of hands, by way of which one is fortified by the Holy Spirit and afforded the endurance to bear witness to the gospel.[60] As such, just as the Apostles were confirmed by the Holy Spirit at Pentecost and imparted the requisite grace to be champions for the faith [Acts 2:1-4], so do we, by way of sacramental confirmation, receive a synonymous spiritual strengthening.[61]

---

58. Catechism of the Catholic Church (1992), Paragraph 1303-1304
59. Ibid., Paragraph 1298
60. Ibid., Paragraph 1304
61. Ibid., Paragraph 1302

Predictably, the sacrament of confirmation is also explicitly attested to throughout the New Testament accounts, wherein we witness the Apostles conferring the reception of the Holy Spirit, via a distinct imposition of hands. Case in point: the book of Acts bespeaks of a confirmatory ritual following the sacrament of baptism, when Peter and John invoke the reception of the Spirit, whilst laying hands upon neophyte Samaritans:

> Now when the apostles at Jerusalem heard that Samaria had accepted the word of God, they sent Peter and John to them. The two went down and prayed for them that they might receive the Holy Spirit (for as yet the Spirit had not come upon any of them; they had only been baptized in the name of the Lord Jesus). Then Peter and John laid their hands on them, and they received the Holy Spirit. (Acts 8:14-17, NRSVCE)

Correspondingly, when Ananias was sent to fortify Paul prior to beginning his ministry, he would impose his hands, apart from baptism, and impart the reception of the Holy Spirit:

> So Ananias went and entered the house. He laid his hands on Saul and said, "Brother Saul, the Lord Jesus, who appeared to you on your way here, has sent me so that you may regain your sight and be filled with the Holy Spirit." And immediately something like scales fell from his eyes, and his sight was restored. Then he got up and was baptized, and after taking some food, he regained his strength. (Acts 9:17-19, NRSVCE)

Furthermore, we then witness Paul conferring the reception of the Spirit in an analogous fashion, as he laid his hands upon Christian converts, following their sacramental baptism:

> Paul said, "John baptized with the baptism of repentance, telling the people to believe in the one who was to come after him, that is, in Jesus." On hearing this, they were baptized in the name of the Lord Jesus. When Paul had laid his hands on them, the Holy Spirit came upon them, and they spoke in tongues and prophesied— altogether there were about twelve of them. (Acts 19:4-7, NRSVCE)

What is more, the Epistle to the Hebrews then explicitly reflects upon the discrete stages of the Christian journey towards heaven, and the imposition of hands is notably depicted as a unique element in the order salvation: [62]

> Therefore let us go on toward perfection, leaving behind the basic teaching about Christ, and not laying again the foundation: repentance from dead works and faith toward God, instruction about baptisms, laying on of hands, resurrection of the dead, and eternal judgment. (Hebrews 6:1-2, NRSVCE)

Wherefore, it is clear that the practice of the laying on of hands so as to confer the reception of the Holy Spirit has been consistently seen as an independent sacrament, which served to fortify Christian conviction. Likewise, it is evident that the sacrament of confirmation, along with faith, repentance, baptism, resurrection, and judgment, has always been viewed as an essential aspect of the Christian journey and a unique element in the order of salvation.

---

[62]. Jimmy Aikin, *The Fathers Know Best: Your Essential Guide To The Teachings Of The Early Church* (San Diego, CA: Catholic Answers Press, 2010), 286

Early Christian Witness
(For the Sacrament of Confirmation)

Saint Theophilus of Antioch

Are you unwilling to be anointed with the oil of God? It is on this account that we are called Christians: because we are anointed with the oil of God. (*Epistle to Autolysis 1:12*, A.D. 181)

Tertullian of Carthage

After coming from the place of washing we are thoroughly anointed with a blessed unction, from the ancient discipline by which [those] in the priesthood . . . were accustomed to being anointed with a horn of oil, ever since Aaron was anointed by Moses. . . So also with us, the unction runs on the body and profits us spiritually, in the same way that baptism itself is a corporal act by which we are plunged in water, while its effect is spiritual, in that we are freed from sins. After this, the hand is imposed for a blessing, invoking and inviting the Holy Spirit. (*On Baptism 7: 1-2, 8*, A.D. 200)

Saint Hippolytus of Rome

The bishop, imposing his hand on them, shall make an invocation, saying, 'O Lord God, who made them worthy of the remission of sins through the Holy Spirit's washing unto rebirth [baptism], send into them your grace so that they may serve you according to your will, for there is glory to you, to the Father and the Son with the Holy Spirit, in the holy Church, both now and through the ages of ages. Amen.' Then, pouring the consecrated oil into his hand and imposing it on the head of the baptized, he shall say, 'I anoint you with holy oil in the Lord, the Father Almighty, and Christ Jesus and the Holy Spirit.' Signing them on the forehead, he shall kiss them and say, 'The Lord be with you.' He that has been signed shall say, 'And with your spirit.' Thus, shall he do to each. (*The Apostolic Tradition 21-22*, A.D. 215)

Saint Cyprian of Carthage

It is necessary for him that has been baptized also to be anointed, so that by his having received chrism, that is, the anointing, he can be the anointed of God and have in him the grace of Christ. (*Epistle 7:2*, A.D. 253)

Council of Carthage

And in the Gospel our Lord Jesus Christ spoke with His divine voice, saying, "Except a man be born again of water and the Spirit, he cannot enter the kingdom of God." This is the Spirit which from the beginning was borne over the waters; for neither can the Spirit operate without the water, nor the water without the Spirit. Certain people therefore interpret for themselves ill, when they say that by imposition of the hand they receive the Holy Ghost, and are thus received, when it is manifest that they ought to be born again in the Catholic Church by both sacraments. (*Session 7*, A.D. 256)

Saint Cyril of Jerusalem

And to you in like manner, after you had come up from the pool of the sacred streams, there was given an Unction, the anti-type of that wherewith Christ was anointed; and this is the Holy Ghost...But beware of supposing this to be plain ointment. For as the Bread of the Eucharist, after the invocation of the Holy Ghost, is mere bread no longer, but the Body of Christ, so also this holy ointment is no more simple ointment, nor (so to say) common, after invocation, but it is Christ's gift of grace, and, by the advent of the Holy Ghost, is made fit to impart His Divine Nature. Which ointment is symbolically applied to your forehead and your other senses ; and while your body is anointed with the visible ointment, your soul is sanctified by the Holy and life-giving Spirit...For as Christ after His Baptism, and the visitation of the Holy Ghost, went forth and vanquished the adversary, so likewise ye, after Holy Baptism and the Mystical Chrism, having put on the whole armor of the Holy Ghost, are to stand against the power of the adversary, and vanquish it, saying, I can do all things through Christ which strengthens me. (*Catechetical Lectures 21: 1,3-4*, A.D. 350)

Saint Serapion of Thmuis

We beseech you, that through your divine and invisible power of our Lord and Savior Jesus Christ, you may effect in this chrism a divine and heavenly operation, so that those baptized and anointed in the tracing with it of the sign of the saving cross of the only begotten... as if reborn and renewed through the bath of regeneration, may be made participants in the gift of the Holy Spirit and, confirmed by this seal, may remain firm and immovable, unharmed and inviolate... (*The Sacramentary of Serapion 25:1*, A.D. 350)

Saint Pacian of Barcelona

If, then, the power of both baptism and confirmation, greater by far than charisms, is passed on to the bishops, so too is the right of binding and loosing. (*Three Letters to the Novatianist Sympronian 1:6*, A.D. 383)

Apostolic Constitutions

How dare any man speak against his bishop, by whom the Lord gave the Holy Spirit among you upon the laying on of his hands, by whom you have learned the sacred doctrines, and have known God, and have believed in Christ, by whom you were known of God, by whom you were sealed with the oil of gladness and the ointment of understanding, by whom you were declared to be the children of light, by whom the Lord in your illumination testified by the imposition of the bishop's hands. (2:4:32, A.D.400)

XI. THE EUCHARIST/HOLY COMMUNION

In conformance with the words of institution, which were laid down by Christ at the last supper [Luke 22:19, 1 Corinthians 11:24], ritualistic communion is habitually observed, in virtually every Christian denomination. However, where the vast majority of protestant denominations celebrate "the Lord's supper" metaphorically, when Catholics commemorate the paschal meal, they do not do so allegorically. On the contrary, commensurate with the words of consecration which Jesus instilled in the twelve disciples, the Church speaks of communion as a propitiatory sacrifice and insists upon Christ's real presence in the sacrament. Indeed, for whilst instituting the celebration of the paschal meal and its memorialization in perpetuity, Christ did not claim that the communion bread was a mere symbol of His body, but rather that it was His body, absolutely [Matthew 26:26-29, Mark 14:22-25, Luke 22:15-20]. Wherefore, whilst celebrating its memorial in the sacrifice of the mass, wherein a priest repeats Christ's words of institution, the Church maintains that the Eucharistic bread truly becomes Christ's body, and therein, that the sacrifice of Calvary is continually revisited. Notwithstanding, this is not to suggest that the material properties of the host are changed or that Jesus is re-sacrificed in perpetuity, but rather that Christ's body is substantially present under the auspices of bread and that His ONE sacrifice is perpetually re-presented.[63] Yet, still, why are Catholics so insistent upon the real presence of Christ in the Eucharist? Can this doctrine be justified by the Scriptures? Moreover, why is it necessary to re-present His sacrifice, when its objectives were thoroughly accomplished [John 19:28]?

To be sure, the Church maintains that the sacrificial offering of Christ once and for all time merited for us the offering of eternal salvation.[64] Nevertheless, she also affirms that the sacrifice on Calvary established a channel via which we might offer the Father perpetual propitiation.[65] As such, in accordance with the prophecy of Malachi, who foresaw the consummation of the Jewish sacrificial practices, the Church continually re-presents Christ's sacrifice to the Father, and thereby, perpetually offers Him a spotless oblation:

> A son honors his father, and servants their master. If then I am a father, where is the honor due to me? And if I am a master, where is the respect due to me? says the LORD of hosts to you, O priests, who despise my name. You say, "How have we despised your name?" By offering polluted food on my altar. And you say, "How have we polluted it?" By thinking that the LORD's table may be despised. When you offer blind animals in sacrifice, is that not wrong? And when you offer those that are lame or sick, is that not wrong? Try presenting that to your governor; will he be pleased with you or show you favor? says the LORD of hosts. And now implore the favor of God, that he may be

---

63. Catechism of the Catholic Church (1992), Paragraph 1366
64. Ibid.
65. Ibid., Paragraph 1367

gracious to us. The fault is yours. Will he show favor to any of you? says the LORD of hosts. Oh, that someone among you would shut the temple doors, so that you would not kindle fire on my altar in vain! I have no pleasure in you, says the LORD of hosts, and I will not accept an offering from your hands. For from the rising of the sun to its setting my name is great among the [Gentile] nations, and in every place incense is offered to my name, and a pure offering; for my name is great among the [Gentile] nations, says the LORD of hosts. (Malachi 1:6-11, NRSVCE)

Furthermore, one must also consider that Christ's institution of communion was prefigured in the Old Testament Exodus account, and, as such, was fittingly depicted by the gospel authors as the New Covenant realization of the Jewish Passover [Matthew 26:17-19, Mark 14:12-16, Luke 22:7-18, 1 Corinthians 5:7]. Subsequently, whilst in the Exodus account of the Passover meal the Israelites slaughtered a spotless lamb, spread its blood on the doors of their households, and then consumed it with unleavened bread [Exodus 12:1-42], in the sacrifice of the mass one is presented Christ's body under the auspices of unleavened bread, he declares his unworthiness for Jesus to enter his household [Matthew 8:8],[66] and then consumes the consummate New Paschal Lamb.

What is more, one must further account for the words of Christ in His discourse on the bread of life, as He foreshadows His presence in the Eucharistic host, and then compels the consumption of His flesh:

> "I am the bread of life. Your ancestors ate the manna in the wilderness, and they died. This is the bread that comes

---

66. Prior to receiving the Eucharist in the Roman Rite, the Catholic faithful recite the following: "I am not worthy that You should enter under my roof, but only say the word and my soul shall be healed."

down from heaven, so that one may eat of it and not die. I am the living bread that came down from heaven. Whoever eats of this bread will live forever; and the bread that I will give for the life of the world is my flesh." The Jews then disputed among themselves, saying, "How can this man give us his flesh to eat?" So Jesus said to them, "Very truly, I tell you, unless you eat the flesh of the Son of Man and drink his blood, you have no life in you. Those who eat my flesh and drink my blood have eternal life, and I will raise them up on the last day; for my flesh is true food and my blood is true drink. Those who eat my flesh and drink my blood abide in me, and I in them. Just as the living Father sent me, and I live because of the Father, so whoever eats me will live because of me. This is the bread that came down from heaven, not like that which your ancestors ate, and they died. But the one who eats this bread will live forever." He said these things while he was teaching in the synagogue at Capernaum. When many of his disciples heard it, they said, "This teaching is difficult; who can accept it?" But Jesus, being aware that his disciples were complaining about it, said to them, "Does this offend you? Then what if you were to see the Son of Man ascending to where he was before? It is the spirit that gives life; the flesh is useless. The words that I have spoken to you are spirit and life. But among you there are some who do not believe." For Jesus knew from the first who were the ones that did not believe, and who was the one that would betray him. And he said, "For this reason I have told you that no one can come to me unless it is granted by the Father." Because of this many of his disciples turned back and no longer went about with him. So Jesus asked the twelve, "Do you also wish to go away?" Simon Peter answered him, "Lord, to whom can we go? You have the words of eternal life." (John 6:48-68, NRSVCE)

In truth, Christ's words were too explicit to be taken symbolically, as attested to by the reaction of His followers, and likewise, He never sought to clarify His statements, even whilst they elected to desert Him. Correspondingly, when His words were misinterpreted elsewhere in John's gospel, He endeavored to resolve the misunderstandings [John 3:1-21, John 4:32-34]. However, in the bread of life discourse He reiterates His teaching, on several consecutive occasions.

Further still, we the see Paul, in his letter to the Corinthians, warning about the unworthy reception of communion, whereon he explicates that a failure to properly discern Christ's body, will bring judgement upon the communicant. However, if Christ's body was not truly present in the bread or it was indeed just a symbolic presentation, it would be absurd to refer to a communicant as undeserving, or to imply that they would be guilty of profanation:

> For I received from the Lord what I also handed on to you, that the Lord Jesus on the night when he was betrayed took a loaf of bread, and when he had given thanks, he broke it and said, "This is my body that is for you. Do this in remembrance of me." In the same way he took the cup also, after supper, saying, "This cup is the new covenant in my blood. Do this, as often as you drink it, in remembrance of me." For as often as you eat this bread and drink the cup, you proclaim the Lord's death until he comes. Whoever, therefore, eats the bread or drinks the cup of the Lord in an unworthy manner will be answerable for the body and blood of the Lord. Examine yourselves, and only then eat of the bread and drink of the cup. For all who eat and drink

without discerning the body, eat and drink judgment against themselves. (1 Corinthians 11:23-29, NRSVCE)

Wherefore, when one is presented with the myriad of scriptural attestations for the Catholic understanding of communion, it is clear why the Church insists upon her teachings and affirms Christ's real presence in the Eucharist. Subsequently, whilst in the Exodus account the Israelites were delivered from Pharaoh through the waters of the Red Sea [Exodus 14:20-23], guided to the promised land by a pillar of fire [Exodus 13:20-22], and sustained via manna from heaven [Exodus 16:4-5], in the New Covenant Israel we are delivered from Satan through the regenerative waters of baptism [John 3:5-8], guided to heaven by the pillar of the Church [1 Timothy 3:15], and sustained by Christ's Eucharistic real presence [John 6:32-35].

Early Christian Witness
(For the Eucharist/Holy Communion)

The Didache
Assemble on the Lord's day, break bread, and offer the Eucharist; but first make confession of your faults, that your sacrifice may be pure. But let no one that is at variance with his fellow come together with you, until they be reconciled, that your sacrifice may not be profaned. For this is that which was spoken by the Lord: In every place and time offer to me a pure sacrifice; for I am a great King, says the Lord, and my name is wonderful among the nations. (14, A.D. 70)

Saint Ignatius of Antioch
I have no taste for corruptible food nor for the pleasures of this life. I desire the Bread of God, which is the flesh of Jesus Christ, who was of the seed of David; and for drink I desire his blood, which is love incorruptible. (*Epistle to the Romans: 7:3*, A.D. 110)

Take note of those who hold heterodox opinions on the grace of Jesus Christ, which have come to us, and see how contrary their opinions are to the mind of God... They abstain from the Eucharist and from prayer, because they do not confess that the Eucharist is the flesh of our savior Jesus Christ, flesh which suffered for our sins and which the Father, in his goodness, raised up again. They who deny the gift of God are perishing in their disputes... (*Epistle to the Smyrnaeans: 7:1*, A.D. 110)

Saint Justin Martyr

We call this food Eucharist, and no one is allowed to partake of it, except the man who believes our teaching to be true, and who has been washed with the washing that is for the remission of sins, and unto regeneration, and who is so living as Christ has enjoined. For not as common bread nor common drink do we receive these; but since Jesus Christ our Savior was made incarnate by the word of God and had both flesh and blood for our salvation, so too, as we have been taught, the food which has been made into the Eucharist by the Eucharistic prayer set down by Him, and by the change of which our blood and flesh is nourished, is both the flesh and blood of that incarnate Jesus. (*First Apology 66*, A.D. 151)

Saint Irenaeus of Lyons

But what consistency is there in those who hold that the bread over which thanks have been given is the body of their Lord, and the cup his blood, if they do not acknowledge that he is the Son of the Creator... How can they say that the flesh which has been nourished by the body of the Lord, and by his blood, gives way to corruption and does not partake of life? ...For as the bread from the earth, receiving the invocation of God, is no longer common bread, but that Eucharist, consisting of two elements, earthly and heavenly. (*Against All Heresies 4:18: 4-5*, A.D. 189)

Saint Hippolytus of Rome
And [Wisdom] has furnished her table' [Prov. 9:2]: This refers to [Christ's] honored and undefiled body and blood, which day by day are administered and offered sacrificially at the spiritual divine table, as a memorial of that first and ever-memorable table of the spiritual divine supper. (*Commentary on Proverbs*, A.D. 217)

Origen of Alexandria
Formerly there was baptism in an obscure way... Now, however, in full view, there is regeneration in water and in the Holy Spirt. Formerly, in an obscure way, there was manna for food; now, however, in full view, there is the true food, the flesh of the Word of God, as he himself says: 'My flesh is true food, and my blood is true drink [Jn 6:56]' (*Homilies on Numbers 7:2*, A.D. 249)

Saint Aphrahat the Persian
After having spoken thus [at the Last Supper], the Lord rose up from the place where he had made the Passover and had given his body as food and his blood as drink, and he went with his disciples to the place where he was to be arrested. But he ate of his own body and drank of his own blood, while he was pondering on the dead. With his own hands the Lord presented his own body to be eaten, and before he was crucified, he gave his blood as drink. (*Treatises 12:6*, A.D. 340)

Saint Cyril of Jerusalem

Then having sanctified ourselves by these spiritual Hymns, we beseech the merciful God to send forth His Holy Spirit upon the gifts lying before Him; that He may make the Bread the Body of Christ, and the Wine the Blood of Christ; for whatsoever the Holy Ghost has touched, is surely sanctified and changed. Then, after the spiritual sacrifice, the bloodless service, is completed, over that sacrifice of propitiation we entreat God for the common peace of the Churches, for the welfare of the world; for kings; for soldiers and allies; for the sick; for the afflicted; and, in a word, for all who stand in need of succor we all pray and offer this sacrifice. (*Catechetical Lectures 23:7-8*, A.D. 350)

Saint Athanasius of Alexandria

You shall see the Levites bringing loaves and a cup of wine and placing them on the table. So long as the prayers of supplication and entreaties have not been made, there is only bread and wine. But after the great and wonderful prayers have been completed, then the bread is become the Body, and the wine the Blood, of our Lord Jesus Christ... Let us approach the celebration of the mysteries. This bread and this wine, so long as the prayers and supplications have not taken place, remain simply what they are. But after the great prayers and holy supplications have been sent forth, the Word comes down into the bread and wine —and thus is His Body confected. (*Sermon to the Newly Baptized from Eutyches*, A.D. 373)

Saint Gregory of Nyssa

The bread again is at first common bread; but when the mystery sanctifies it, it is called and actually becomes the

Body of Christ. So too the mystical oil, so too the wine; if they are things of little worth before the blessing, after their sanctification by the Spirit each of them has its own superior operation. This same power of the word also makes the priest venerable and honorable, separated from the generality of men by the new blessing bestowed upon him. (*Sermon on the Day of Lights or On the Baptism of Christ*, A.D. 394)

Theodore of Mopsuestia

When [Christ] gave the bread, he did not say, 'This is the symbol of my body,' but, 'This is my body.' In the same way, when he gave the cup of his blood he did not say, 'This is the symbol of my blood,' but, 'This is my blood'; for he wanted us to look upon the [Eucharistic elements] after their reception of grace and the coming of the Holy Spirit not according to their nature, but receive them as they are, the body and blood of our Lord. We ought... not regard [the elements] merely as bread and cup, but as the body and blood of the Lord, into which they were transformed by the descent of the Holy Spirit. (*Catechetical Homilies 5:1*, A.D. 405)

Saint Augustine of Hippo

What you see is the bread and the chalice... But what your faith obliges you to accept is that the bread is the Body of Christ and the chalice the Blood of Christ. Take, then, and eat the Body of Christ... You have read that, or at least heard it read, in the Gospels, but you were unaware that the Son of God was that Eucharist. (*Sermon 272*, A.D. 411)

Council of Ephesus

We will necessarily add this also. Proclaiming the death, according to the flesh, of the only begotten Son of God, that is Jesus Christ, confessing his resurrection from the dead, and his ascension into heaven, we offer the unbloody sacrifice in the churches, and so go on to the mystical thanksgivings, and are sanctified, having received his holy flesh and the precious blood of Christ the Savior of us all. And not as common flesh do we receive it . . . but as truly the life-giving and very flesh of the Word himself. (*Session 1 [Epistle of Cyril to Nestorius]*, A.D. 431)

XII. THE SACRAMENT OF CONFESSION

Inasmuch as original sin and personal transgressions are remitted through the waters of baptism, what are we to do when we inevitably fall short of our baptismal renunciations of Satan? To be sure, the New Testament states that if we confess our sins, then God will be faithful and just and, as such, forgive us our trespasses/cleanse our souls from all unrighteousness [1 John 1:9]. However, to whom exactly are we supposed to confess? Do all sins compel formal reconciliation? Moreover, what is the scriptural foundation for the sacrament of confession and why does it require human/priestly mediation?

In truth, as sensory and scrupulous beings, it is expedient for us to have recourse to a means of reconciliation that both aligns with our nature and assures us of the fact that we are indeed forgiven. Notwithstanding, this is not to imply that we lack a scriptural foundation that bespeaks of sacramental confession, for there are a myriad of passages that evince its investiture and testify to its essentiality. Case in point: in the gospel accounts, Christ goes out of His way to manifest His authority to forgive sins [Matthew 9:4-

8, Mark 2:1-12, Luke 5:17-26], whereafter He entrusts said authority to the remaining disciples, prior to His heavenly ascension:

> When it was evening on that day, the first day of the week, and the doors of the house where the disciples had met were locked in fear of the Jews, Jesus came and stood among them and said, "Peace be with you." After he said this, he showed them his hands and his side. Then the disciples rejoiced when they saw the Lord. Jesus said to them again, "Peace be with you. As the Father has sent me, so I send you." When he had said this, he breathed on them and said to them, "Receive the Holy Spirit. If you forgive the sins of any, they have forgiven them; if you retain the sins of any, they are retained. (John 20:19-23, NRSVCE)

Accordingly, we also read in the Gospel of John that God desires to reside within us as in a holy temple. However, this indwelling is ultimately predicated upon a devout following of Jesus's commandments; for how could God dwell in a temple of sin or be subjected to our grievous transgressions [1 Corinthians 3:16-17]? Subsequently, we must strive to remain in a state of grace and avoid committing grave moral offenses:

> "They who have my commandments and keep them are those who love me; and those who love me will be loved by my Father, and I will love them and reveal myself to them." Judas (not Iscariot) said to him, "Lord, how is it that you will reveal yourself to us, and not to the world?" Jesus answered him, "Those who love me will keep my word, and my Father will love them, and we will come to them and make our home with them. Whoever does not love me does not keep my words; and the word that you hear is not mine

but is from the Father who sent me." (John 14:21-24, NRSVCE)

Furthermore, John then pointedly expounds upon said mortal offenses, which separate us from God's grace, and distinguishes them from lesser transgressions, which do not lead one permanently astray:

> If you see your brother or sister committing what is not a mortal sin, you will ask, and God will give life to such a one—to those whose sin is not mortal. There is sin that is mortal; I do not say that you should pray about that. All wrongdoing is sin, but there is sin that is not mortal. (1 John 5:16-17, NRSVCE)

Correspondingly, Paul also reinforces, to the Romans and Galatians, that we can indeed have a falling from grace [Galatians 5:4, Romans 11:19-22] and, as such, we are to work out our salvation with fear and trembling [Philippians 2:12], for even he risked disqualification from the salvific race:

> Do you not know that in a race the runners all compete, but only one receives the prize? Run in such a way that you may win it. Athletes exercise self-control in all things; they do it to receive a perishable wreath, but we an imperishable one. So I do not run aimlessly, nor do I box as though beating the air; but I punish my body and enslave it, so that after proclaiming to others I myself should not be disqualified. (1 Corinthians 9:24-27, NRSVCE)

Wherefore, if we find ourselves, via an examination of conscience, in a state of mortal sin, we ought to avail ourselves of the sacrament of confession, wherein we can be assured our transgressions are forgiven. As such, the Church teaches that it is prudent to make regular examinations, through the lens of seven capital vices, wherein one assesses his guilt through the channels by way of which our iniquities so often flow.[67] Subsequently, through the purview of pride, envy, greed, sloth, lust, wrath, and gluttony, one is able to adequately evaluate the state of their conscience, and seek reconciliation if:[68]

1. They have committed a sin with willful intent, and of a sufficient gravity to separate themselves from God's sanctifying grace.

2. They are truly contrite and have a firm intention to amend their lives.

3. They are willing to do penance in the form of prayer, works of mercy, service of neighbors, and other such sacrifices as a remedial action against any incurred temporal punishment.

In summation, throughout history the form of sacramental confession has been, admittedly, organically regulated and altered, developing along with the growth of the Church. However, amidst this change we can nevertheless discern unchanging core aspects of the sacrament: it was never performed as a merely personal or solitary act apart from the Church, but rather, always in an ecclesial setting.[69] To be sure, whether publicly or privately, sins were confessed to a priest, who then granted the penitent absolution, and likewise, penances were always assigned as a remedial action against any incurred temporal punishment. Furthermore, in certain circumstances, penances could later be mitigated by ecclesial

---

67. Catechism of the Catholic Church (1992), Paragraph 1454
68. Ibid., Paragraph 1450
69. Jimmy Aikin, *The Fathers Know Best: Your Essential Guide To The Teachings Of The Early Church* (San Diego, CA: Catholic Answers Press, 2010), 305

authorities as an act of mercy (Lat. *indulgentiam*), from which the practice of indulgences was ultimately derived, clarified, and then doctrinally articulated.

Wherefore, given that Scripture explicitly attests to the possibility of a fall from grace, the expediency of confession, and the apostolic authority to forgive sins, it behooves us to frequent the sacramental means through which we are reconciled and forgiven.

Early Christian Witness
(For the Sacrament of Confession)

The Didache
In the Church you shall acknowledge your transgressions, and you shall not come near for your prayer with an evil conscience. This is the way of life... But every Lord's day gather yourselves together and break bread and give thanksgiving after having confessed your transgressions, that your sacrifice might be pure. (4:14, A.D. 70)

Saint Ignatius of Antioch
For where there is division and wrath God does not dwell. To all those who repent, the Lord grants forgiveness, if they turn in penitence to the unity of God, and communion with the Bishop. (*Epistle to the Philadelphians 3:8*, A.D. 110)

Saint Irenaeus of Lyons
(The Gnostic disciples of Marcus) have deluded many women, who's consciences have been branded with a hot iron. Some of these women make a public confession, but

others are ashamed to do this, and in silence, as if withdrawing from themselves the hope of the life of God, they either apostatize entirely or hesitate between the two courses. (*Against All Heresies 1:22*, A.D. 189)

Tertullian of Carthage

[Regarding confession, some] flee from this work as being an exposure of themselves, or they put it off from day to day. I presume they are more mindful of modesty than of salvation, like those who contract a disease in the more shameful parts of the body and shun making themselves known to the physicians; and thus, they perish along with their own bashfulness. (*Repentance 10:1,* A.D. 203)

Saint Hippolytus of Rome

The bishop conducting the ordination of the new bishop shall pray: God and Father of our Lord Jesus Christ... Pour forth now that power which comes from you, from your royal Spirit, which you gave to your beloved Son, Jesus Christ, and which he bestowed upon his holy Apostles... and grant this your servant, whom you have chosen for the episcopate, [the power] to feed your holy flock and to serve without blame as your high priest, ministering night and day to propitiate unceasingly before your face and to offer to you the gifts of your holy Church, and by the Spirit of the high priesthood to have the authority to forgive sins, in accord with your command. (*The Apostolic Tradition 3*, A.D. 215)

Origen of Alexandria

[A final method of forgiveness], albeit hard and laborious [is] the remission of sins through penance: when the sinner washes his pillow with tears [Ps 6:7], when his tears are nourishment day and night [Ps 41:4], and when he does not shrink from declaring his sin to a priest of the Lord and from seeking medicine. (*Homilies on Leviticus 2:4*, A.D. 249)

Saint Cyprian of Carthage

Of how much greater faith and salutary fear are they who... confess their sins to the priests of God in a straightforward manner and in sorrow, making an open declaration of conscience... I beseech you, brethren, let everyone who has sinned confess his sin while he is still in this world, while his confession is still admissible, while the satisfaction and remission made through the priests are still pleasing before the Lord. (*Epistle 28,29*, A.D. 250)

Saint Aphrahat the Persian

You [priests], then, who are disciples of our illustrious physician [Christ], you ought not deny a curative to those in need of healing. And if anyone uncovers his wound before you, give him the remedy of repentance. And he that is ashamed to make known his weakness, encourage him so that he will not hide it from you. And when he has revealed it to you, do not make it public, lest because of it the innocent might be reckoned as guilty by our enemies and by those who hate us. (*Demonstrations 7:4*, A.D. 340)

Saint Basil of Caesarea

It is necessary to confess our sins to those to whom the dispensation of God's mysteries is entrusted. Those doing penance of old are found to have done it before the saints. It is written in the Gospel that they confessed their sins to John the Baptist [Matt. 3:6], but in Acts [19:18] they confessed to the Apostles. (*Rules Briefly Treated 288*, A.D. 374)

Saint Jerome

If the serpent, the devil, bites someone secretly, he infects that person with the venom of sin. And if the one who has been bitten keeps silence and does not do penance and does not want to confess his wound ... then his brother and his master, who have the word [of absolution] that will cure him, cannot very well assist him. (*Commentary on Ecclesiastes 10:11*, A.D. 388)

Saint Augustine of Hippo

When you shall have been baptized, keep to a good life in the commandments of God so that you may preserve your baptism to the very end. I do not tell you that you will live here without sin, but they are venial sins which this life is never without. Baptism was instituted for all sins. For light sins, without which we cannot live, prayer was instituted... But do not commit those sins on account of which you would have to be separated from the body of Christ. Perish the thought! For those whom you see doing penance have committed crimes, either adultery or some other enormities. That is why they are doing penance. If their sins were light, daily prayer would suffice to blot them out... In the Church, therefore, there are three ways in which sins are forgiven: in baptisms, in prayer, and in the greater humility of penance. (*Sermon to Catechumens on the Creed 7:15, 8:16*, A.D. 395)

XIII. THE SACRAMENT OF EXTREME UNCTION
(Anointing of the sick)

The anointing of the sick is another visible sign of the imparting of invisible grace, wherein one sacramentally unites to the passion of Christ, both for his own benefit and for that of the Church.[70] Respectively, if it is conducive to salvation, this sacramental anointing may invoke a restoration of health; however, irregardless, it confers the requisite strength, peace, and courage so as to faithfully endure the sufferings of illness or old age.[71] What is more, if one is unable to receive the absolution of sins via the sacrament of confession, they may also receive absolution by way of extreme unction, and, as such, be prepared for passing to life eternal.[72] Correspondingly, this anointing and absolution is also typically accompanied by the reception of the Eucharist, or *viaticum*, which strengthens us in our trial and provides all the spiritual nourishment characteristic of the Blessed Sacrament.

---

70. Catechism of the Catholic Church (1992), Paragraph 1521, 1522
71. Ibid., Paragraph 1520, 1532
72. Ibid., Paragraph 1532

Further still, the anointing of the sick and its sacramental effects are not just a speculative transmission of grace; they are explicitly practiced within the New Testament and established by Christ, himself.[73] Case in point: in the Gospel of Mark, we see the disciples go forth in conformance with the dictates of Jesus to ritualistically anoint the sick with oil and alleviate their illnesses:

> And he called the twelve; and began to send them two and two and gave them power over unclean spirits. He ordered them to take nothing for their journey except a staff; no bread, no bag, no money in their belts; but to wear sandals and not to put on two tunics. He said to them, "Wherever you enter a house, stay there until you leave the place. If any place will not welcome you and they refuse to hear you, as you leave, shake off the dust that is on your feet as a testimony against them." So they went out and proclaimed that all should repent. They cast out many demons, and anointed with oil many who were sick and cured them. (Mark 6:8-13, NRSVCE)

Accordingly, James would record a synonymous practice in his epistle to the twelve tribes of Israel, wherein he instructs sick laymen to call a priest, to be anointed for healing and forgiveness:

> Is any of you sad? Let him pray. Is he cheerful in mind? Let him sing. Is any man sick among you? Let him bring in the priests of the church, and let them pray over him, anointing him with oil in the name of the Lord. And the prayer of faith shall save the sick man: and the Lord shall raise him up: and if he be in sins, they shall be forgiven him. (James 5:13-15, NRSVCE).

---

73. Ibid., Paragraph 1511

Wherefore, inasmuch as He provided alternative means for the imparting of forgiveness, sustenance, and grace, Christ, in His mercy, granted us last rites so as to strengthen us in our final days. As such, it is befitting, when possible, to be anointed by a priest when threatened by grave illness or death, to be healed, comforted, fortified, forgiven, and prepared for the journey ahead.[74]

---

74. Ibid., Paragraph 1523

Early Christian Witness
(For the Sacrament of Extreme Unction)

Saint Hippolytus of Rome

If someone makes an offering of oil, the bishop shall give thanks in the same manner as for the oblation of the bread and wine. He does not give thanks with the same words, but quite similar, saying, "Sanctify this oil, God, as you give holiness to all who are anointed and receive it, as you anointed kings, priests, and prophets, so that it may give strength to all who taste it, and health to all who use it." (*The Apostolic Tradition 5:1-2*, A.D. 215)

Council of Nicaea

Concerning the departing, the ancient canonical law is still to be maintained, to wit, that, if any man be at the point of death, he must not be deprived of the last and most indispensable Viaticum. (*Canon 13*, A.D. 325)

Saint Aphrahat the Persian

Of the sacrament of life, by which Christians [in baptism], priests [in ordination], kings and prophets are made perfect; it illuminates darkness [in confirmation], anoints the sick, and by its secret sacrament restores penitent. (*Treatises 23:3*, A.D. 345)

Saint Serapion of Thmuis

We beseech you, Savior of all men, you that have all virtue and power, Father of our Lord and Savior Jesus Christ, and we pray that you send down from heaven the healing power of the only begotten [Son] upon this oil, so that for those who are anointed... it may be effected for the casting out of every disease and every bodily infirmity... for good grace and remission of sins. (*The Sacramentary of Serapion* 29:1, A.D. 350)

Saint Jerome

There also came Constantia a holy woman whose son-in-law and daughter he [Saint Hilarion] had anointed with oil and saved from death. (*Life of Saint Hilarion 44*, A.D. 392)

Saint Cyril of Alexandria

If some part of your body is suffering...recall also the saying in the divinely inspired Scripture: "Is anyone among you ill? Let him call the presbyters of the Church and let them pray over him, anointing him with oil in the name of the Lord. And the prayer of faith will save the sick man, and the Lord will raise him up, and if he be in sins they shall be forgiven" [James 5:14-15] (*Worship and Adoration 6*, A.D. 412)

Pope Saint Innocent I

In the epistle of the blessed Apostle James...'If anyone among you is sick, let him call the priests... There is no doubt that this anointing ought to be interpreted or understood of the sick faithful, who can be anointed with the holy oil of chrism...it is a kind of sacrament. (*Epistle to Decentius, 25:8:11, 6*, A.D. 416)

Saint Hillary of Arles

Whenever some illness comes upon man, he should hurry back to the Church. Let him receive the body and blood of Christ, be anointed by the presbyters with consecrated oil and ask them and the deacons to pray over him in Christ's name. If he does this, he will receive not only bodily health but also forgiveness of his sins. (*Sermon 19:5*, A.D. 440)

Saint Caesarius of Arles

As often as some infirmity overtakes a man, let him who is ill receive the body and blood of Christ; let him humbly and in faith ask the presbyters for blessed oil, to anoint his body, so that what was written may be fulfilled in him: 'Is anyone among you sick? Let him bring in the presbyters, and let them pray over him, anointing him with oil; and the prayer of faith will save the sick man, and the Lord will raise him up; and if he be in sins, they will be forgiven him... See to it, brethren, that whoever is ill hasten to the church, both that he may receive health of body and will merit to obtain the forgiveness of his sins. (*Sermon 13, 325:3*, A.D. 542)

Cassiodorus of Rome

A priest is to be called in, who by the prayer of faith and the unction of the holy oil which he imparts will save him who is afflicted [by a serious injury or by sickness]. (*Complexions in Epp. Apostolorum*, A.D. 570)

XIV. THE SACRAMENT OF MATRIMONY

Insofar as God is the author of the natural world and the divine architect of Scripture, we should not be surprised that the sacrament of matrimony is consistent with both revelation and the teleology of nature. Case in point: human sexuality has structure, intelligibility, and an objective end to which it is ultimately ordered, and, as such, it is evident that a fully integrated expression of a sexual act is both unitive, and procreative.[75] Accordingly, the innate differences between male and female counterparts serve to transform and elevate one another, and thus, their sacramental fusion in the form of a permanent union creates an optimal foundation for the raising and education of children. [76] Subsequently, the Church teaches in line with natural teleology and the revelation of Scripture, that the sacrament of matrimony confers an indissoluble bond and is reserved for one man and one woman.[77] Furthermore, she maintains that the sacrament is also mirrored by the relation of Christ to the Church, and, as such, it is sanctifying,

---

75. Catechism of the Catholic Church (1992), Paragraph 2363
76. Ibid., Paragraph 1652,1653, 2333
77. Ibid., Paragraph 1644, 1645, 1646

sacrificial, enduring, life giving, and marked by service and pious submission [Ephesians 5:20-33].

Predictably, Christ would bespeak the permanence of sacramental marriage throughout the gospel accounts and bear witness to its objective ends of unity and procreativity. For example, in the Gospel of Mark He would divulge to the Pharisees that divorce was granted to them as an indult and that male and female counterparts were tailored to become one flesh, in the form of an indissoluble union:

> He left that place and went to the region of Judea and beyond the Jordan. And crowds again gathered around him; and, as was his custom, he again taught them. Some Pharisees came, and to test him they asked, "Is it lawful for a man to divorce his wife?" He answered them, "What did Moses command you?" They said, "Moses allowed a man to write a certificate of dismissal and to divorce her." But Jesus said to them, "Because of your hardness of heart he wrote this commandment for you. But from the beginning of creation, 'God made them male and female.' 'For this reason a man shall leave his father and mother and be joined to his wife, and the two shall become one flesh.' So they are no longer two, but one flesh. Therefore what God has joined together, let no one separate." Then in the house the disciples asked him again about this matter. He said to them, "Anyone who divorces his wife and marries another commits adultery, and whoever marries a woman divorced from her husband commits adultery." (Mark 10:5-10, NRSVCE)

Furthermore, in the Gospel of Luke He would reaffirm His teaching whilst preaching to the twelve disciples, stating that whomever divorced a valid spouse so as to marry another committed the sin of adultery:

> It is easier for heaven and earth to pass away, than for one stroke of a letter in the law to be dropped. Anyone who divorces his wife and marries another woman commits adultery, and the man who marries a divorced woman commits adultery. (Luke 16:17-18, NRSVCE)

What is more, inasmuch as Christ bears witness to the permanent and procreative nature of marriage throughout the gospel accounts, Paul is even more explicit within his instructive epistles. For instance, in his letter to the Romans, he would emphatically state that sacramental marriage was only dissoluble by death and that those who elected to remarry, whilst their spouse still lived were culpable of an adulterous union:

> Thus a married woman is bound by the law to her husband as long as he lives; but if her husband dies, she is discharged from the law concerning the husband. Accordingly, she will be called an adulteress if she lives with another man while her husband is alive. But if her husband dies, she is free from that law, and if she marries another man, she is not an adulteress. (Romans 7:2-3, NRSVCE)

Correspondingly, in his letter to the Corinthians, Paul reiterates his teaching on the permanence of a sacramental union by maintaining that if a valid marriage had become irreconcilable, one was bound to a life of chastity and virtue:

> To the married I give this command—not I but the Lord—that the wife should not separate from her husband. But if she does, she must remain unmarried or else be reconciled

to her husband. And a husband must not divorce his wife.
(1 Corinthians 7:10, NRSVCE)

Notwithstanding, this is not to deny that there can be sufficient cause for two spouses to legally separate.[78] However, due to the immutable and indissoluble character of sacramental marriage, it is no longer licit to remarry and/or procreate.[79] Subsequently, the Church maintains that God imparts sufficient grace to those who have been sacramentally married to either fulfill their vows or endure in continence, so long as their spouse remains living:

> No testing has overtaken you that is not common to everyone. God is faithful, and he will not let you be tested beyond your strength, but with the testing he will also provide the way out so that you may be able to endure it.
> (1 Corinthians 10:13, NRSVCE)

In summation, whereas the vast majority of Christian denominations have reformed their teachings on marriage to align with modern culture, the Church is faithful to the principles of natural teleology and to the instructions of Christ and the Apostles. Wherefore, just as the early Church Fathers opposed the sensualism of the Greco-Romans and Pope Clement VII resisted King Henry VIII, the Church remains true to her perennial teachings on matrimony and does not compromise for popularity's sake.

---

78. Ibid., Paragraph 1649
79. Ibid., Paragraph 1650

Early Christian Witness
(For the Sacrament of Matrimony)

Hermas of Rome

What then shall the husband do if the wife continues in this disposition [adultery]? Let him divorce her, and let the husband remain single. But if he divorces his wife and marries another, he too commits adultery. (*The Shepherd 2:4:1*, A.D. 80)

Saint Justin Martyr

In regard to chastity, [Jesus] has this to say: 'If anyone look with lust at a woman, he has already before God committed adultery in his heart.' And, 'Whoever marries a woman who has been divorced from another husband, commits adultery.' According to our Teacher, just as they are sinners who contract a second marriage, even though it be in accord with human law, so also are they sinners who look with lustful desire at a woman. He repudiates not only one who actually commits adultery, but even one who wishes to do so; for not only our actions are manifest to God, but even our thoughts. (*First Apology 15*, A.D. 151)

Saint Clement of Alexandria

That Scripture counsel's marriage, however, and never allows any release from the union, is expressly contained in the law: 'You shall not divorce a wife, except for reason of immorality.' And it regards as adultery the marriage of a spouse, while the one from whom a separation was made is still alive. 'Whoever takes a divorced woman as wife commits adultery,' it says; for 'if anyone divorce his wife, he debauches her'; that is, he compels her to commit adultery. And not only does he that divorces her become the cause of this, but also, he that takes the woman and gives her the opportunity of sinning; for if he did not take her, she would return to her husband. (*Miscellanies 2:23*, A.D. 207)

Origen of Alexandria

Just as a woman is an adulteress, even though she seems to be married to a man, while a former husband yet lives, so also the man who seems to marry her who has been divorced does not marry her, but, according to the declaration of our Savior, he commits adultery with her. (*Commentaries on Matthew 14:24*, A.D. 249)

Council of Elvira

Likewise, women who have left their husbands for no prior cause and have joined themselves with others, may not even at death receive Communion. (*Canon 8*, A.D. 300)

Saint Basil of Caesarea

A man who marries after another man's wife has been taken away from him will be charged with adultery in the case of the first woman; but in the case of the second he will be guiltless. (*Epistle 199:37*, A.D. 375)

Saint Ambrose of Milan

You dismiss your wife, therefore, as if by right and without being charged with wrongdoing; and you suppose it is proper for you to do so because no human law forbids it; but divine law forbids it. Anyone who obeys men ought to stand in awe of God. Hear the law of the Lord, which even they who propose our laws must obey: 'What God has joined together let no man put asunder.' (*Commentary on Luke 8:5*, A.D. 389)

Saint Jerome

Do not tell me about the violence of the ravisher, about the persuasiveness of a mother, about the authority of a father, about the influence of relatives, about the intrigues and insolence of servants, about household losses. So long as a husband lives, be he an adulterer... be he guilty of every kind of vice, if she left him on account of his crimes, he is her husband still and she may not take another. (*Epistle 55:3*, A.D. 398)

Pope Saint Innocent I

[T]he practices is observed by all of regarding an adulteress woman who marries a second time while her husband yet lives, and permission to do penance is not granted her until one of them is dead. (*Epistle 2:13:15*, A.D. 408)

Saint Augustine of Hippo

A women begins to be the wife of no later husband unless she has ceased to be the wife of a former one. She will cease to be the wife of a former one, however, if that husband should die, not if he commits fornication. A spouse, therefore, is lawfully dismissed for the cause of fornication; but the bond of chastity remains. That is why a man is guilty of adultery if he marries a woman who has been dismissed even for this very reason of fornication. (*Adulterous Marriages 2:4:4*, A.D. 419)

XV. THE SACRAMENT OF HOLY ORDERS

Inasmuch as the New Testament authors conscientiously depict Christ as the new and eternal Davidic king [2 Samuel 7:12-17, Matthew 1:6-16, Luke 1:32-33], they also present Him as a New Covenant realization of Moses and the Jewish exodus from Egypt [Acts 3:20-22]. For, in truth, Moses had prophesied that a commensurable prophet was to rise up from the nation of Israel [Deuteronomy 18:15], and thus, as Christ began to mirror his actions and words, it became an undeniable typological parallel. Case in point:[80] where Moses was rescued as an infant in Egypt from the genocidal decree of Pharaoh [Exodus 1:22], Jesus sought refuge in Egypt as an infant from an analogous decree by King Herod [Matthew 2:13]. Likewise, where Moses came out of Egypt to the desert, through the waters of the Red Sea [Exodus 14:26-30. 15:22-24], Jesus left Egypt and proceeded to the desert through the baptismal waters of the Jordan

---

80. The subsequent typological examples have been summarized from: Dr. Scott Hahn, "Is Jesus the New Moses," August 13, 2020, The Road to Emmaus Podcast, https://stpaulcenter.com/audio/the-road-to-emmaus/is-jesus-the-new-moses/

[Matthew 2:19-20, 3:13-17, 4:1]. Furthermore, Moses then fasted for 40 days in God's presence [Exodus 34:28], whereon Israel was tempted and failed [Exodus 32:1-35], whereas Jesus would fast for 40 days, amidst the Spirit, to be tempted by Satan and pass [Matthew 4:1-11]. In point of fact, Christ would go so far as to explicitly quote Moses whilst combatting the temptations of Satan [Deuteronomy 6:13, 6:16, 8:3], and, as such, by recounting the commands that were given to Israel, He succeeded precisely where they had failed. What is more, Moses then proceeded to receive God's laws on Mount Sinai and deliver them to the nation of Israel [Exodus 34:29], whilst Jesus delivered His sermon on the mount and thereon consigned the New Covenant to His disciples [Matthew 5:1-48]. To be sure, Moses had Aaron, Nadab, and Abihu, whilst Jesus had Peter, James, and John, and where Moses appointed 12 chiefs over the tribes of Israel [Numbers 1:1-16], Jesus appointed 12 disciples [Matthew 10:1-4, 19:28]. Accordingly, Moses then anointed 72 priestly elders so as to serve under his 12 chief phylarches [Exodus 24:1-18], and Jesus appointed 72 priestly disciples to minister under the 12 Apostles [Luke 10:1-20].

Wherefore, when one views the actions of Christ in the Gospels through the lens set forth by Moses, one should not be surprised that the structure and function of the New Testament priesthood came to parallel those of ancient Israel's. Indeed, for where the Old Testament priesthood had a threefold structure of high priest, priest, and Levite [Numbers 18:1-7, Hebrews 5:4], an analogous structure of bishop, priest, and deacon unfolded under the guidance of Jesus and the Holy Spirit [1 Timothy 3:1-10, 5: 17-19, Titus 1:5, James 5:14]. Likewise, where the Old Testament priests and high priests offered animal sacrifices [Numbers 18:7-10], whilst the Levites ministered and managed the sanctuary [Numbers 18:2], so too did the New Testament bishops and priests offer Eucharistic oblations [Hebrews 13:10, 1 Corinthians 10:16-21, 1 Clement 44:4-5] whilst the deacons performed works of service [Acts 6:1-6]. What is more, where the Old Covenant priests piously practiced continence prior to experiencing God's presence [Exodus 19:10-15], celibacy was promoted in the New Covenant priesthood, which encountered Christ daily in the Eucharist [Matthew 19:12, 1 Corinthians 7:27-34]. Correspondingly, just as the Mosaic priesthood was restricted to the male descendants of Aaron [Exodus 28:1, Numbers 3:1-4] and the Levite ministry to the sons of the tribe Levi [Numbers 3: 5-13], so too were sacramental ordinations reserved for men within the New Covenant priesthood [1 Corinthians 14:34-45, 1 Timothy 2:8-15].

Regrettably, the regulation of celibacy in the New Covenant priesthood has been depicted as unnecessary, unjustified, and extreme; however, it is a discipline routed in the writings of the Apostles [1 Corinthians 7:27-35] and affords one the requisite flexibility to further Christ's kingdom [Matthew 19:12]. Accordingly, whereas the all-male hierarchy within the New Covenant priesthood has been seen as misogynistic and unjust, the Church is bound by the fundamental constitutions of Jesus and the Apostles, and their resolution to reserve ordination for men [Ordination Sacerdotalis 1-4]. Notwithstanding, the Church has always upheld the dignity of women and their essentiality in its mission and ministry, so much so, that her female saints are frequently among the most venerated, and several have been granted titles of the highest esteem [Teresa of Avila, Catherine of Siena, Therese of Lisieux, Hildegard of Bingen].[81] What is more, the priesthood is not an institution where power is consolidated, or where one seeks to acquire fortune or fame, but rather, it is an institution committed to a life of evangelization, service, sacrifice, and aid.[82]

---

81. Declared a "Doctor of the Church" in 1970, 1970, 1997, and 2012 respectively.
82. Catechism of the Catholic Church (1992), Paragraph 1599

Early Christian Witness
(For the Sacrament of Holy Orders)

Saint Ignatius of Antioch,

Now, therefore, it has been my privilege to see you in the person of your God-inspired bishop, Damas; and in the persons of your worthy presbyters, Bassus and Apollonius; and my fellow-servant, the deacon, Zotion. What a delight is his company! For he is subject to the bishop as to the grace of God, and to the presbytery as to the law of Jesus Christ. (*Epistle to the Magnesians* 2, A.D. 110)

I cried out while I was in your midst, I spoke with a loud voice, the voice of God: 'Give heed to the bishop and the presbytery and the deacons.' Some suspect me of saying this because I had previous knowledge of the division certain persons had caused; but he for whom I am in chains is my witness that I had no knowledge of this from any man. It was the Spirit who kept preaching these words, 'Do nothing without the bishop, keep your body as the temple of God, love unity, flee from divisions, be imitators of Jesus Christ, as he was imitator of the Father.' (*Epistle to the Philadelphians 7:1-2*, A.D. 110)

Saint Clement of Alexandria

A multitude of other pieces of advice to particular persons is written in the holy books: some for presbyters, some for bishops and deacons; and others for widows, of whom we shall have opportunity to speak elsewhere. (*The Instructor of Children 3:12*, A.D. 197)

Saint Hippolytus of Rome

When a deacon is to be ordained, he is chosen after the fashion of those things said above, the bishop alone in like manner imposing his hands upon him as we have prescribed. In the ordaining of a deacon, this is the reason why the bishop alone is to impose his hands upon him: he is not ordained to the priesthood, but to serve the bishop and to fulfill the bishop's command. He has no part in the council of the clergy but is to attend to his own duties and is to acquaint the bishop with such matters as are needful. (*The Apostolic Tradition* 9, A.D. 215)

Origen of Alexandria

Not fornication only, but even marriages make us unfit for ecclesiastical honors; for neither a bishop, nor a presbyter, nor a deacon, nor a widow is able to be twice married. (*Homilies on Luke 17*, A.D. 235)

Council of Elvira

Bishops, presbyters, and deacons may not leave their own places for the sake of commerce, nor are they to be traveling about the provinces, frequenting the markets for their own profit. Certainly, for the procuring of their own necessities they can send a boy or a freedman or a hireling or a friend or whomever, but, if they wish to engage in business, let them do so within the province. (*Canon 19*, A.D. 300)

Council of Nicaea I

It has come to the knowledge of the holy and great Synod that, in some districts and cities, the deacons administer the Eucharist to the presbyters, whereas neither canon nor custom permits that they who have no right to offer should give the Body of Christ to them that do offer. And this also has been made known, that certain deacons now touch the Eucharist even before the bishops. Let all such practices be utterly done away, and let the deacons remain within their own bounds, knowing that they are the ministers of the bishop and the inferiors of the presbyters. Let them receive the Eucharist according to their order, after the presbyters, and let either the bishop or the presbyter administer to them. Furthermore, let not the deacons sit among the presbyters, for that is contrary to canon and order. And if, after this decree, any one shall refuse to obey, let him be deposed from the diaconate. (*Canon 18*, A.D. 325)

Saint Cyril of Jerusalem

Consider, I pray, of each nation, Bishops, Presbyters, Deacons, Solitaries, Virgins, and laity besides; and then behold their great Protector, and the Dispenser of their gifts;—how throughout the world He gives to one chastity, to another perpetual virginity, to another almsgiving, to another voluntary poverty, to another power of repelling hostile spirits. And as the light, with one touch of its radiance sheds brightness on all things, so also the Holy Ghost enlightens those who have eyes; for if any from blindness is not vouchsafed His grace, let him not blame the Spirit, but his own unbelief. (*Catechetical Lectures 16:22*, A.D. 350)

Saint Epiphanius of Salamis

It is true that in the Church there is an order of deaconesses, but not for being a priestess, nor for any kind of work of administration, but for the sake of the dignity of the female sex, either at the time of baptism or of examining the sick or suffering, so that the naked body of a female may not be seen by men administering sacred rites, but by the deaconess... From this bishop [James the Just] and the just-named Apostles, the succession of bishops and presbyters [priests] in the house of God have been established. Never was a woman called to these. (*Against Heresies 78:13*, A.D. 377)

Saint Jerome

In fact, as if to tell us that the traditions handed down by the Apostles were taken by them from the old testament, bishops, presbyters and deacons occupy in the church the same positions as those which were occupied by Aaron, his sons, and the Levites in the temple... (*Epistle 146:2*, A.D. 390)

Saint John Chrysostom

[In Philippians 1:1 Paul says,] 'To the co-bishops and deacons.' What does this mean? Were there plural bishops of some city? Certainly not! It is the presbyters that [Paul] calls by this title; for these titles were then interchangeable, and the bishop is even called a deacon. That is why, when writing to Timothy, he says, 'Fulfill your diaconate' [2 Tim. 4:5], although Timothy was then a bishop. That he was in fact a bishop is clear when Paul says to him, 'Lay hands on no man lightly' [1 Tim. 5:22], and again, 'Which was given you with the laying on of hands of the presbytery' [1 Tim. 4:14], and presbyters would not have ordained a bishop. (*Homilies on Philippians 1:1*, A.D. 402)

XVI. JUSTIFICATION BY GRACE, THROUGH FAITH, FORMED BY CHARITY

Whereas the vast majority of Protestant denominations view justification as a finite legal exchange, the Church has perennially taught that it is an ongoing process wherein Christ transforms us into His image [Romans 8:29].[83] Case in point: Martin Luther would assert that humanity was totally depraved and thus could only be justified by the imputation of Christ's righteousness, as accepted through faith. However, the Church ardently maintained that grace was operative within the soul, actively transforming, sanctifying, and perfecting it.[84] Correspondingly, Martin Luther would avow that humanity was justified by grace alone, through faith alone, once and for all time. However, the Church conscientiously insisted that we were compelled to cooperate with God's grace and to continue to grow in righteousness via faith working through charity [John 15:1-9].[85] Subsequently, inasmuch as she condemns the belief that we can strictly earn our salvation, or that we can grow in

---

83. Catechism of the Catholic Church (1992)., Paragraph 2012
84. Ibid., Paragraph 2000
85. Ibid., Paragraph 2001

justification apart from God's grace, the Church also rejects the proposition that we are justified by faith alone, or that we are simply imputed righteousness, as opposed to actively transformed [Romans 6:1-23].

Notwithstanding, the Church does readily confess that each and every individual is called to the Christian life by God's grace alone and that no action or deed that precedes our baptism could merit the grace of this initial justification [Titus 3:4-8, Romans 3:24-25, Ephesians 2:8-10].[86] However, through baptism, we are not merely imputed righteousness by the acceptance of Christ's merits through faith; on the contrary, we are regenerated, sanctified, made anew, and absolved of original and personal sins [Acts 2:38, Acts 22:15-16, 1 Peter 3:21-22]. Furthermore, our salvific race is not complete at our initial justification, nor are we rendered righteous once and for all time, in that Scripture charges us to cooperate with God's sanctifying grace, and to increase in justification over the course of our Christian life.[87] For instance, James would submit that true faith in Christ required far more than mere intellectual assent and that a man was not justified by faith alone, but rather, by a faith continuously working through the virtue of charity:

> What good is it, my brothers and sisters, if you say you have faith but do not have works? Can faith save you? If a brother or sister is naked and lacks daily food, and one of you says to them, "Go in peace; keep warm and eat your fill," and yet you do not supply their bodily needs, what is the good of that? So, faith by itself, if it has no works, is dead. But someone will say, "You have faith and I have works." Show me your faith apart from your works, and I by my works will show you my faith. You believe that God

---

86. Council of Trent, *Decree on Justification* (13, January 1547), Ch. 8
87. Catechism of the Catholic Church (1992), Paragraph 2013

is one; you do well. Even the demons believe—and shudder. Do you want to be shown, you senseless person, that faith apart from works is barren? Was not our ancestor Abraham justified by works when he offered his son Isaac on the altar? You see that faith was active along with his works, and faith was brought to completion by the works. Thus the scripture was fulfilled that says, "Abraham believed God, and it was reckoned to him as righteousness," and he was called the friend of God. You see that a person is justified by works and not by faith alone. Likewise, was not Rahab the prostitute also justified by works when she welcomed the messengers and sent them out by another road? (James 2:14-25, NRSVCE)

Accordingly, Paul would maintain that the salvific race was to be run to its natural end [1 Corinthians 9:24-27, Philippians 2:12, Galatians 5:7, Romans 11:19-22] and that man could not be justified by the Mosaic law, but rather, a faith expressing itself through charity and love:

You who want to be justified by the law have cut yourselves off from Christ; you have fallen away from grace. For through the Spirit, by faith, we eagerly wait for the hope of righteousness. For in Christ Jesus neither circumcision nor uncircumcision counts for anything; the only thing that counts is faith working through love. (Galatians 5:4-6, NRSVCE)

What is more, Paul explicitly asserts that we were created in Christ for the express purpose of performing charitable works [Ephesians 2:10], and, as such, we will inevitably be judged by the extent to which we do so, in cooperation with God's sanctifying grace:

For he will repay according to each one's deeds: to those who by patiently doing good seek for glory and honor and immortality, he will give eternal life; while for those who are self-seeking and who obey not the truth but wickedness, there will be wrath and fury. There will be anguish and distress for everyone who does evil, the Jew first and also the Greek, but glory and honor and peace for everyone who does good, the Jew first and also the Greek. For God shows no partiality. All who have sinned apart from the law will also perish apart from the law, and all who have sinned under the law will be judged by the law. For it is not the hearers of the law who are righteous in God's sight, but the doers of the law who will be justified. (Romans 2:6-13, NRSVCE)

Subsequently, when one views the context set forth by Scripture, as it relates to justification by grace, through faith, it is clear that it is a continual process, wherein Christ transforms us into His image. Wherefore, insofar as men are justified apart from works of the law [Galatians 2:15-21, Romans 3:27-31], it is not by faith alone [James 2:24], but rather, by a faith which is formed through the virtue of charity [James 2:18, Galatians 5:6, James 1:22-25], for faith without works is dead [James 2:17, 20].[88]

---

88. Jimmy Akin, "Faith and Works: Understanding Ephesians 2:8-9," September 1, 1999, Catholic Answers, https://catholic.com/magazine/print-edition/faith-and-works

Early Christian Witness
(For Justification by Grace, Through Faith, Formed by Charity)

Pope Saint Clement I

Let us therefore join with those to whom grace is given by God. Let us clothe ourselves in concord, being humble and self-controlled, keeping ourselves far from all backbiting and slander, being justified by works and not by words... Why was our Father Abraham blessed? Was it not because of his deeds of justice and truth, wrought in faith?... So, we, having been called through his will in Christ Jesus, were not justified through ourselves or through our own wisdom or understanding or piety or works which we wrought in holiness of heart, but through faith, whereby the almighty God justified all men. (*Epistle to the Corinthians 30:3, 31:2, 32:3-4*, A.D. 95)

Saint Ignatius of Antioch

Give heed to the bishop, that God also may give heed to you. My soul be for theirs that are submissive to the bishop, to the presbyters, and to the deacons, and may my portion be along with them in God! Labor together with one another; strive in company together; run together; suffer together; sleep together; and awake together, as the stewards, and associates, and servants of God. Please Him under whom you fight, and from whom you receive your wages. Let none of you be found a deserter. Let your baptism endure as your arms; your faith as your helmet; your love as your spear; your patience as a complete panoply. Let your works be the charge assigned to you, that you may receive a worthy recompense. Be long-suffering, therefore, with one another, in meekness, as God is towards you. May I have joy of you forever! (*Epistle to Polycarp and Smyrna 6,* A.D. 110)

Saint Theophilus of Antioch
Give studious attention to the prophetic writings, and they will lead you on a clearer path to escape the eternal punishments and to obtain the eternal good things of God. He who gave the mouth for speech and formed the ears for hearing and made eyes for seeing will examine everything and will judge justly, granting recompense to each according to merit. To those who seek immortality by the patient exercise of good works, he will give everlasting life, joy, peace, rest, and all good things, which neither has eye seen nor ear heard, nor has it entered into the heart of man. (*Epistle to Autolycus 1:14*, A.D. 181)

Saint Irenaeus of Lyons
[Paul], therefore, exhorts us to the struggle for immortality, that we may be crowned, and may deem the crown precious, namely, that which is acquired by our struggle, but which does not encircle us of its own accord. And the harder we strive, so much is it the more valuable; while so much the more valuable it is, so much the more should we esteem it.

And indeed, those things are not esteemed so highly which come spontaneously, as those which are reached by much anxious care. (*Against All Heresies, 4:37:7,* A.D. 189)

Saint Clement of Alexandria

When we hear, 'Your faith has saved you,' we do not understand the Lord to say simply that they will be saved who have believed in whatever manner, even if works have not followed. To begin with, it was to the Jews alone that he spoke this phrase, who had lived in accord with the law and blamelessly and who had lacked only faith in the Lord. (*Stromata 6:14,* A.D. 202)

Saint Hippolytus of Rome

And being present at His judicial decision, all, both men and angels and demons, shall utter one voice, saying, Righteous is Your judgment. Of which voice the justification will be seen in the awarding to each that which is just; since to those who have done well shall be assigned righteously eternal bliss, and to the lovers of iniquity shall be given eternal punishment. (*Against Plato 3,* A.D. 220)

Lactantius

Let everyone train himself to justice, mold himself to self-restraint, prepare himself for the contest, equip himself for virtue, that if by any chance an adversary shall wage war, he may be driven from that which is upright and good by no force, no terror, and no tortures, may give himself up to no senseless fictions, but in his uprightness acknowledge the true and only God, may cast away pleasures, by the attractions of which the lofty soul is depressed to the earth, may hold fast innocence, may be of service to as many as possible, may gain for himself incorruptible treasures by good works, that he may be able, with God for his judge, to gain for the merits of his virtue either the crown of faith, or the reward of immortality. (*Divine Institutes 73,* A.D. 317)

Saint Cyril of Jerusalem

The root of all good works is the hope of the resurrection; for the expectation of the recompense nerves the soul to good works. For every laborer is ready to endure the toils if he sees their reward in prospect. (*Catechetical Lectures 18:1,* A.D. 350)

Saint Gregory of Nyssa

Paul, joining righteousness to faith and weaving them together, constructs of them the breastplates for the infantryman, armoring the soldier properly and safely on both sides. A soldier cannot be considered safely armored when either shield is disjoined from the other. Faith without works of justice is not sufficient for salvation; neither is righteous living secure in itself of salvation if it is disjoined from faith. (*Homilies on Ecclesiastes* 8, A.D. 394)

Saint Prosper of Aquitaine

Indeed, a man who has been justified, that is, who from impious has been made pious, since he had no antecedent good merit, receives a gift, by which gift he may also acquire merit. Thus, what was begun in him by Christ's grace can also be augmented by the industry of his free choice, but never in the absence of God's help, without which no one is able either to progress or to continue in doing good. (*Responses on Behalf of Augustine 6,* A.D. 431)

XVII. PURGATORY

Although the vast majority of Christians concede that heaven will not permit iniquity or dysfunction, there is a disparity of opinion on what exactly occurs between earthly existence and final glorification.[89] To be sure, Scripture explicitly states that no form of impurity can coexist with God's omnibenevolence [Habakkuk 1:13, Revelation 21:26-27], and, as such, between the sinfulness of this life, and heavenly glory, it would seem requisite to be purged of all remnant imperfections.[90] Wherefore, inasmuch as those who have died in a state of grace are assured of their eternal salvation, if they have been imperfectly sanctified within their lives, it is fitting that they undergo a final purification.[91] Nevertheless, this remedial purgation is in no way synonymous with the punishment of the damned, but rather, it is an obligatory cleansing of residual impurity, so as to achieve the requisite holiness to enter God's kingdom.[92]

---

    89. Jimmy Aikin, *The Fathers Know Best: Your Essential Guide To The Teachings Of The Early Church* (San Diego, CA: Catholic Answers Press, 2010), 385
    90. Ibid.
    91. Catechism of the Catholic Church (1992), Paragraph 1030
    92. Ibid., Paragraph 1030, 1031

Unsurprisingly, the biblical texts repeatedly speak of a final purification and avow that all human imperfections require expiation prior to receiving the beatific vision. For instance, the book of Maccabees evinces ancient Israel's belief in postmortem expiations and presumes that those in need of a final purgation can be assisted by the living:

> On the next day, as had now become necessary, Judas and his men went to take up the bodies of the fallen and to bring them back to lie with their kindred in the sepulchers of their ancestors. Then under the tunic of each one of the dead they found sacred tokens of the idols of Jamnia, which the law forbids the Jews to wear. And it became clear to all that this was the reason these men had fallen. So they all blessed the ways of the Lord, the righteous judge, who reveals the things that are hidden; and they turned to supplication, praying that the sin that had been committed might be wholly blotted out. The noble Judas exhorted the people to keep themselves free from sin, for they had seen with their own eyes what had happened as the result of the sin of those who had fallen. He also took up a collection, man by man, to the amount of two thousand drachmas of silver, and sent it to Jerusalem to provide for a sin offering. In doing this he acted very well and honorably, taking account of the resurrection. For if he were not expecting that those who had fallen would rise again, it would have been superfluous and foolish to pray for the dead. But if he was looking to the splendid reward that is laid up for those who fall asleep in godliness, it was a holy and pious thought. Therefore he made atonement for the dead, so that they might be delivered from their sin. (2 Maccabees 12:39-46, NRSVCE)

Accordingly, in the Gospel of Matthew we witness Christ allude to the reality of a postmortem prison, wherein no one is permitted to a reprieve, until their debt has been paid in full:

> So when you are offering your gift at the altar, if you remember that your brother or sister has something against you, leave your gift there before the altar and go; first be reconciled to your brother or sister, and then come and offer your gift. Come to terms quickly with your accuser while you are on the way to court with him, or your accuser may hand you over to the judge, and the judge to the guard, and you will be thrown into prison. Truly I tell you, you will never get out until you have paid the last penny. (Matthew 5:23-26, NRSVCE)

What is more, in his letter to the Corinthians, Paul explicitly acknowledges the reality of postmortem purgatory fires, which are allotted to test our toils, bring forth sufferings and rewards, and vanquish residual impurities:

> For no one can lay any foundation other than the one that has been laid; that foundation is Jesus Christ. Now if anyone builds on the foundation with gold, silver, precious stones, wood, hay, straw— the work of each builder will become visible, for the Day will disclose it, because it will be revealed with fire, and the fire will test what sort of work each has done. If what has been built on the foundation survives, the builder will receive a reward. If the work is burned up, the builder will suffer loss; the builder will be saved, but only as through fire. (1 Corinthians 3:11-15, NRSVCE)

Subsequently, as much as the precise nature and extent of our final purification has been largely left to the realm of theological speculation, it is clear that we must be cleansed of all remnant imperfections before we obtain our final glorification. Indeed, for heaven forbid that we would allow our impurities to defile God's heavenly kingdom or be content to receive our eternal reward whilst persisting in earthly iniquities.

Early Christian Witness
(For Purgatory)

Saint Americus of Hierapolis

The citizen of a prominent city, I erected this while I lived, that I might have a resting place for my body. Abercius is my name, a disciple of the chaste Shepherd who feeds his sheep on the mountains and in the fields, who has great eyes surveying everywhere, who taught me the faithful writings of life. Standing by, I, Abercius, ordered this to be inscribed: Truly, I was in my seventy-second year. May everyone who is in accord with this and who understands it pray for Abercius. (*Epitaph of Abercius*, A.D. 190)

Saint Clement of Alexandria

Accordingly, the believer, through great discipline, divesting himself of the passions, passes to the mansion, which is better than the former one, viz., to the greatest torment, taking with him the characteristic of repentance from the sins he has committed after baptism. He is tortured then still more—not yet or not quite attaining what he sees others to have acquired. Besides, he is also ashamed of his transgressions. The greatest torments, indeed, are assigned to the believer. For God's righteousness is good, and His goodness is righteous. And though the punishments cease in the course of the completion of the expiation and purification of each one, yet those have very great and permanent grief who are found worthy of the other fold, on account of not being along with those that have been glorified through righteousness. (*Stromata 6:14*, A.D. 202)

Tertullian of Carthage

A woman, after the death of her husband... prays for his soul and asks that he may, while waiting, find rest; and that he may share in the first resurrection. And each year, on the anniversary of his death, she offers the sacrifice. (*Monogamy 10:1-2*, A.D. 216)

Origen of Alexandria

If a man departs this life with lighter faults, he is condemned to fire which burns away the lighter materials, and prepares the soul for the kingdom of God, where nothing defiled may enter. For if on the foundation of Christ you have built not only gold and silver and precious stones (I Cor., 3); but also wood and hay and stubble, what do you expect when the soul shall be separated from the body? Would you enter into heaven with your wood and hay and stubble and thus defile the kingdom of God; or on account of these hindrances would you remain without and receive no reward for your gold and silver and precious stones? Neither is this just. It remains then that you be committed to the fire which will burn the light materials; for our God to those who can comprehend heavenly things is called a cleansing fire. But this fire consumes not the creature, but what the creature has himself built, wood, and hay and stubble. It is manifest that the fire destroys the wood of our transgressions and then returns to us the reward of our great works. (*The Greek Fathers 8*, A.D. 220)

Saint Cyprian of Carthage

The strength of the truly believing remains unshaken; and with those who fear and love God with their whole heart, their integrity continues steady and strong. For to adulterers even a time of repentance is granted by us, and peace is given. Yet virginity is not therefore deficient in the Church, nor does the glorious design of continence languish through the sins of others. The Church, crowned with so many virgins, flourishes; and chastity and modesty preserve the tenor of their glory. Nor is the vigor of continence broken down because repentance and pardon are facilitated to the adulterer. It is one thing to stand for pardon, another thing to attain to glory: it is one thing, when cast into prison, not to go out thence until one has paid the uttermost farthing; another thing at once to receive the wages of faith and courage. It is one thing, tortured by long suffering for sins, to be cleansed and long purged by fire; another to have purged all sins by suffering. It is one thing, in fine, to be in suspense till the sentence of God at the day of judgment; another to be at once crowned by the Lord. (*Epistle 51:20*, A.D. 252)

Lactantius

But when He shall have judged the righteous, He will also try them with fire. Then they whose sins shall exceed either in weight or in number, shall be scorched by the fire and burnt but they whom full justice and maturity of virtue has imbued will not perceive that fire; for they have something of God in themselves which repels and rejects the violence of the flame. So great is the force of innocence, that the flame shrinks from it without doing harm, which has received from God this power, that it burns the wicked, and is under the command of the righteous (*Divine Institutes 7:21*, A.D. 307)

Saint Cyril of Jerusalem

Then we make mention also of those who have already fallen asleep: first, the patriarchs, prophets, Apostles, and martyrs, that through their prayers and supplications God would receive our petition; next, we make mention also of the holy fathers and bishops who have already fallen asleep, and, to put it simply, of all among us who have already fallen asleep, for we believe that it will be of very great benefit to the souls of those for whom the petition is carried up, while this holy and most solemn sacrifice is laid out. (*Catechetical Lectures 23:5:9*, A.D. 350)

Saint Gregory of Nyssa

If a man distinguishes in himself what is peculiarly human from that which is irrational, and if he be on the watch for a life of greater urbanity for himself, in this present life he will purify himself of any evil contracted, overcoming the irrational by reason. If he has inclined to the irrational pressure of the passions, using for the passions the cooperating hide of things irrational, he may afterward in a quite different manner be very much interested in what is better, when, after his departure out of the body, he gains knowledge of the difference between virtue and vice and finds that he is not able to partake of divinity until he has been purged of the filthy contagion in his soul by the purifying fire. (*Sermon on the Dead*, A.D. 382)

Saint John Chrysostom

Let us help and commemorate them. If Job's sons were purified by their father's sacrifice [Job 1:5], why would we doubt that our offerings for the dead bring them some consolation? Let us not hesitate to help those who have died and to offer our prayers for them. (*Homilies on First Corinthians 41:5*, A.D. 392)

Saint Augustine of Hippo

Temporal punishments are suffered by some in this life only, by some after death, by some both here and hereafter, but all of them before that last and strictest judgment. But not all who suffer temporal punishments after death will come to eternal punishments, which are to follow after that judgment. (*The City of God 21:13*, A.D. 419)

XVIII. THE COMMUNION OF SAINTS

Via the Incarnation, Christ established Himself as the unique arbiter between God and man [1 Timothy 2:5]. However, this does not preclude us from asking our Christian brethren to pray with us and on our behalf [James 5:16].[93] In fact, this is even more so the case with the angels and saints, who, having already received their eternal reward, are perfected in righteousness, freed from sin, and reside with God in all His glory.[94] Indeed, for our God is not the God of the dead but rather the God of the living [Matthew 22:32, Mark 12:27, Luke 20:38], and, as such, given that the prayers of the righteous availeth much [James 5:16], it behooves us to solicit their intercession. What is more, insofar as the Church and her elect have been incorporated into the mystical body of Christ [1 Corinthians 12:12-23, Ephesians 1:22-23, Colossians 1:18], then it is fitting that we remain spiritually united to those have completed their earthly struggles. As such, the Church militant on earth remain united to the Church suffering, who are being purged of their imperfections.

---

93. Jimmy Aikin, *The Fathers Know Best: Your Essential Guide To The Teachings Of The Early Church* (San Diego, CA: Catholic Answers Press, 2010), 354

94. Ibid.

Likewise, we also remain united to the Church triumphant, who are beholding the beatific vision in heaven. Wherefore, just as the eternal became finite in the Incarnation and in perpetuity via the institution of the Paschal supper, through Christ we unite to the elect in eternity and access their intercessory power.

To be sure, the biblical texts repeatedly bear witness to the efficacy of the intercessory power of the angels and saints, and whilst, admittedly, there are express prohibitions on practices such as necromancy [Leviticus 19:26, Leviticus 20:5-8, Deuteronomy 18:10], there are no such condemnations of rightly ordered supplications. Case in point: the book of Revelation evinces that the heavenly elders offer prayers for the earthly saints, and thus, those who have been adorned in glory actively petition for those still running the Christian race:

> When he had taken the scroll, the four living creatures and the twenty-four elders fell before the Lamb, each holding a harp and golden bowls full of incense, which are the prayers of the saints. (Revelation 5:8, NRSVCE)

Accordingly, Revelation also bespeaks of the presence of angels at the foot of God's heavenly throne, who offer up prayers on behalf of the faithful, who still toil for their eternal reward:

> Another angel with a golden censer came and stood at the altar; he was given a great quantity of incense to offer with the prayers of all the saints on the golden altar that is before the throne. And the smoke of the incense, with the prayers of the saints, rose before God from the hand of the angel. (Revelation 8:3-4, NRSVCE)

What is more, in the Gospel of Matthew Christ goes out of His way to caution those who would disparage the young, for their guardian angels are in the presence of the Father, actively interceding on their behalf:

> See that you despise not one of these little ones: for I say to you, that their angels in heaven always see the face of my Father who is in heaven. (Matthew 18:10, NRSVCE)

Subsequently, given that Scripture compels us to pray for one another—for forgiveness, healing, and aid [James 5:16]— let us heed the inspired words of the Apostles so as to be strengthened, renewed, and sustained. Further still, let us seek the assistance of those perfected in glory—those who have triumphed in their Christian race; let us entreat the petitions of the righteous and holy; let us solicit the intercession of the angels and saints.

Early Christian Witness
(For The Communion of Saints)

Hermas of Rome
[The Shepherd said:] 'But those who are weak and slothful in prayer hesitate to ask anything from the Lord; but the Lord is full of compassion and gives without fail to all who ask him. But you, [Hermas,] having been strengthened by the holy angel [you saw], and having obtained from him such intercession, and not being slothful, why do not you ask of the Lord understanding, and receive it from him?' (*The Shepherd 3:5:4*, A.D. 80)

Saint Clement of Alexandria
In this way is he [the true Christian] always pure for prayer. He also prays in the society of angels, as being already of angelic rank, and he is never out of their holy keeping; and though he prays alone, he has the choir of the saints standing with him [in prayer] (*Miscellanies* 7:12, A.D. 208)

Origen of Alexandria

But not the high priest [Christ] alone prays for those who pray sincerely, but also the angels... as also the souls of the saints who have already fallen asleep. (*Prayer 11*, A.D. 233)

Saint Cyprian of Carthage

Let us remember one another in concord and unanimity. Let us on both sides [of death] always pray for one another. Let us relieve burdens and afflictions by mutual love, that if one of us, by the swiftness of divine condescension, shall go hence first, our love may continue in the presence of the Lord, and our prayers for our brethren and sisters not cease in the presence of the Father's mercy. (*Epistle 56:5*, A.D. 252)

Saint Methodius of Philippi

Therefore, we pray [ask] you, the most excellent among women, who glories in the confidence of your maternal honors, that you would unceasingly keep us in remembrance. O holy Mother of God, remember us, I say, who make our boast in you, and who in august hymns celebrate the memory, which will ever live, and never fade away. (*Oration on Simon and Anna 14*, A.D. 300)

Saint Cyril of Jerusalem

Then [during the Eucharistic prayer] we make mention also of those who have already fallen asleep: first, the patriarchs, prophets, Apostles, and martyrs, that through their prayers and supplications God would receive our petition. (*Catechetical Lectures 23:9*, A.D. 350)

Saint Ephrem of Syria

You victorious martyrs who endured torments gladly for the sake of the God and Savior, you who have boldness of speech toward the Lord himself, you saints, intercede for us who are timid and sinful men, full of sloth, that the grace of Christ may come upon us, and enlighten the hearts of all of us so that we may love him. (*Commentary on Mark*, A.D. 370)

Saint Gregory of Nazianz

Yes, I am well assured that [my father's] intercession is of more avail now than was his instruction in former days, since he is closer to God, now that he has shaken off his bodily fetters, and freed his mind from the clay that obscured it and holds conversation naked with the nakedness of the prime and purest mind. (*Orations 17*, A.D. 380)

Saint Augustine of Hippo

A Christian people celebrates together in religious solemnity the memorials of the martyrs, both to encourage their being imitated and so that it can share in their merits and be aided by their prayers. (*Against Faustus the Manichean*, A.D. 400)

Saint Jerome

You say in your book that while we live, we are able to pray for each other, but afterwards when we have died, the prayer of no person for another can be heard...But if the Apostles and martyrs while still in the body can pray for others, at a time when they ought still to be solicitous about themselves, how much more will they do so after their crowns, victories, and triumphs? A single man, Moses, oft wins pardon from God for six hundred thousand armed men; and Stephen, the follower of his Lord and the first Christian martyr, entreats pardon for his persecutors [Acts 7:59-60]; and when once they have entered on their life with Christ, shall they have less power than before? The Apostle Paul says that two hundred and seventy-six souls were given to him in the ship [Acts 27:37]; and when, after his dissolution, he has begun to be with Christ, must he shut his mouth, and be unable to say a word for those who throughout the whole world have believed in his Gospel? Shall Vigilantius the live dog be better than Paul the dead lion? (*Against Vigilantius 6*, A.D. 406)

XIX. THE UNIQUENESS OF MARY

Whereas the vast majority of Protestant denominations view Marian devotion as contemptible, erroneous, and extreme, the Church vigorously denounces all conflations of God with creatures; however, she also resolves to hold Mary in the highest of esteem. Case in point: she thoroughly condemned the ancient heresy of the Collyridians, who exalted Mary beyond what was due;[95] however, she also rebuked the Anticomarianists, who degraded Mary's status and virtue.[96] Indeed, for the proper reverence of Mary neither obscures nor diminishes the adoration which is due to God alone; on the contrary, it evinces His honor, His glory, and His power, in that her soul doth magnify the Lord [Luke 1:46]. Correspondingly, one cannot diminish Mary's status and virtue without inexplicitly diminishing the status of Christ, and, as such, the Church duly honors her as "immaculate" [Luke 1:28-30, Luke 1:46-50, Genesis 3:15] "the mother of God" [Luke 1:43, Isaiah 7:14], and "the queen mother" of the eternal king [Revelation 12:1-2]. Furthermore, inasmuch as her merits are ultimately predicated upon the merits of

---

95. Saint Epiphanius of Salamis, *Panarion 78:13-23, 19:1-4*, A.D. 374
96. Saint Epiphanius of Salamis, *Panarion 78:1*, A.D. 374

her incarnate Son, in a wholly unique way, Mary cooperated with God's grace and His resolution to bring salvation to souls.[97] As such, via her complete adherence to the will of the Father and to the redemptive work of the Son, and via her total cooperation with every prompting of the Spirit, she is an ideal example of faith, charity, and obedience to model ourselves upon.[98] Accordingly, just as the sacramental priesthood participates in the high priesthood of Jesus and the created order in God's omnibenevolence, via her distinct maternal relation to the Incarnate Word, she uniquely participates in Christ's one mediation.[99] Wherefore, just as Christ heeded Mary's words at the wedding of Canna [John 2:1-10] and King Solomon avowed to acquiesce to his queen mother [1 King 2:18-20], we likewise solicit the intercession of Mary, our queen, as Jesus duly honors both His mother and Father [Exodus 20:12, Matthew 5:17].

To be sure, Scripture also attests to Mary's uniqueness and her distinct role in the order of grace, and likewise, it evinces her as the providential conduit through which God chose to redeem the human race. For instance,[100] where mankind would be plunged into sin and death by the disobedience of the virgin Eve [Genesis 3:6], salvation would come through the virgin Mary and her acceptance of what God had decreed [Luke 1:38]. Consequently, whilst Eve was led astray by the words of an angel, transgressed God, and then fled from his presence [Genesis 3:1-24], Mary received faith and joy from Gabriel, became obedient, and bore God her belly [Luke 1:26-38]. Correspondingly, where Eve became an ancestral mother to all humans after partaking of the forbidden tree [Genesis 4:1-32], Mary

---

97. Catechism of the Catholic Church (1992), Paragraph 970
98. Ibid., Paragraph 967
99. Ibid., Paragraph 970
100. The subsequent typological examples have been summarized from: Dr. Scott Hahn, "Dawn of the New Eve," January 26, 2022, The Road to Emmaus Podcast, https://stpaulcenter.com/audio/the-road-to-emmaus/treat-her-like-a-queen-part-1/

became a spiritual mother to all Christians as Christ hung on the cross at Calvary [John 19:25-27].

What is more, Luke also goes to great lengths in his gospel account to present Mary as the Ark of the New Covenant, and thereon, he bears witness to her status, splendor, and holiness, as well as her unique capacity to bear within her God's presence. Case in point:[101] whilst in Exodus we read that the glory of the Lord came via a cloud to "overshadow" the Ark of the covenant [Exodus 40:34-35], Luke would describe the power of the most-high "overshadowing" Mary in analogous fashion [Luke 1:35]. Likewise, whilst in Samuel we read that David "arose and went to Judah" so as to bring up Ark of God [2 Samuel 6:2], Luke would record that Mary "arose and went to Judah" after consenting to give birth to God's Son [Luke 1:39]. In point of fact, the book of Samuel explicitly states that the Ark of the Covenant remained in the hill country for three months in the house of Obed-Edom, the Gittite [2 Samuel 6:11], whilst Mary remained in the hill country for three months in the house of her cousin Elizabeth [Luke 1:56]. Further still, David then admits his unworthiness to receive the Ark, via his exclamation, "How can the Ark of the Lord come onto me" [2 Samuel 6:9], whilst Elizabeth exclaims her unfitness to receive Mary via a synonymous decree [Luke 1:43]. Correspondingly, David then shouted and leaped for joy as the Ark was brought into his presence [2 Samuel 6:15-16], whilst Elizabeth would shout, as John leaped in her womb, at the sound of Mary's salutation [Luke 1:41-42].

Wherefore, when one views the significance of Mary in Scripture and her utter uniqueness in the order of grace, it is clear why the Church honors her so fervently and incessantly calls upon her mediation. Indeed, for she is the mother of God [Luke 1:43,

---

[101] The subsequent typological examples have been summarized from: Dr. Scott Hahn, "The New Ark," December 14, 2015, St. Paul Center for Biblical Theology, https://stpaulcenter.com/the-new-ark/

Isaiah 7:14], the Ark of the New Covenant [Luke 1:35-56, Revelation 11:19], the new Eve [Luke 1: 26-38], and our spiritual mother [John 19:25-26]; she is our heavenly queen [Revelation 12:1-2], the immaculately conceived [Luke 1:28-30, Luke 1:46-50, Genesis 3:15], our unique advocate, and intercessor.

Early Christian Witness
(For The Uniqueness of Mary)

Saint Justin Martyr

[Jesus] became man by the Virgin so that the course which was taken by disobedience in the beginning through the agency of the serpent might be also the very course by which it would be put down. Eve, a virgin and undefiled, conceived the word of the serpent and bore disobedience and death. But the Virgin Mary received faith and joy when the angel Gabriel announced to her the glad tidings that the Spirit of the Lord would come upon her and the power of the Most-High would overshadow her, for which reason the Holy One being born of her is the Son of God. And she replied, 'Be it done unto me according to your word' [Luke 1:38]. (*Dialogue with Trypho 100*, A.D. 155)

Saint Irenaeus of Lyons

Consequently, then, Mary the Virgin is found to be obedient, saying, 'Behold, O Lord, your handmaid; be it done to me according to your word.' Eve, however, was disobedient, and, when yet a virgin, she did not obey. Just as she, who was then still a virgin although she had Adam for a husband—for in paradise they were both naked but were not ashamed; for, having been created only a short time, they had no understanding of the procreation of children, and it was necessary that they first come to maturity before beginning to multiply—having become disobedient, was made the cause of death for herself and for the whole human race; so also Mary, betrothed to a man but nevertheless still a virgin, being obedient, was made the cause of salvation for herself and for the whole human race... Thus, the knot of Eve's disobedience was loosed by the obedience of Mary. What the virgin Eve had bound in unbelief, the Virgin Mary loosed through faith. (*Against All Heresies 3:22:24*, A.D. 189)

Tertullian of Carthage

It was while Eve was still a virgin that the word of the devil crept in to erect an edifice of death. Likewise through a virgin the Word of God was introduced to set up a structure of life. Thus what had been laid waste in ruin by this sex was by the same sex reestablished in salvation. Eve had believed the serpent; Mary believed Gabriel. That which the one destroyed by believing, the other, by believing, set straight. (*The Flesh of Christ 17:4*, A.D. 210)

Origen of Alexandria

This Virgin Mother of the Only begotten of God, is called Mary, worthy of God, immaculate of the immaculate, one of the one. (*Homily* 1, A.D. 244)

SPIRITUM SANCTUM, DOMINUM

Saint Ephrem of Syria

You alone, and your Mother are more beautiful than any others, for there is no blemish in you nor any stains upon your Mother. Who of my children can compare in beauty to these? (*Nisibene Hymns 27:8*, A.D. 361)

Saint Athanasius of Alexandria

O noble Virgin, truly you are greater than any other greatness. For who is your equal in greatness, O dwelling place of God the Word? To whom among all creatures shall I compare you, O Virgin? You are greater than them all O Covenant, clothed with purity instead of gold! You are the Ark in which is found the golden vessel containing the true manna, that is, the flesh in which divinity resides. (*Homily of the Papyrus of Turin 71:216*, A.D. 373)

Saint Ambrose of Milan

The first thing which kindles ardor in learning is the greatness of the teacher. What is greater [to teach by example] than the Mother of God? What more glorious than she whom Glory Itself chose? What more chaste than she who bore a body without contact with another body? For why should I speak of her other virtues? She was a virgin not only in body but also in mind, who stained the sincerity of its disposition by no guile, who was humble in heart, grave in speech, prudent in mind, sparing of words, studious in reading, resting her hope not on uncertain riches, but on the prayer of the poor, intent on work, modest in discourse; wont to seek not man but God as the judge of her thoughts, to injure no one, to have goodwill towards all, to rise up before her elders, not to envy her equals, to avoid boastfulness, to follow reason, to love virtue. When did she pain her parents even by a look? When did she disagree with her neighbors? When did she despise the lowly? When did she avoid the needy? (*The Virgins 2:2:7*, A.D. 377)

The prophet David danced before the Ark. Now what else should we say the Ark was but holy Mary? The Ark bore within it the tables of the Testament, but Mary bore the Heir of the same Testament itself. The former contained in it the Law, the latter the Gospel. The one had the voice of God, the other His Word. The Ark, indeed, was radiant within and without with the glitter of gold, but holy Mary shone within and without with the splendor of virginity. The one was adorned with earthly gold, the other with heavenly. (*Sermon 42:6*, 382 A.D)

Saint Augustine of Hippo

Having excepted the holy Virgin Mary, concerning whom, on account of the honor of the Lord, I wish to have absolutely no question when treating of sins—for how do we know what abundance of grace for the total overcoming of sin was conferred upon her, who merited to conceive and bear him in whom there was no sin?—so, I say, with the exception of the Virgin, if we could have gathered together all those holy men and women, when they were living here, and had asked them whether they were without sin, what do we suppose would have been their answer? (*Nature and Grace 36:42*, A.D. 415)

Saint Proclus of Constantinople

She who called us here today is the Holy Mary; the untarnished vessel of virginity; the spiritual paradise of the second Adam; the workshop for the union of natures; the marketplace of the contract of salvation; the bridal chamber in which the Word took flesh in marriage; the living bush of human nature, which the fire of a divine birth-pang did not consume; the veritable swift cloud who carried in her body the one who rides upon the cherubim; the purest fleece drenched with the rain which came down from heaven, whereby the shepherd clothed himself with the sheep; handmaid and mother, virgin and heaven, the only bridge for God to mankind; the awesome loom of divine economy upon which the robe of union was ineffably woven. (*Homily 1,* A.D. 446)

XX. CONCLUSION

Inasmuch as the New Testament writings are inspired by God and are profitable for teaching and reproof, Christ did not explicitly leave us these texts, but rather a singular, authoritative, hierarchical, and successional Church, which then produced and preserved said Scriptures. Likewise, insofar as Scripture is an invaluable and authoritative source which bears witness to Christian truths, it is neither self-defining nor easily interpreted, nor does it contain every apostolic teaching. On the contrary, Scripture explicitly bespeaks of complementarity authorities such as Sacred Tradition and the Magisterium of the Church, which help guide us to orthodox scriptural interpretations and provide supplemental teachings when necessary. In point of fact, it would be difficult to have confidence in Christianity at all without acknowledging these complimentary authorities, in that they were foundational in establishing dogmas like the Trinity, the Hypostatic union, and affixing the biblical canon. What is more, if Scripture was indeed intended to be the supreme and final Christian authority, then what are we to make of the first 1500 years of pre-reformation Christian history? Are we to disregard the fact that there was widespread illiteracy and an extreme scarcity of Scripture until the end of the fifteenth century? Correspondingly, the authority of Tradition and the Magisterium of the Church are attested to throughout Church history, as are Catholic doctrines, dogmas, a three-fold hierarchy, apostolic succession, the seven sacraments, and sacrificial liturgies.

Furthermore, just as the Church was visible in every age, so too was its visible head, relentlessly guiding and preserving the new and eternal Israel under its heavenly Davidic king. In fact, both Scripture and Tradition not only extensively attest to the reality and validity of Petrine supremacy but also to its divine mandate, its unique charism, Peter's travels to Rome, his subsequent martyrdom, and his possession of dynastic keys. Accordingly, so as to guarantee the orthodoxy of Christian doctrine, and to give assurance to all those who believe, they also bespeak of the infallibility of his office and the incorruptibility of the Roman see. What is more, history has made manifest what invariably occurs in the absence of Petrine authority, namely, endless schisms, rampant heresy, unfettered sectarianism, as well as widespread doctrinal and moral uncertainty.

Further still, both Scripture and Tradition also bear witness to seven channels of grace, through which we might access the mercy of God and receive spiritual strengthening on a daily basis. To be sure, the sacraments afford us a visible sign of the imparting of invisible grace, wherein we are sanctified, fortified, made anew, and absolved from original and personal sins. Notwithstanding, the seven sacraments are also in no way extraneous or arbitrary offerings of grace; rather, they are the providential culmination of Old Testament ritualistic practices, which penetrate into all areas of the Christian lived experience. Indeed, for via baptism, confirmation and the Eucharist we are born into the Christian life, and via extreme unction and confession, we are spiritually healed. Accordingly, via matrimony and holy orders, we are called to lives of Christian service, which are formed through the virtue of charity.

Subsequently, if our aspirations are to complete our salvific race and obtain our eternal reward, then it behooves us to access these visible channels, which afford us reconciliation, renewal, and sustenance.

Wherefore, when one considers the testimony of Sacred Tradition, alongside the witness of Holy Scripture, it is evident that Christ established a visible Church which is one, holy, Catholic, and apostolic. Likewise, it is clear He inaugurated a visible head in the person of Simon Peter, whom He also entrusted the keys to a dynastic office, which is protected by the Holy Spirit. Furthermore, it is clear that Christ invested His visible Church with seven sacraments that align with our sensory and scrupulous natures, and which visibly impart us invisible grace, so as to reconcile us, transform us, and sustain us. Correspondingly, it is clear that God compels us to cooperate with His grace and to continue to increase in justification, and that we are not simply imputed the righteousness of Christ but rather undergo a radical transformation. What is more, He also implores us to entreat the petitions of the angels and saints who are residing with Him in His glory, for they are perfected in righteousness, freed from earthly attachments, and rendered impeccably holy.

In summation, no other institution in the history of the world can lay claim to the Church's pedigree, ascendency, or splendor, and likewise, no other institution can match its longevity, despite centuries of persecution and repression. Subsequently, to what do we credit 2000 years of continuance in the face of such fierce opposition? How do we explain her ability to endure despite the personal failures and faults of her clerics and adherents? Further still, how are we to explain her soundness of doctrine, her philosophical preeminence, and her global influence? How could one Church and her saints have surmounted the world, apart from Christ's divine institution?

Yet, though your greatness terrifies me, your kindness attracts me. From the priest I demand the safe keeping of the victim, from the shepherd the protection due to the sheep. Away with all that is overweening; let the state of Roman majesty withdraw. My words are spoken to the successor of the fisherman, to the disciple of the cross. As I follow no leader save Christ, so I communicate with none but your blessedness, that is with the chair of Peter. For this, I know, is the rock on which the church is built [Matthew 16:18]! This alone is the house where the paschal lamb can be rightly eaten [Exodus 12:22]. This is the Ark of Noah, and he who is not found in it shall perish when the flood prevails [Genesis 7:23]. (Saint Jerome, *Epistle 15:2 [Epistle to Pope Saint Damasus]*, A.D. 372)

BOOK III BIBLIOGRAPHY

Akin, Jimmy. *The Fathers Know Best: Your Essential Guide to the Teachings of the Early Church*. San Diego, CA: Catholic Answers Press, 2010.

Albright, W.F and Mann, C.S. *The Anchor Bible: Matthew*. Garden City, NY: Doubleday, 1971.

Bloomberg, Craig. *From Pentecost to Patmos: an Introduction to Acts through Revelation*. Nashville, TN: B&H Academic, 2006.

Catechism of the Catholic Church (1992), http://www.vatican.ca/archiveENG0015/_INDEX.HTM

Catholic Answers, http://www.catholic.com/

Evidence Unseen, http://www.evidenceunseen.com/

France, R.T. *The Gospel of Matthew*. Grand Rapids, MI: Wm. B. Publishing Co., 2007.

Hahn, Scott. *Answering Common Objections: Talk 1- The Pope*. Sycamore, Il: Saint Joseph Communications, 2004.

National Catholic Register, http://www.ncregister.com/

New Advent, http://www.newadvent.org/fathers

St. Paul Center for Biblical Theology, https://stpaulcenter.com

Suan Sonna, https://hds.academia.edu/SuanSonna

Ybarra, Erick. *The Papacy: Revisiting the Debate between Catholics and Orthodox*. Steubenville, OH: Emmaus Road Publishing, 2022.

www.ingramcontent.com/pod-product-compliance
Lightning Source LLC
Chambersburg PA
CBHW030243010526
44107CB00030B/1314/J